Department of Health and Social Security
Scottish Education Department
(Social Work Services Group)
Welsh Office

Working Party on Fostering Practice

Guide to Fostering Practice

London: Her Majesty's Stationery Office

ISBN O 11 320187 7

Contents

Appendices

Working Party on Fostering Practice

MEMBERSHIP

Mrs. Janie Thomas (Chairman)	Lecturer in Social Work Studies, London School of Economics and Political Science
Miss Fiona Abington	Social Worker, Child Guidance Clinic, London Borough of Waltham Forest
Mr. Jack Bates	Senior Social Worker, Social Services Department, Gwent County Council
Miss Celia Downes	Senior Social Worker, The Tavistock Clinic
Miss Mary James	Director, Independent Adoption Society
Miss Mary Joynson	Director of Child Care, Dr. Barnardo's
Miss Ermyne Lee-Kin	Development Officer, Department of Social Services, London Borough of Waltham Forest
Mrs. Raissa Page	Development Officer, Children's Centre, National Children's Bureau
Mr. Brian Roycroft	Director of Social Services, City of Newcastle upon Tyne
Mr. Edward Thomas	Depute Director of Social Work, The Fife Regional Council

Assessors

Miss Myra Copleston	Social Work Service, Welsh Office
Miss Dorothy Morgan	Social Work Services Group, Scottish Education Department
Miss Joan Vann	Social Work Service, Department of Health and Social Security

Observer

Miss Mabel Hill	Social Work Advisory Group, Department of Health and Social Services, N. Ireland

Joint Secretaries

Miss Margaret Evans	Department of Health and Social Security
Mr. John Booth	Department of Health and Social Security

Assistant Secretary

Miss Pamela Green	Department of Health and Social Security

Preface

Working Party on Fostering Practice

MEMBERSHIP

i. This Guide was prepared during a period of re-examination and redefinition of foster care, at a time when changes in legislation were under discussion and in a climate of conflicting and even confusing views as to the nature of children's needs and rights and those of adults in relation to them.

ii. The differing views prevailing when preparing the Guide were reflected within the Working Party membership. Some members base their practice on specific theories whilst others take a more eclectic view. There is inevitable conflict between the various schools of thought and we recognised the controversial nature of much on which we were being asked to advise. We accepted that, as attitudes affect conclusions, the product of any working group must be in the form of a consensus document. Nevertheless, although any one member might have emphasised points somewhat differently from others we discovered that within a spectrum of opinion it is possible to identify a central core of principles and the implications which flow from them.

iii. What follows is a combination of research findings, the 'practice wisdom' obtainable within the Working Party (every member has experience in child care social work and, between us, in statutory and voluntary agencies both before and after the 'Seebohm' reorganisation) and the evidence and expert opinion submitted.

iv. We are immensely grateful to the many people who shared their experiences and opinions with us. There was a generous response to our invitation for written comment from foster parent groups, individual foster parents, foster children, other individuals and from various bodies. We invited certain people, either in their own right or as representatives of organisations, to meet us in session. In addition, members of the Working Party journeyed about the country, talking with groups of foster parents, with staff at differing levels in local authority social services departments and in voluntary child care agencies and with other individuals. A list of those who helped us is given in Appendix V. We acknowledge their help with thanks whilst accepting full responsibility for the final outcome.

v. We could not have undertaken our task without a commitment to fostering as a positive form of care for some children. In planning for children unfortunate enough to be deprived of their families for varying periods of time, there is growing flexibility as to who might benefit from foster care, renewed appreciation of its value and versatility and enhanced awareness of its place in a total care context. All this we welcome, not least because the focus on foster care sharpens concern with practice standards.

vi. Much of the necessary investment required to promote successful fostering has been identified over the years or has been indicated by recent research studies. But those same studies confirm that a considerable gap exists between theory and practice in foster care. Our hope is that this Guide will go some way towards reducing that discrepancy.

September 1975   Janie Thomas

Introduction

The purpose and use of the guide

1. The Working Party on Fostering Practice was set up in 1974 by the Secretary of State for Social Services. This was in response to the wish expressed by the Departmental Committee on the Adoption of Children at paragraph 150 of their Report (Cmnd 5107) that 'the central departments will consider as a matter of urgency what else can be done to secure improvements in fostering practice, whether by the issue of written guidance . . . or by other means'. Accordingly, the terms of reference of the working party were:— 'to compile a code of good fostering practice for the guidance of local authorities and voluntary organisations in boarding-out children in their care, in the form of a guide which could be published for the use of social workers and others'.

2. The terms of reference make clear the boundaries to our task. We were not asked to propose changes in the law, nor to make major policy recommendations. Furthermore, consideration of private fostering and of foster care for groups other than children was not in our remit. However, many of the proposals which follow may usefully be adapted to fostering situations generally. In preparing the Guide we have worked within the legal framework existing at the time, drawing on basic principles which apply whatever the circumstances and which will stand the test of time. This is in no sense a definitive document and we recognise the need for periodic updating.

3. We are aware that the Guide is being published at a time of intense interest and concern across a wide spectrum of child care policy and practice. Expectations of this publication, therefore, may go beyond its limited perspective. It seems important to state at the outset that this is not a child care manual. There are various methods of care for children who cannot live with their families and these, together with services aimed at enabling children to remain in their own homes, make up a total child care context. Although an integrated consideration of the various elements needs to be undertaken it is a separate and more comprehensive task than that given to us. We are only looking in detail at the part of child care practice relating to fostering.

4. The primary purpose of the Guide is to aid social workers who are involved in face-to-face work with children, parents, foster parents and with all others who have a part to play in this form of care. During our discussions with staff in agencies responsible for fostering services, the need of social workers coming new to work in foster care for basic guidance was urged upon us. We have been mindful of that, but at the same time we have tried to produce a guide helpful to practitioners with varying degrees of training, experience and departmental support.

5. Although primarily directed at social workers, we hope that the Guide will be useful to others involved in fostering: both those directly involved in the caring team—foster parents, social work supervisors and allied professionals—and those with training, managerial and administrative responsibilities whose policies and procedures affect practice.

6. Whatever group is using the Guide they will not find it a procedural manual which gives instruction at each stage in the fostering process. There is a place for more detailed commentary but this, we suggest, is a matter for local effort. We liken this document to a travel guide. The territory as a whole is taken account of, certain areas are mapped out for exploration and some essentials, not to be missed at all costs, are highlighted. We hope it will start people thinking, whet the appetite for further investigation and stimulate individual initiative. From a travel guide a particular itinerary can be worked out, tailored to individual requirements. Similarly we hope that individual departments or areas will use this document as a base for more detailed guidance taking into account local factors.

7. The Guide has been written from the standpoint of our culture with its emphasis on the nuclear family group. We recognise that within our overall culture, sub-cultural patterns exist, that we are being enriched by the addition of groups from other cultures, and that in any event cultural norms change over time. We have tried to take account of these factors in a general way, but they need to be given specific consideration in any particular instance.

8. Throughout the preparation of the Guide we have been influenced by the outcomes of research but at the same time we have had to accept that some aspects of foster care are untested, or even untestable. Where research findings have passed into practice knowledge, these have been incorporated without specific reference in the text. However, the bibliography is designed to facilitate the further examination of specific studies and of other relevant literature.

9. The Guide is divided into three main parts. In Part I the versatility of foster care is recognised and set in an historical perspective. Consideration is given to the fostering situation from the stand-point of the main participants—child, parents, foster parents, agency staff and others who share in the care of the child. The purpose of these chapters is to provide, in some measure, a frame of reference for the practice of foster care. Part II is the essence of the Guide in that it is concerned with the social work task throughout the fostering process. It is, in particular, the material given in this part which could form the basis for departmental manuals and handbooks. Part III points up some guide lines to policies and procedures, both to facilitate good practice in particular instances and to maintain the resource of fostering generally. The various emphases are interdependent and the index highlights key subjects and provides some cross-reference of aspects which are necessarily referred to in more than one part of the Guide. In the Appendices we have included a summary of some aspects of a child's emotional development and the implications for fostering practice. This has been provided by Miss Celia Downes, a member of the Working Party and is an individual statement based on one specific theoretical viewpoint. We have also included a detailed developmental chart provided by Dr. Mary Sheridan and a list of the statutes relevant to children in foster care.

10. The word 'child' is subject to variable interpretations in statute. For ease of reference we have chosen it to encompass children and young persons up to the age of 18 unless otherwise stated. Finally, we have called the social worker 'she' and the child 'he', not because we have preference for either to be of the sex chosen, but simply because the English language requires a choice to be made.

Part I
Sharing the care of a child

Chapter 1
Fostering — A means of care

11. The agencies caring for children all seek to provide a form of care which is in the best interests of the individual child. When children are unable to live with their own parents various alternatives become available: some may be adopted but in the majority of situations the agency needs to accept responsibility for either short or long term care. Of these children some will be best placed in a residential setting but for others the most positive caring environment will be within a foster home. Whatever provision is made for a child in care his total care is always shared between several interested parties. Each has his specific role to play and all are interdependent on one another for the ultimate success of their joint purpose. This is to enable the child to grow and develop towards his maximum potential as a healthy, loving, creative human being.

12. In foster care the nuclear group which shares the care of the child includes the foster parents, the social worker supervising the child and his parents. In a minority of cases, the parents will not be present, for example, in situations where the child has been orphaned or abandoned. Around this nuclear group is an ever-widening circle of those who participate in his care. This circle will include: the social work agency and its staff especially those residential child care staff who may have cared for the child in the past, his extended family, the extended foster family, the health visitor, the general practitioner and the staff of the school. Children in care may also have a need for religious practices and cultural experiences which are not part of the daily life of those responsible for their immediate care and in these situations the circle of care-sharers will be extended to include those who can provide these missing essentials.

13. Sharing the care of a child is a difficult undertaking for it is work in a field full of emotion and of subjective judgement. It could not be otherwise for it involves the constant interaction between human beings. Fostering is the term used to describe situations in which a child is cared for in a family setting, that is in a private home, usually but not necessarily by a married couple who may or may not have children of their own. There are many forms of foster care for its purpose is to meet the individual needs of children.

14. There are many kinds of children in foster homes. They may need to stay in their foster homes for only a few days or for many years, for fostering is a means of providing both short and long term* care and it can play a vital part in creating a caring environment for a child. In the terms of previous legislation it can 'further his best interests' and 'afford him the opportunity for the proper development of his character and abilities'. Its purpose is to care for some of the many children who, for various reasons, have been deprived of a normal family life.

15. The circumstances in which children may be received into the care of a local authority are laid down by Act of Parliament. Voluntary organisations are free to make their own criteria as to when they will accept responsibility for a child and a high proportion of the children cared for by some voluntary societies are in fact in the legal care of local authorities. Children come into care for a variety of reasons and may be of any age from a few days old to late adolescence. Some children are in care at the request of their parents, some may have been abandoned by their families. Others may have been committed to care by a court or children's panel either following the judicial separation or divorce of their parents, or because they have committed an offence or have been found in need of care or control.

16. Children may remain in care until the age of eighteen years or, if committed to care after the age of sixteen years, until they reach nineteen years and in certain circumstances the local authority may assume the right of the parents of a child received into voluntary care. It is however the minority of children who spend most of their childhood in care for the majority only stay for short periods of time.

17. Because of these variations in the ages of the children and in the reasons for their being in care, it is necessary for there to be a wide range of provision available from which the one most suited to an individual child's needs can be selected. The success of any plan for a child is dependent on the quality of earlier work in assessing his needs. This is particularly true of foster care. Fostering is only one way, albeit a very important one, of providing for a child who is separated from his parents and it is important to recognise from the outset that fostering is not in itself a single identifiable method of care. It offers a range of placements which have in common only the fact that they provide care in a family

---

* In the Boarding Out Regulations for England and Wales short term care is for a period of boarding out up to eight weeks and long term care for a period exceeding eight weeks. There is no similar provision in the Scottish Regulations.

setting. There are even more types of foster homes than there are of residential homes. Each foster family is unique and each has different qualities to offer to the child who comes into its care.

18. The range of fostering situations which exist derive from the personalities, abilities, strengths, weaknesses, hopes and expectations of the foster families themselves. In practice, the social worker needs to develop the skill to identify which fostering situation is appropriate if the plan for the individual child is to be carried out successfully. She must also ensure that as far as possible all those involved in the fostering situation—his parents, foster family and, if he is old enough to understand, the child himself—are fully aware of the basis on which the choice of placement has been made and are in full agreement with it. Many difficulties, which can result in a request for a foster child to be removed, stem from the fact that the aim of the placement has been perceived differently by the various people involved. All concerned in the fostering situation need to be aware too of the fact that foster parents' attitudes both towards fostering and towards a particular child may change with time as also may the child's ability to leave his foster parents and thrive with his own parents. Some of these variations are described below.

19. Legal adoption is the only situation in which a child becomes in law almost as though he had been born to his new parents. Through this process all the rights and duties of the original parents are transferred permanently and completely to the adopters and the child ceases to be in the care of the agency.* Whilst some foster children may be adopted into their foster families, most remain in the care of the agency until they return home or reach adulthood. Where children remain in foster care the extent of parental contact varies considerably. In some cases they continue to feel part of their natural family. In others there may be little parental contact and, especially where children were placed at a young age, they may come to look upon their foster family as their own. The foster parents in their turn then see themselves more as parents than as participating in an agency's caring role. At the other extreme there is the child fostered for a few weeks whilst his mother goes into hospital for confinement or because of illness. In these circumstances there is no question of the child coming to be looked upon nor of regarding himself as a member of the foster family.

---

* When the 1975 Children Act is implemented the foster parents may become legal custodians of the child; here again the child goes out of the care of the agency. A custodianship order will not however, permanently deprive the parents of all rights as it may subsequently be revoked.

20. Sometimes, for example in one-parent families, where the father or mother is in employment, foster home placement during the school holidays will often prevent the need for the children to come into care on a long-term basis. Similarly, Monday to Friday foster care, when combined with effective family casework, may be of more help to a child than a residential placement. This form of care may be particularly helpful to a delinquent child or one who has problems over school attendance.

21. Many handicapped children benefit from long term foster care but some children in care may have such a severe mental, emotional or physical handicap that a 'permanent' foster home cannot readily be found for them. Such children can however benefit considerably from a regular holiday foster home, and from subsequent visits by their foster parents during term time. Fostering links can in addition benefit children in long term hospital care where the local authorities have assumed responsibility for their social care.

22. Foster parents may also look after a child whose mother is mentally ill. They not only do this each time the mother's health breaks down and she is admitted to hospital, but they also offer practical support and companionship to the mother when she is at home. In these situations foster parents can come to be regarded more as friends or as members of the extended family. Their acceptance of the mother can be very reassuring to a child who is not only facing separation from home but also having to come to terms with the illness of his parent.

23. Babies are sometimes boarded out with foster parents whilst awaiting placement for adoption, and some foster mothers gain great satisfaction from looking after such children and later seeing them settled into loving adoptive homes.

24. There is also an increasing use of foster care for the placement of children during a period of assessment or whilst on remand by a court. In both these situations a foster home may, for some children, be a more satisfactory placement than a residential establishment.

25. Fostering will mean differing things to different children depending upon their individual circumstances. For example, it may enable the child coming into care whilst his mother is ill to remain within his familiar neighbourhood, to attend the same school and see his friends each day. The similarity of the foster family and their home to his own will help to lessen the natural upsets of separation from his parents. It may also mean

that he and a brother or sister can remain together. Fostering enables the child in long term care to experience life in a setting which is accepted as the normal environment for every child who is brought up by his own parents. This goes some way towards conteracting that sense of 'being different' which is felt by most children who are brought up away from their own families.

26. In fostering there is a long continuum of types of placement ranging from the short stay through long stay, with or without rehabilitation, on to near adoption. In all stages of this continuum there may be elements which actually overlap. It is important that the practitioner is able to differentiate between these various stages and to apply the appropriate practice skills.

27. The differing fostering situations call for considerable practice skills in all those who work together to provide this form of care for a child. But whatever the reason for their need for care, all foster children have experienced separation from their parents and this fact of separation affects not only the child but also his parents and extended family, his foster family and the social worker in the agency which has taken responsibility for the child. This is the dynamic context of fostering practice and the practitioner must be sensitive to its ever-changing nature if he is to do his best for the child in care.

Chapter 2
An historical perspective

28. For a long time society has shown concern about the needs of children who are separated from their families and deprived of a normal home life. Society has also exhibited conflict and ambivalence in its attitudes towards the parents of such children and towards the children themselves when they have been seen by some as being more sinning than sinned against. The tendency towards separating the deserving from the undeserving and the delinquent from the orphan has shown itself in recurring themes throughout the history of child care. These themes are still with us today and the practitioner in fostering practice will meet them in all those concerned with her work and not least within the social work agency itself. For this reason a brief consideration of fostering from an historical perspective will identify some of the roots of our current attitudes and debates.

29. The social policy of boarding out children became formalised in the 17th century when 'poor law' children were made apprentices and when Christ's Hospital in London placed out younger children with wet nurses in the London suburbs. Later, in 1834 the Poor Law Amendment Act recognised boarding out as a means of providing a more healthy and beneficial training than that which could be provided in either a workhouse or school. Foster parents had to satisfy boarding out committees as to their moral character, religion, health, housing and economic status. They were judged to be 'good' or 'bad' by whether they boarded children as a charitable act or for pecuniary gain, and allowances payable for this work were based upon the cost of maintaining the child within the poor law institution. The quality of the supervision of boarded out children was usually very poor and its primary aim was to see that children were not neglected or ill treated.

30. These early schemes for the boarding out of children were only concerned with children who were parentless or who had been totally deserted. Parents who were unable to care for their children were considered to be feckless and might be threatened that, if they abandoned their children at the workhouse, the children would be fostered outside the Union's boundary and so would lose all contact with them. Both parents and

relatives were seen as undesirable contacts for children in the boarding out system and in 1870 a Poor Law Inspector recommended that children should not be boarded out with relatives. Parents were regarded as being worthless and public or voluntary care came to be seen as 'saving' children and as giving them a fresh start. Thus boarding out was given an air of permanency so that many fostering arrangements became quasi-adoptive.

31. The literature of the 19th century vividly illustrates both the plight of deprived children and the growing concern of philanthropists. This was the age when the voluntary organisations pioneered schemes for helping these children. Public care through the Poor Law Unions was often kindly but it was firmly based on the deterrent principles of the 1834 legislation. Foster care was seen as a charitable act, the level of payments made for children were very low and the children in receipt of care were expected to show gratitude to those who gave them help.

32. In the early 20th century boarding out was being practised by the Poor Law authorities and voluntary societies in a very modest way. However, following the first world war the Ministry of Pensions became responsible for large numbers of children of ex-servicemen and founded a progressive system of boarding out. Relatives were frequently used and no age limits were applied. A system of supervision was included and the welfare of the children was reviewed at regular intervals. In 1933 the Children and Young Persons Act enabled delinquent children to be placed in the care of the local authority and made boarding out obligatory, subject to exceptions in special cases. The number of children boarded out was then increasing, but the quality of their supervision varied and the quality of care likewise.

33. The end of the second world war saw a great deal of concern for children deprived of a normal home life. The experiences of evacuation had increased public awareness of the needs of these children, and the death of Denis O'Neil whilst in a foster home highlighted the dangers inherent in a system which failed to provide for the skilled and efficient supervision of children in public care. Subsequently two committees concerned with the care of children, Curtis in England and Clyde in Scotland, both expressed confidence in the boarding out system as being potentially the best substitute for children deprived of a normal home life.

34. As a result of these two reports, the local authority Children's Departments were set up in 1948 and Children's Officers appointed. The staff of each Children's Department included Boarding Out Officers, later called

Child Care Officers, who were obliged by law to board out all children in the care of the local authority except those whom it was considered impracticable or undesirable to place in foster homes. This obligation continued until the passing of the Children and Young Persons Act 1969.

35. One of the major results of the second world war was the opening up of society so that its problems no longer remained isolated and encapsulated in quiet corners well out of the public eye. Evacuation had evoked considerable sympathy for children deprived of a normal family life and this sympathy was extended to the many children who were found to be in residential homes and nurseries when the Children's Departments came into being in 1948. At this time there was a strong movement against institutional care and boarding out was seen to be a way of meeting the need of these children for some experience of family life. It was also seen as having the advantage of being cheaper than institutional care.

36. With the coming of the welfare state the public not only became more aware of the needs of children in public care, they also began to use Children's Departments as a service to the community as a whole. More families, who would not have dealt with the old Poor Law authorities, now began to ask for short term reception into care for their children.Public care at the time of illness or a confinement became possible and there was an increase in the number of children under five who came into short term care.

37. During the early 1950s it was realised that those young children whose parents were not able to look after them for short periods, would often receive a more appropriate form of care in a foster home rather than in a residential nursery. Such an arrangement, by providing a similar environment to the child's home, helped to reduce to a minimum the ill effects of the family crisis. This practice brought the child care services into contact with a different 'set' of foster parents and circumstances for which the service had to adopt new methods of working.

38. As a result, in the 1950s there was a rapid development in the provision of foster care with its drive to give institutional children the experience of family life and its use of foster homes for short term care. In addition, social workers in Children's Departments continued to seek further ways which would help to relieve some of the distress which children experienced when their parents were unable to care for them. Many situations were found where relatives were in a position to care for such children and in some cases were already doing so, but due to financial difficulties such

arrangements were sometimes of short duration. By recognising the relatives as foster parents and the child as boarded out, local authorities became able to give financial assistance and, in addition, they could help with any emotional problems arising in the child. This reception into care and boarding out with relatives often prevented the traumatic event of a child being removed from the caring environment of his own family.

39. The idealism which characterised the early 1950s however, was soon challenged by the large number of boarding out placements which failed. There was a growing realisation that foster care was not a simple system whereby a substitute could be provided for the parent-child relationship. There was also a growth of practice wisdom and skill which was built on an appreciation of the complex dynamics of the inter-relationships between a child, his family and his foster home. Paralleled with this, however, was the questioning of the need for the child to be in care and a rapid move towards work designed to prevent reception into care. Where reception into care was inevitable, there was a growing acknowledgement of the positive value of residential care for some children.

40. The trends in the 1960s therefore brought a slowing down in the number of children being boarded out. There was an increased awareness that to provide a substitute home was only a partial answer for children in care and, along with this, was the continuing recognition that fostering required not only a foster home but also the back-up support of the placing agency and its social work staff. The deployment of staff on preventive work, however, tended to divert some resources of skilled personnel from foster care work. Before the problems arising from these two factors could be worked out, the reorganisation of the local authority social services created yet another change in the field of foster care.

41. Despite the overall decrease in the number of children fostered, up to the 1970s the finding of foster homes was still a major part of the Children's Department's task and a great deal of time and resources were devoted to this work. In recent years the reorganisation of the work of the local authority Health, Welfare and Children's Services and the formation of large Social Services Departments have resulted in social workers being responsible for a very wide range of duties. This reorganisation involved many staff in changing their areas of work and resulted in the dispersal of the body of knowledge concerning fostering. Additional legislation also brought a further increase in the number of duties of a social worker, so that in some departments less time and a smaller commitment have been given both to the task of finding foster homes and to that of supporting

13

foster parents and foster children. Unlike the statutory agencies, the voluntary organisations have tended to increase their use of foster care and have continued to develop their professional skills in this work.

42. The swing of the pendulum in the mid-1970s may well go once more in favour of increased resources being given to foster care. Once again there is increased community interest and the establishment of organisations of foster parents has been an important development. Foster care associations are striving to improve the standards of foster care and the status of foster parents. They are asking that they should be seen as equal partners with the staff of social work agencies in their work of caring for children. More experiments are taking place in the provision of foster care for children with exceptional needs. Many agencies are actively promoting schemes which aim to develop the particular skills of some foster parents, and these schemes are attracting flexible rates of payments and allowances. It will be the task of social work agencies to encourage this growth of community involvement and to ensure that the positive use of fostering is one of the main provisions of a family orientated service.

Chapter 3
Children separated from their parents

43. All foster children have experienced separation from their parents. Some may also have been separated from others who have cared for them, either as foster parents or as residential staff in community homes, and some may have experienced many separations in a short space of time. Their tolerance, however, is not inexhaustible and too many separations in his life can adversely affect a child's capacity to develop to his full potential as an adult. All separation results in stress and children need help at this time. Whilst separation from those to whom a child is attached can interrupt his growth, this separation is sometimes unavoidable. There is, however, the paradox that in a limited number of situations where a child moves from a pathological or negative relationship to the care of a person who is able to respond in a positive personal way, he is enabled to grow emotionally following the separation where he could not develop previously. There is, however, a very long continuum from the wholly good to the totally bad relationship and it requires considerable skill to decide whether or not a child would, in the long term, benefit from such a move. It is a decision not be be taken without a full assessment of the situation and it is a decision never to be taken by one person alone.

44. A pre-requisite to all social work with children is an understanding of their physical, emotional, social and intellectual developmental needs. In this wider field of child care, there is continuous debate and research as to the ways in which needs should be met, on the effects of separation and on the results of a lack of continuity in the care of the child. It is not within the compass of this Guide to analyse the work done in this field but the bibliography includes some essential reading for child care practitioners. Two individual statements have been given in Appendix I and Appendix II and may provide helpful background material for further study.

45. In foster care part of the social work task is to help a child through the stress of separation and to provide him with substitute caregivers who can enable him to develop and grow. It may also be concerned with seeing the child through a further experience of separation if he moves back to his own family, or to a change of foster home or into a residential place-

ment. Human beings are resilient creatures, but they need someone available to whom they can relate deeply and with whom they can feel safe if they are to retain their capacity for growth in a stressful situation, and with children this needs to be the person actually looking after them. The skill of the social worker is in trying to ascertain and provide the most positive environment which meets the developmental needs of each child in care.

46. In the context of separation and foster care, one need can be isolated for special discussion. This is a child's need to make and maintain relationships. In considering the development of a child's capacity to relate to others, we have given special consideration to the early years of a child's life. There are a number of reasons for this, of which two are given at this point. Firstly, this is a sensitive period when a child's capacity to form relationships develops and separation from the person who matters most to him can be most damaging. The child is at a vulnerable stage but there are a number of ways in which good foster care and skilled social work can mitigate the effects of such damage. Secondly, older children, teenagers and adults, when separated from their families and those to whom they relate most closely, seem to experience many of the same basic emotions as the small child does in a similar situation. So an understanding of some aspects of what separation means to a young child should extend a social worker's ability to work with other age groups.

How do children form attachments?

47. A child does not automatically become emotionally attached to the person who gave birth to him, and not even to those who feed him and care for his bodily needs. An attachment forms when the adult caring for the child is personally and emotionally involved with him. Normally the person who meets the child's physical needs also cares for him in a personal way, so that these two aspects of parenthood are not separated. However, it is the intensity, quality and reciprocity of the interaction which seems to be more important than the mere duration of contact or the giving of physical care.

48. A young child's capacity to form relationships develops in his day to day interaction with a caring adult and as adult and child share their experience together, a 'fit' develops between the child's needs and the adult's responses. Both will experience the emotional bond growing stronger with time, as both become increasingly emotionally involved with each other. Although the adult concerned is frequently referred to here as

16

'mother', it could equally well be father, another relative, a foster mother, a residential child care officer or whoever has had the care of the child long enough for an emotional relationship of primary significance to form. An absent or inactive mother cannot meet this essential need for her child, and unless someone else provides this personal care, the child will not develop towards his best potential.

49. There are no set rules for parenting. In order to understand and meet the needs of her baby, a mother must be able to respond not only to his physical needs but to the way he is experiencing these inwardly. This is to say, she must have empathy with him. She will learn the meaning of his various different cries, the way he holds on to her, and later what his smiles and babbling are about. Usually a mother experiences a heightened sense of anxiety in the first few weeks after child birth and is able to use this in developing a highly sensitive response to her baby's signals. This is useful to bear in mind when considering the difficult job we ask of foster mothers in caring for babies. They are expected to adapt to the different subtle signals of children they have not carried, given birth to nor looked after from the start. It has implications for the selection of foster mothers to care for babies as it cannot be assumed that every potential foster parent has this capacity. The positive qualities of a foster home will not always match with the needs of a specific child.

50. Through a sensitive response to her baby an intense interaction builds up between a mother and her child. When both parents are directly involved in a baby's care, it is usual in the early months for a baby to be more strongly emotionally attached to one of them and his total behaviour will be geared to maintaining a degree of proximity with the person to whom he is attached and who makes him feel safe. A baby will summon his mother by particular cries, cling to her, suck her breast or her clothes; later he will keep track of his mother's movements by watching her and listening to her moving about in the next room and then hold her attention through smiles and babbling. Later still, when he can crawl or walk, he will move closer or further away from her himself, so that he is no longer solely dependent on these early instinctive powers of summoning her.

51. As well as providing him with an essential sense of security by the proximity on which his emotional development depends, a baby's first attachment figures will provide him with 'working models' of how he thinks people are likely to behave towards him in a variety of situations. The extent to which he can be confident that the person to whom he is primarily attached is available to him will determine the security of the

17

base from which he can explore, play and gradually relate to other people. The way his attachment behaviour becomes organised sets a pattern which influences the way he subsequently behaves as an adult. His expectations will be based on these early models. In view of this it follows that a very inadequate quality of care or discontinuity of care can have long term consequences for a child.

52. If development has progressed normally, a marked personal attachment will be established between a baby and his mother by the time he is around six months old. In contrast to dependent behaviour which is at its height at birth and which gradually diminishes with age, attachment behaviour is absent at birth. It develops gradually so that by the age of six months it is strongly in evidence. It is at its greatest intensity between one and three years, and continues throughout life, especially in conditions of danger and disaster when people feel a strong need to be near those to whom they are most deeply attached. In these terms it is misleading to regard every manifestation of this need in older children as being regressive.

53. The relationships between a baby and his mother figure will lay the foundations for his future development. If for some reason the child is cared for by someone who is incapable of forming a relationship with him, or if he is placed in an institution organised in such a way that no adult can become his primary attachment figure, then he will experience greater difficulty in forming relationships. In extreme cases he may have a permanently impaired capacity to relate. This of course has very important implications for social work with children and particularly with those in the first few years of life. High priority must be given to promoting work with mothers and children which is aimed at maintaining the developing attachment bond or, when this is impossible, providing an adequate quality of substitute care with the minimum disruption of experience. This is not a luxury for there can be no better investment of time in safeguarding the emotional health of a new generation.

Transferring attachments

54. Young children will form an emotional attachment to whoever is caring for them whether this is a relative, a foster mother or a residential social worker and they must do this for the sake of healthy development. Often the speed and intensity at which babies and young children relate wholeheartedly to a satisfactory caretaker can be embarrassing to social workers who may wish that it were possible to put a toddler in 'cold

18

storage' for a year until they could find him a suitable permanent home. Unfortunately the situation can never be a static one and the implications for social work practice are far reaching. The speed and intensity at which a young child transfers his primary attachment will depend on a number of factors including his age, stage of emotional development, the meaning of other relationships and the nature of the substitute care he receives. This means that the return home after a period of years or even months in care will inevitably involve a further disturbance for the child. Parents and children will need considerable help at this time. This is described in more detail in Chapter 15.

Factors hindering emotional attachments developing

55. Firstly, this can happen when the quality of care given by a child's own parent or a caretaker is inadequate. If adults have not been emotionally well cared for themselves as children they may have more than the usual amount of difficulty in understanding and responding to a child's needs and heavy demands. The same may apply to a parent or foster parent who is severely depressed. She may be unable to respond to the child with warmth, to comfort him and to identify with him intuitively. She may be inhibited in bodily contact with her baby, avoiding picking him up, cuddling him or even touching him. Foster mothers who are caring for a number of babies or who are continuously withholding themselves emotionally 'for fear of getting too attached' may experience similar difficulties. In the early weeks and months of life, inadequate interaction with another person will mean that a baby's capacity to start forming emotional attachments is delayed and impoverished. Some clues that this is happening may be seen in babies who at eight to ten weeks have a low quality or quantity of body movement. They have slow responses, serious expressions and incongruously watchful eyes. This special quality of 'looking' is almost as though the baby takes over part of his mother's role as protector. On the mother's part, there is often a noticeable absence of any kind of pleasure in mothering. Some disturbed mothers may be able to care responsively for very young babies but, because of their inability to experience themselves and their babies as separate people, they are unable to allow their child to develop an awareness of himself as a separate being.

56. The second factor which will delay or impair a child's capacity to form emotional attachments is the situation where no one person has the responsibility for his emotional care. A child who loses contact with the adult to whom he is attached will try to find a substitute. If he cannot find a person with whom he can relate, he may then turn away from people

and live in a world of his own. The longer he remains in this state the more difficult it will be for him to turn to people for comfort and for him to form new relationships in the future. He will probably submit to being moved from place to place without further protest, having lost touch with his feelings of anxiety and loss. If a child has to be moved, the aim should be to provide a substitute caregiver in such a way as to minimise the disruption to his previous experience. Surroundings, routines, food and handling which are as familiar as possible, will all help to reduce his anxiety when provided in the context of personal substitute care. As far as possible, this care should be given by one person who is sensitive in the response to his cues and communications.

57. A third factor which will hinder the development of emotional attachments is that of frequent moves from one person to another, so that the child experiences many changes of care. Such disruption in the continuity of care has different consequences for different ages, but the net effect may be to undermine the quality of future attachments. When this happens, then a child's capacity to relate to others may be adversely affected so that he becomes less trusting, increasingly shallow and lacking in discrimination.

Why do children react in different ways to separation?

58. Whatever the age of a child, separation from the person to whom he has the strongest personal attachment may in itself be distressing. No two children will react to their experiences in the same way and each situation is unique. For example, some children will have reached a developmental stage where they are able to retain their attachment to an absent adult. The extent to which separation is accompanied by a sense of loss depends on the age of the child, his stage of development and in particular whether he is able to hold an inner memory and attachment to an absent person who then needs to be mourned. Differences in temperament will also affect his response. If the child's physical needs are not being satisfied with the expected degree of warmth and sensitivity, this too will be distressing and add to his anxiety.

59. But anxiety may also be due to subjective, internal fears. For instance, he may feel that he has destroyed his mother or is being punished by her. This is more easily understood when the child has been subject to threats from his mother or foster mother—'If you don't behave I'll send you away' or 'You'll be the death of me'. But, whether because these threats are more widespread than is realised or for other reasons, these fears and

the accompanying sense of rejection are almost universal, even though the child knows at a rational level that, for instance, his mother has gone to hospital to have another baby.

60. In the first few months of life, separation, unless carefully handled, may leave a baby disorientated, but without this state being obvious to the casual observer. An older child may have similar experiences of disorientation but to this will be added the conscious sense of having lost the most important person in his life and an instinctive sense of fear with strangers. His reactions to loss are likely to be more obvious, and will be very distressing to those providing substitute care, to social workers and, of course, to visiting parents. He may, for instance, start wetting or soiling after a period of control. A child will need to mourn his loss and if he is not supported at the time he may develop a mistrust in himself and other people, provoking them to reject him, so that his early experience of rejection becomes further confirmed.

61. The length of time before parental absence is experienced by children as permanent and the degree to which it is accompanied by feelings of helplessness and profound deprivation, depends on a number of factors. Firstly his age; an infant or toddler can only be separated from his mother for a very short period before he sees this as a permanent breach of continuity of care. The same period of time would, however, have no significance for a school-age child who can hold on to memories of his parents for much longer and will gradually mourn their loss. Secondly, it will depend on his capacity to cope with the anxiety aroused by breaches of coninuity of care. If he has 'lost' his mother in the past he will fear that it may happen again, and his capacity to manage his anxiety will be diminished. Thirdly, it will depend on the immediate factors in the situation which either support or destroy his continuity of experience. If in the absence of his mother he is being cared for by someone who is already familiar to him and to his mother, and if he is in a place that he first explored with his mother, then he will have much greater confidence in her return. His continuity of experience will be supported by the presence of his brothers and sisters. Furthermore, if care is taken to provide him with familiar food, familiar routines and with his own clothes and possessions; if he is not expected to behave in ways that were not asked of him at home, for example to use a pot for the first time or to ask for things by names when he is still using non-verbal means of communication; these factors will lessen his anxiety. They are particularly crucial with babies and toddlers but the principle is still remarkably important with much older children. With young children in particular this puts heavy

demands on the social worker's attention to detail, as well as on the foster parent's sensitivity to a child's unique pattern of communication.

62. All these factors will have a bearing on how much distress a child will experience during separation, how much upset behaviour he shows on his return home, and what are the long term effects of his separation. For example, an emotionally healthy toddler who has not previously been separated from his mother, is not usually unduly distressed by a brief separation which is carefully managed and will show little evidence of emotional disturbance when he returns home. If he protests loudly and angrily it may serve to draw attention to some factor in the situation which could be modified to lessen his distress. This situation needs to be distinguished from that of a baby or older child who is already emotionally deprived, and shows no obvious sign of disturbance during separation, but may later show evidence of mistrust of people. He may appear superficially to settle well with a foster family or with his parents when back at home. However, once he begins to feel safe with them he may start to test out the safety and permanence of his new home by behaviour which would provoke rejection—this may go on for years. Sometimes he may return for a time to the babyish behaviour and demands appropriate to the age when he experienced separation. If this can be accepted and understood, then he may eventually free himself to enter into more mature relationships, involving concern for others.

63. The discussion in this chapter has emphasised the child's need to form attachments. It has also considered the stress experienced by children separated from those to whom they are attached. This stress is inevitable and unless recognised the adults involved cannot begin to help the child. But to acknowledge that a child is experiencing stress is a painful experience for adults and our culture tends to encourage a philosophy of the stiff upper lip. Failure to support a child in a time of stress can lead to distress, for distress occurs when stress is unrecognised, rejected, denied or mishandled. Awareness of the stress factors in separation therefore is a vital necessity for all those engaged in foster care. Such awareness can promote a positive basis for understanding the needs of the individual child, and it should underpin all work with children when they are experiencing separation from the adults who have been fulfilling a parental role.

Chapter 4
Parents separated from their children

64. In focusing on the needs of children and in giving priority to measures designed to prevent family breakdown, relatively little attention has so far been paid to the effect on parents when they are separated from their children. All parents of children in care have experienced this separation and an understanding of the individual parent's perception and experience is a prerequisite to social work practice in this field. Parenting is a dynamic process. Whilst parents may have a consistent overall pattern of relationship with their children, the actual relationship with each child in the family will be both ever-changing and individual. The effect of separation, therefore, will vary in its nature and intensity in relation to each child in the family. Any plan for the care of a child must take into account this changing relationship, whether his stay is for a short or long period of time.

65. In may ways the parents' view of themselves as parents predetermines their performance in the parental role. Society may confirm this self-image and make it difficult for change to take place. How then do adults come to perceive themselves as parents and in what ways is this parental self-image confirmed by others? Whilst the fact of physically becoming a parent is significant in itself, the moment of birth does not automatically confer a capacity for good parenting. Attachments and the capacity to form them are a developmental necessity, but it cannot be assumed that a primary attachment between parent and child will invariably take place. Most children received into care will feel a sense of loss, the extent of this varying with their previous experiences. It does not necessarily follow, however, that their parents will share the intensity of this experience. For many parents, feelings of loss, guilt and personal failure will be overwhelming; for others a sense of release will predominate and with it the urgency to retreat from the child both physically and psychologically. What is relevant to practice is the parents' unique response in relation to an individual child, especially where there are several children in the family. Neither child nor parent is a mere adjunct to the world of the other. Each will interact with his immediate environment on the basis of his own innate characteristics and propensity for growth; the child in response to his changing developmental needs, the parent according to his personal and social needs.

23

66. In this chapter the focus is on the parents' experience of separation and the conflicts which arise when, to the parents, their child becomes 'someone else's child'. This is not to imply that under no circumstances should parents and children be separated. For a number of children separation is unavoidable and for some it may prove positively helpful. For others it is seriously damaging. What needs to be kept in mind is that, unless they consistently share their experiences, it becomes increasingly difficult for parents and children to relate to each other in a realistic way.

Assuming the parental role

67. The process of assuming the parental role has particular relevance in considering the parent separated from the child and the appropriate focus of the social work help which should be made available to parents. Establishing yourself as a parent and finding that you are able to meet your child's needs with a reasonable degree of competence takes time. This process may be said to take place in four main ways. Firstly, when the adult does those things which parents do, such as providing food and shelter. Secondly, when the child responds to the adult as a parent. Thirdly, when the adult and child interact as parent and child. Fourthly, when other people reinforce the parental self-image by treating the adult socially as parent of the child. When all four concur and persist, then the adult can be said effectively to have assumed the parental role. This process is common to all parent-child relationships, irrespective of whether or not the adult concerned is a biological parent. In this context the term 'parent' applies to father or substitute father as well as mother or substitute mother. In normal family circumstances fathers have a close and important relationship even with their young children and at all ages their role, though often different from that of the mother, is still significant. The nature of their relationship with the mother, in addition, has an important effect on the child.

What does society expect of parents?

68. The basic child rearing unit in our society is that of the nuclear family: father, mother and child. The term one parent family illustrates our acceptance of a variation in this unit but also indicates that it is not wholly acceptable as a norm. Society makes exacting demands of adults who beget children, reinforcing its assumption by law and social policy that parents should assume full responsibility for the care of their children. Stigma attaches, therefore, to the parent who does not fulfil society's expectations: the parent of a child in public care may be seen as a 'poor' or 'failed'

parent. This disapproval in turn mobilises defences, often in a self-defeating or frustrating manner. It is important that social workers recognise that parents may be vulnerable in this respect.

Why are parents unable to care for their children?

69. The parents of children in care are parents with problems. Many, if not most, live in materially deprived circumstances and poverty itself can be a primary reason for care. It may not be the main problem but, when it is experienced by those who are already subjected to other stresses, it can be the catalyst in creating a family breakdown. Many parents have serious marital and personal problems and may themselves as children have been deprived of secure and loving relationships. A number of children in care have been born out of wedlock and/or have been brought up in one parent households. At the time the child comes into care, the single parent may not have a stable relationship with the child's mother or father and is likely to be isolated within the community, with only very fragile support from transitory or casual acquaintances. In some cases the agency is taking over the child's care at a time of crisis or emergency in an otherwise self supporting family. In others reception into care stems from an extremely disturbed family situation. There are many gradations in between, and the possibility of resuming or establishing normal family functioning depends on the severity of the problem and the quality of help provided by the agency.

Filial deprivation

70. The concept of maternal deprivation is now generally accepted, not only by professional workers, but also to a large extent, by the general public. The concept of filial deprivation, however, has only recently begun to gain credence and recognition. The term is used to describe and explain the separation experiences and responses of parents when separated from their children. It indicates that when this occurs, parents experience anxiety, depression and detachment comparable to that experienced by the children. These responses may occur spontaneously in the parent as a normal defence against the pain of separation. Such defences can impair and thwart their attempts at a successful resumption of the parental role. Depending on circumstances, reception into care may result in the parent experiencing a sense of acute loss, although this may alternate with feelings of relief. The parent's anxiety and concern to act positively on the child's behalf will be most intense when separation is either imminent or has just occurred. But within a very short time anxiety and the very real opportunity

if affords for positive social work intervention will give way to depression, soon to be counter-acted and rationalised by detachment. Once detachment establishes itself, the parents may begin to reorganise their lives so that they actively exclude the child or reduce the number of practicable opportunities for including the child in their new life style. They may, for example, take up shift work, change their employment, set up house with a partner who 'does not want the child', or the mother may become pregnant and so replace the child in care. It is for this reason that social workers often find it hard to re-involve the parents of children in long term care.

71. The concept of filial deprivation affords many practical applications to social work practice with regard to the parents of children in care. It does not seek to minimise the problem of assessing a person's capacity to be a parent to his or her child. It does however go some way in enabling social workers to understand the dynamics of the separation experience, in so far as they affect and define the scope of social work with the parents of children in care. As a practice concept it stresses the importance of working intensively with parents about to be or very recently separated from their children. Concentration of social work services at this point is a realistic way of promoting parental responsibility, and of ensuring the involvement of parents in meeting the needs of children whose normal development may be thwarted or seriously impaired by reception into care.

Sharing parental responsibilities

72. Sharing parental roles and responsibilities is a delicate, demanding operation, even in the best and happiest of families. Sharing the parenting of a child with a public agency is complex and demanding in the extreme. It requires those skills and personal reserves and resources that most elude parents who are in trouble, and it is not surprising therefore if they should shy away from such an enterprise. The parent will be obliged to share some aspects of his parental duties and responsibilities, whether the child comes into care as a result of a voluntary agreement between the parent and the agency, or whether he comes into care involuntarily as the consequence of a decision by a legal institution such as a court or children's panel.

73. The parents' part in this sharing will include understanding and acting within the constraints of their legal situation; being assessed for maintenance; reorganising their finances; understanding agency arrangements for visiting their child and accepting the unfamiliar world of case conferences or the fact that others may perceive their child's needs differently

26

from themselves. They will be asked for information which they may not at the time remember and for documents which they may not be able to find. All this comes at a time when the stress of separation is added to the stress of the basic causes for the child coming into care. Some parents at this time worry unduly that they may 'lose' their children if they are too vocal in questioning arrangements made for the child. Other parents, unable or unwilling to resume their parental role and to make a home, fear that social workers will compel them to discharge their children from care. The majority of parents, however serious their problems and curtailed their capacities, expect to do whatever they can for the child. They wish to meet prospective caretakers, whether residential staff or foster parents. Most parents are painfully aware that if their child is looked after by someone else, that person may receive the child's affection and in time his feelings of attachment and loyalty. Parents may feel powerless to contribute much to the child's welfare, yet at the same time they are expected to supply considerable information about the child, about themselves and their circumstances. As clients they are very much in need of support and help.

74. Attitudes to care will be complicated and sometimes influenced by the parents' role handicap. How do you behave socially and as a parent when someone else is looking after your child? In helping families who are unable to meet the needs of their children, it is important to establish what the individual parent(s) and family are experiencing as a result of the child being away from home. What do they experience as difficult and painful? What are their fears and expectations? How do they explain the child's absence from home to the child, themselves, their neighbours and their friends?

Implications of fostering

75. When a foster care placement has been chosen for their child, parents then have to understand the emotional and legal implications of fostering at the particular stage of their child's development. In the case of infants and pre-school age children parents may soon find themselves displaced by the substitute parents. However good the parents' understanding of the effects of separation, any awareness that they are being displaced in the child's affections by foster parents will arouse feelings of guilt, anxiety and hostility. Reaction to these feelings may well result in the defences of 'fight' or 'flight'. Feelings of failure and lack of personal worth tend to be compounded at this time. Many parents hitherto actively involved with their child may lapse into apathy or withdraw almost unnoticed from his

27

life. Others may make unrealistic demands on the child for proof of affection, criticising the foster parents and being seen as attempting to 'sabotage' the placement, so necessitating considerable support to all concerned.

76. For parents whose own childhoods were emotionally deprived, the loss of their child is likely to reactivate and enhance feelings of deprivation. They may be unable to see the child as other than an extension of themselves; and the child, looked after by someone else, may become an object of envy. They may then vie with their children for the foster parents' concern and attention. Such behaviour can be exceedingly destructive with the parents actively though unwittingly contributing to the breakdown of the placement. They can leave disruption in the wake of their visits to the foster home.

Implications of prolonged separation

77. In planning her work with the parents of children who are likely to remain in long term care, the social worker has to assess the extent to which they are capable of either establishing or maintaining their parental role. Such an assessment is fundamental to decisions about the future of the children involved: whether they should ultimately be rehabilitated with their parents, whether they should remain in their foster home but maintain links with their parents, whether such links are impossible to establish or maintain or whether, in extreme cases, links with parents should be severed. Parents separated from their children very early in the children's lives will have had little opportunity to build up the shared experience and learned competence that are so necessary for establishing the parental role; these are also the parents most likely to leave their children in care. Where parents have established their role but later relinquish or hand over the day to day care of their children for prolonged periods of time, they may become less and less parents both in their own eyes and in the eyes of their children.

78. When it is proposed that the child shall return home, parents need special help in the preparatory period. This help will be geared to meeting both practical and emotional needs. No child should remain separated from his family solely on the grounds of material hardship, and agencies have a responsibility for ensuring that all available resources are used to meet the needs of such families. For example, local authorities are empowered to assist parents, in cash or kind, in order to facilitate the discharge of a child from care. When parents and children have been

separated for a considerable length of time both will inevitably encounter stresses and problems. Neither parent nor child will be the same after, as before, separation each having had experiences the other has not shared. The process of rehabilitation is a gradual one and parents may need considerable help in understanding their children's behaviour, their changed standards and different expectations. Both parents and children are likely to experience considerable conflict and be subject to strong feelings of ambivalence about each other.

79. When very early separation has precluded the building up of experience and competence in the parental role, this, coupled with prolonged separation militates strongly against a smooth resumption of the child's care. In these circumstances the social worker has a difficult task. She cannot undo the fact of the earlier separation nor can she create a magic attachment between child and parent. But she may be able to help the parent and child to work through some of their problems at this time and can at least help them to acknowledge some of their mixed feelings about each other. A supportive social work service may make all the difference between success and failure.

80. In many situations where rehabilitation is not possible, parents continue to be important to their children as links with their origins and part of their self-identity; for this reason alone maintaining some degree of contact between parent and child is likely to be beneficial. In some cases, however, the parents' capacities for maintaining contact are extremely limited or even non-existent and all efforts to engage their positive involvement will remain fruitless.

81. There will always be a small but taxing number of parents who are so disturbed that contact with their children is positively harmful. Some of these parents can be helped to withdraw from their children's lives. Others will not accept this situation and considerable conflict can occur; the most that social work help may sometimes be expected to achieve is to ensure that these parents are fully aware of their legal rights. In these, as in other situations the agency's main focus of work must remain on its primary responsibility for the child's long term welfare.

Chapter 5
On being a foster parent

82. 'Foster parents' and 'fostering' are terms which are not self-explanatory and some of the misunderstandings between social workers, foster parents and the general public arise because people are talking about totally different situations whilst calling them by the same name. Any definition of the role of foster parents is dependent upon the permutations of many variable factors—the motivations and situations of the foster parents, the needs and circumstances of the children and their families, current social work policy and practice, and the contemporary perception by society of accepted standards. Each group which shares the care of a child will be unique in its operation and in its expectations of the role of each participant.

83. This chapter considers what it is like to experience life as a foster parent and is based on comments made by individual foster parents to the Working Party.

84. Foster families as representatives of society will inevitably reflect a cross section of the feelings of society towards both children in care and towards their parents. As human beings, foster parents will have their own individual reactions to the stresses of separation and grief, to anti-social behaviour and to cultural mores which are alien to their own. The entry of a foster child into their home will call for many readjustments both in their social life and in the internal network of relationships within the family.

85. Their expectations on becoming foster families will vary from family to family also between individuals, both adult and child, within the family. Expectations do not always match with experience. Foster parents have commented:

'From our experience no amount of talking can ever really prepare you for the problems involved in fostering. We were warned that our two girls were problem children, but the only real problem is that they are not ordinary problems. Fostering is very hard work and maybe if I had known of the problems before we started I might not have done it.

30

However, it can be very rewarding too. When we think back to how they were and then see how they are now, the improvement is fantastic, so we really feel we are doing something worthwhile and we do hope that one day they will feel that they can trust us.'

'Fostering is far better than we expected. It is very rewarding because the children seem to appreciate everything you do for them. You can see the difference a little love and care makes to their personalities. In a nursery they all seem to act in the same way but when they get into a family home, their own personality shines through. You can see the results for a little effort.'

'Do not expect too much. Learn to give. In their teens they seem to reject you and resent you. But when fully mature, they do fulfil all you expected. But you must wait for them to show it first. My foster-daughter at twenty five has just this last two years started to send Mother's Day flowers.'

'After the initial moment of panic it was almost all with a couple of exceptions truly enjoyable. Children are very adaptable once they have accepted their new situation. As far as emergency fostering is concerned, it is very tiring. Not so much physically as emotionally.'

'Our expectations of fostering were and are to give love, security and understanding to a child when it needs them at a time which could be very confusing for it, and to see a speedy and happy reunion with its parents. Unfortunately we have been disillusioned more than once. We feel that a lot of the children we have had should never have been in care in the first place, this is no fault of the local authority but of the system. Irresponsible parents take advantage of the system, then after a couple of weeks decide they want the children back. By then the damage could already have been done. We feel proud and happy to be able to see a child rejoin its family, knowing that perhaps we have helped the child by keeping it in a family environment, also helping to maintain its emotional, mental and physical development. Our only reservation is that sometimes the child is being returned to the same environment which originally ended in the child being put into care. Then you think how long until next time?'

'We expected to be heart-broken when it came for the children to go home. However, although the first time was very hard it was not as bad as we thought it would be. We enjoyed every experience and although we hated parting from them, we accepted the situation for what it was— to give a temporary home to a child in need.'

'Fostering is very like parenthood—you have little conception of just what is involved before you start—and it is just as well because if you really knew what you were letting yourself in for you would run a mile. Nevertheless I feel fostering is probably one of the most enriching jobs possible and I think that all my children have gained by sharing their home and their parents with others.'

86. The ambivalence of the general public towards fostering is demonstrated by foster parents' comments on the attitudes of people outside the family:

'To anyone wanting to find out more about their acquaintances and neighbours, I would suggest they take up fostering. During bad weather people I have hardly spoken to have knocked and offered to take a child to school. Other people have sorted out toys, books and clothes for various children. One neighbour said she thought fostering was not very nice. She did not like the thought of children 'like that' living here.'

'People tend to think you are marvellous or peculiar without any thoughts of helping in any way or of offering to do fostering themselves. They tend to think that if the foster children affect ones own children at all, they should go i.e. the foster children come last.'

'. . . Either sickly sentiment or downright antagonism. My mother disapproves of our fostering and considers that we have ruined our own children's lives by making them mix with 'those terrible girls'. People blame everything on to the fact that we foster.'

'Living in largely a middle class area, without any coloured children and city children's problems, also being the only foster mother in the village, one can envisage the problems that city children, regardless of colour or creed, can create. City children seem to create problems with neighbouring children by their destructiveness etc. This does not endear them to the parents in the village. Where the child has reasonable behaviour they mix in very well. We found all our long-term children did rather well as they came younger and grew up as part of the family.'

'Most friends admire the job I do but admit they could not do it themselves. Few can see beyond the emotional upheaval involved in returning a child to its natural parents. My in-laws were worried about the effect it would have on our children. Friends and neighbours are a great help.'

'On the whole the people we have met have been sympathetic—I think some have queried our sanity—some have been given to expressing admiration, some even envious. Schools are very tolerant of our

32

changing population and all the foster children have been members of brownies, scouts, boys brigade, guides, church or chapel and as far as the village is concerned, they belong.'

'My experience was generally favourable with friends regarding themselves as foster aunts and uncles and treating children as they would my own. Outsiders however tended sometimes to display pitying attitudes and undue sentimentality. This is a matter of more public education.'

'Attitudes vary considerably. On the whole I would suggest people regard a foster mother as a crank—something anyone could do if they wanted. Very seldom the praise which I would consider welcome—simply that one was doing a job of work which is extremely responsible and worthwhile. So many people never realise that it is in fact a task like nursing, teaching or social work.'

87. One of the most difficult tasks of a foster parent is sharing the care of a child with his own family. In considering parents separated from their children, we have already commented on their problems and reactions. But there is another side to these reactions and foster parents too have a difficult role to play. However understanding they may be of the child's need for his parents and the parents' need for their child, parental visiting to the foster home can be a trying and even stressful experience needing adequate support from the social worker. In some situations foster parents can themselves support parents in facing their problems. In foster parents' own words:

'This can be one of the most difficult parts of fostering. There can be two extremes of one mother never visiting, the other visiting every day. I think foster parents could be helped with some sort of training in dealing with natural parents. We have to welcome into our homes all sorts of people who have varying degrees of problems. All of these can be very hard for a layman to cope with.'

'Amicable all round contact can help the child enormously. Natural parents can be irritating but they are very important and must be encouraged to visit the child. A temporary upset child after his parents have gone is preferred to a child who might feel abandoned.'

'I think the two lots of parents should meet because it helps the foster parent understand the things the children are worried about. The real parents can be very disturbing and upsetting to the children when they see them.'

33

'Whenever we have had contact with the natural parents it has been a constant source of irritation. The natural parents are on the defensive when they are unable to care for their own children. They resent the foster parents who are able to. As foster parents we are apt to judge the natural parents and I think it is virtually impossible to form a relationship. I have found the most satisfactory way of dealing with this is for the natural parents to hand over the children personally to us. Thereafter I find it more satisfactory if the social worker takes the child to visit its parents.'

'I welcome the natural parents but it places a huge strain on the foster parents when the child's parents visit and stay for long periods of time and expect to be given meals. I always feel that it is in fact the parents that need my guidance just as much as their children.'

'Do social workers realise what it is like to have a child's mother visit for several hours at week-ends when she too probably needs mothering; and what it is like to hand over a screaming child for a week-end visit and then mop up the emotional disturbance on return? We feel we need help that we never get.'

'The more the natural parents are encouraged by the foster parents to visit the child and feel welcome at any time the better. But natural parents should realise they have not the right to just come and go as they please but should make arrangements which are mutually acceptable. Foster parents must guard against any natural antagonism towards natural parents as this often has a deep effect on the child.'

'We have had our long-term foster-boy, now fourteen years old, since he was three. His natural parents had no contact with him until about two and a half years ago. Since then we have had to call in child guidance experts to sort him out. We feel they should have kept in touch from a very early age or not at all.'

'Our opinion is that we are fostering to help the family, but we are fostering the child, not the parents, so our only contact with the parents is confined to their visiting the children. It can be upsetting to the children if the parents are always popping in and out. We try to keep it to pre-arranged times, then we can make sure we are in. Sometimes parents pour their troubles out to us and we are prepared to listen, but if they need help we try to get them in touch with the Council. We do not encourage any visits once the child has left our care as we feel it is better for children and parents to get things going again without living in the past.'

34

'We believe it is far better to keep children in contact with their parents whenever possible, with reservations in certain extreme cases. We have encouraged our youngsters in care not to neglect their natural parents while encouraging parents to contact their children. Where the children are likely to return home it is very necessary to have regular parental contact. The hardest task is to foster children where parents' standards are very different from those of your household or even neighbourhood. Particularly if their behaviour is violent and unreasonable. It is equally difficult to take the foster child to visit his family home if you are obliged to take the rest of your children with you. A centre where natural parents could meet their children on neutral grounds in these extreme cases would help. The worst experience of long-term care is where the parents are clearly content for you to bring up their child and then in early teens begin a campaign to capture the child's affection and overall loyalty.'

'If possible, contact should definitely be made with the child's natural parents. I think that if the parents can see the home his child is in and have an idea that he is being looked after properly, then a load is surely lifted from the parent's mind.'

'Foster parents have an important part to play in the return of children to their natural families. A good supportive relationship must be encouraged with the foster mother if possible being a crutch to the natural mother for the first month after the return of the child. Too often a child goes home and the foster family hear no more. I think the foster family should be encouraged to act as real support to the natural family—taking the child back at week-ends to ease the pressure, etc. We must work as a team—foster parents, natural parents, and social workers for the sake of the children.'

88. The foster parent is the full-time member of this caring team and there is no doubt that may would prefer the social workers to take a more active role in promoting a professional relationship between the agency and the foster home. Their contact should be not only in relation to the child but also as a support to the foster home. Again in the words of the foster parents:

'Ideally this should be a partnership with everyone working for the benefit of the child. I think foster parents should be included more in decisions affecting the children in their care. If they have had the child for some time they know that child better than the social worker. If foster parents are included in case conferences they are in a better position to co-operate with the social worker in carrying out the plans made for the child.'

'There should be a friendship between foster parent and social worker, keeping each other informed on health and welfare of the child, but not for social workers to interfere and pry into family life. The social worker should be always in the background as someone to rely on for help and guidance when needed.'

'I find that the social workers vary a great deal but most do not call as often as they say they will. They seem to think that as all foster homes are vetted before approval that is good enough for them. How often I have wished one would call to discuss a case and how often I have telephoned the office only to find that the social worker in charge of that particular case is out and that no-one else knows anything about it.'

'We need more contact in the early days with social departments and workers. More confidence must be given to the new foster parent and the knowledge that the Department is there to help with little things as well as big problems.'

89. The reorganisation of the local authority social services in 1971 has highlighted the difficulties of the social worker in fulfilling her role in the caring group. Unfortunately this has come about due to the inability of field staff to meet all the calls on their time. The situation is recognised by the foster parents, but it is one which shifts the balance of responsibility for care so that it often rests too heavily on the foster family. As social services departments become established, the question of specialisation for their social work staff is increasingly a matter for debate. Here is the situation when viewed from the perspective of the foster parents:

'I have always got on extremely well with my social worker. Opinions and ideas even of social workers differ. I do not like personal prejudice. If foster parents were suitable then they should be used by all social workers. We have not had any complaints regarding the old Children's Department when a children's officer was exactly that, but since it became social services and they became social workers, we are all dissatisfied. Social workers have far too much to do trying to visit problem homes, the aged, the handicapped, etc. What may seem a trivial matter to social workers can be a big problem with the foster parent.'

'Relationships have improved. When we first became foster parents (sixteen years ago) we were made to feel that the Department was doing us a favour. However social workers now are grateful if one of their children gets a decent home and their visits are enjoyed by parents and children.'

'Relationships could, I think, be greatly improved upon. I think that the social workers who visit regularly the homes where foster children are placed, should take more notice of what the foster parents are telling them about the children and not adopt the attitude—we'll wait and see what happens. It took my husband and I all of eighteen months before someone at the Council sat up and took notice of what we were telling them about one of our foster children.'

'In all cases but one we have had a very good relationship with the social workers who have brought children into our care. Our local social services department does try to arrange informal meetings and discussions between foster parents and social workers but it is difficult to find evenings when many can attend. On the odd occasions when we have been able to attend these meetings we have found it useful to meet the social workers in a different atmosphere to the one in which we normally meet them. It has also been valuable to find that other foster parents have problems exactly like our own.'

'We had four different social workers during a nine month fostering of a little girl. Both she and we found this difficult as each social worker had different ideas. The fostering should be apart from other social services and have social workers who deal with nothing else but fostering and adoption.'

'I have found I do not get on so well since the child care officer changed to the Joint Social Services Department. Some of the workers were trained for other than children's work and do not know too much about the Children's Department. They also seem too busy and when the children are settled in we do not see them very often.'

'We look forward to social workers' visits but have quite often felt that they were too hurried and we could not really burden them with our problems or ask their advice, although they have been pleasant and friendly. There is somehow the feeling that clients need the attention that foster parents know it all, which is not the case.'

'A social worker should be able to be regarded as a friend of the family. You need a social worker who at times will just sit and listen to your problems and then suggest some line of action that you can discuss together. The lack of communication between foster parents and the Social Work Department is, I think, terrible.'

'The main problem seems to be lack of contact both in frequency of visits and in personal communication. We would suggest regular case studies in small groups with social workers and foster parents since communication with a social worker on a home visit is difficult as he comes basically to visit the child. We feel, as experienced parents, we can help and advise the social workers on treatment of particular children. There is also a lack of communication through the different departments of the local authority, e.g. education department and social services department. A handbook supplied to each family, by the social services department, containing information on allowances, responsibilities, medical welfare, position of the foster parent in law and in relation to the social services department, could ease much misunderstanding and help the social worker in his job.'

'Foster parent and social workers should feel equal. They work together, one by placing the child, the other by caring. Ideally foster parents should have their own social worker, apart from the social worker connected with the children, who is interested in their needs, to reassure and guide them.'

'The relationship between foster parents and social workers and their departments has deteriorated since the 'Seebohm' set-up. When you have been fostering for a number of years your experience is often greater than the social worker's. As foster parents we regard ourselves as equal in the triangle social worker-child-foster parent. Unfortunately very few social workers accept this and you, as foster parents, are expected to show respect to the social worker, just because they are social workers. The Social Services Department are overworked and this means that unless there is a crisis you never hear from them. This is very destructive to the foster children as they realise that the only way to receive attention is to be naughty. As one child of fourteen told me— it doesn't pay to be good, they just are not interested in you then.'

90. The latter chapters of this book will formulate a guide to practice in the field of foster care. But the comments of foster parents illustrate the fact that there is far more to caring than the actual physical care of the child. In responding to the need for care, a foster family becomes involved in a highly complex task. This, in its turn, demands considerable skills from its practitioners.

Chapter 6
Caring for children from different cultures

91. In considering the wider circle of those who share in the care of a child, reference was made to those who might help to preserve the cultural identity of a child. Children placed with their relatives are able to live within the broad cultural patterns of their own nuclear family. Children placed outside their own families always have to adapt to the differences related to, firstly, the social behaviour of the foster home and, secondly, to the social environment of that home. In the search for foster homes, children have often been placed in an alien setting. They have had to adapt to a twin culture, that of their foster home and that of their parental home, and whilst these experiences can be enriching, they can also cause conflict, a confusion of identity and feelings of insecurity which can follow a child into adult life.

92. The wartime experience of town children evacuated to the country alerted the community to the problems which such a move can create. Subsequently, in the post war era, there has been a movement towards ensuring that children who have to be separated from their families are placed in substitute homes which match as nearly as possible with their home of origin. This matching process is still an ideal which has not been fully formulated nor assessed. However there is agreement that if a child has to tolerate the stress of an unpreventable separation he should not also be subjected to the unnecessary stress of adaptation to a sub-culture which is alien to his own or to a setting in which negative attitudes exist. This is particularly relevant if there are feelings of hostility or discrimination within the host community.

93. There are however many children in care whose families are recent immigrants to Britain, and in this situation not only the child but also the parents are living through a period of adaptation and change. Their extended families are unlikely to be in this country and, when separated from his family, a child may also have to experience the stress of separation from the culture of his ethnic group.

94. Social care agencies, therefore, should consider the proposition that the more recent the arrival of an ethnic group, the more need there is to

look to the group itself as a participant in providing for the overall care of its children who, for one reason or another, are inevitably separated from their families. This is an added dimension to caring, for if the day to day care of a child has to be given by foster families from a different culture or even sub-culture, then additional living experiences must also be arranged. An example of this might be facilitating social contact with members of the child's own ethnic group.

95. Two of the largest and most recent ethnic minority groups to come to Britain have been the Asian and West Indian communities and this chapter will consider some aspects of their situations. Its wider implications however may also apply to other immigrants from distant lands, to those who have re-settled within the smaller world of the British Isles and to the significant minority of black and mixed race people born in the United Kingdom.

96. In the present century several immigrant groups have settled in this country. They have come from vastly differing cultural backgrounds and these are reflected in their family patterns and ways of adapting to life in Britain. One feature of life in Britain is the multiplicity of cultural and sub-cultural organisations which co-exist within the overall cultural structure; examples of these are the Scottish, Irish and Welsh organisations which exist in major conurbations in England. All seek to promote the ethnic identities of their membership.

97. Some ethnic groups establish distinct communities in this country which are insular and supportive, while still playing an essential part in the support of the family and community in the home country. The Asian immigrants form such a group. Their pattern of migration has differed from that of other immigrant groups. For example married men have arrived with their adolescent sons, joining up with relatives to form the basis of a village community in Britain. Later, as changes in immigration legislation have forced them to settle, they have started to send for their wives and children to join them in this country. Today the majority of Indian immigrants have their wives and children with them in Great Britain, whilst in the Pakistani and Bangladeshi communities many wives are still in their own countries. Asian wives and children joining their husbands in Great Britain, immediately become part of a community group which provides support in everyday matters and serves as a protection from 'premature' contact with the host society and culture.

98. It is this cohesiveness, characteristic of the Asian community as well as some other ethnic groups, which accounts for the small proportion of

their young children being in need of substitute care. Those who come into care appear to do so on a short term basis because of mother's illness, or because of her temporary absence from home for family reasons. It is these children who may now be placed in foster homes; many of which will be in the host community. But as the families become more established the need for care may change.

99. The Community Relations Commission has commented:—

There are already small indications of a changing situation. Change is likely to come from two angles: by the threat to the mother's health and confidence arising from her loneliness and isolation; and secondly, by the influence of English society, which operates most strongly on the children. There are increasing signs of a readiness to look outside the family for support, particularly in situations of marital strife. It is however, particularly hard for an Asian woman to separate from her husband and to cope adequately on her own in caring for her family. Not least of the difficulties is that of removing herself and the children from the husband's home through lack of alternative accommodation. An increase in the number of children of broken Asian marriages in care can be foreseen.

The children of Asian immigrants who grow up in England to some extent live in separate worlds, one at home and one at school. There is growing concern over the Asian generation gap, particularly in such respects as adolescents' claiming freedom to retain their wages and mix socially. In future, therefore, there may be a rise in the incidence of children of Asian descent being in long term care of local authorities. Such children will share to some extent in the position of mixed race children, with regard to a duality of culture, and problems of relating differing values in a coherent identity.

It is not difficult to appreciate difficulties that can arise when an Asian child is fostered in an English home. The language, the food, the organisation and the whole atmosphere of the home will be alien and confusing to him, even those aspects of the foster home which can be said to be 'better' than his own home will be a cause of distress, for example, even the practice of insisting that a child should have his own room could be a cause of further anxiety in the Asian community, as it is unusual for an Asian child to have his own bedroom and be left to sleep alone. We would strongly recommend in short term fostering cases that Asian children are only fostered in homes which closely approximate to their natural homes; undoubtedly, a fair amount of informal and unofficial fostering takes place among Asian families as part of community self help, but each local authority could take steps immediately to draw up a list of potential Asian foster homes, covering Hindu, Sikh and Moslem households of the different language groups, so that in time of need suitable foster parents can be provided for Asian families in crisis.

100. In contrast to the Asian situation, many immigrants from the West Indies arrive as single persons needing to provide for themselves the essentials of life—a home, employment and a partner. They hope to achieve these whilst adapting to a new style of living. They are semi-skilled or unskilled, coming from what has been described as the 'rural colonial proletariat' and so fall within the lower income groups. The majority settle in urban centres and industrial areas and are subject to the

social and economic pressures of unsatisfactory race relations, poor housing, and isolation. These are some of the pressures which later create strain and predispose their family life to breakdown and change. Because of the pattern of common law unions in the West Indies, many of these single people are already parents, responsible at least financially for their children who have been left behind with relatives. For the couple who have married in England, this is one factor which creates the need for two independent incomes. After a long period of separation many of these 'outside'* children eventually rejoin their parent. Subsequently they find it difficult to adjust to the 'new' family and social environment. The existence of 'outside' children born to the West Indian parent can also create an economic and emotional burden. Some parents who find it difficult to cope with the children living with them, have an added responsibility for others left behind in the West Indies. Apparent neglect or inadequacy on their part may in fact be a manifestation of the intolerable burden of providing for two families separated by distance and culture. In addition, the feature of the dominant woman household, in the form of the single-parent family with the man only marginally involved, is still present.

101. The agency must be aware of these cultural differences at all times. At the stage of assessment and reception into care, in particular, they will need the answer to such questions as—Does the child come from a one parent family and if so, what does this really mean? Is the mother solely responsible for his upbringing, or is there a common law union or is there a visiting relationship in which both parents share the responsibility for him? It is not unusual to find West Indian fathers who contribute voluntarily to their children's support and form strong bonds with them which may be maintained with encouragement. A useful indicator of a father's interest is the entry of his name on the child's birth certificate. Where this interest is evident, it should be encouraged and supported for the long term security and identity needs of the child.

102. The young unmarried mother is likely to find it particularly hard to care for herself and her child if she is isolated from her family. The cause of any drift away from her parents should be explored. There may have been conflict with her parents as a result of differing adaptation to life in this country. An approach to them which is seen as an acknowledgement of their parental role and authority may make it possible to effect a reconciliation. It is worth remembering that part of the cultural pattern

---

* Outside the current union of marriage.

in most black Commonwealth countries is that grandparents are usually prepared to assume the care of their grandchildren, in spite of any disappointment which they may have experienced with their own children. Their active interest may only be successfully achieved gradually, but securing the involvement of grandparents can provide a means of rehabilitating the child with his own family.

103. The incidence of black children in the long term care of local authorities is sometimes erroneously interpreted as a displacement of the parents' cultural dependence on the extended family to assist with the care of their children. Leaving a child in care may be more an act of despair. Knowledge of the parents' life situation leads to greater sensitivity and can enable a better understanding of the crisis which has precipitated the request for reception into care. Plans can then be made with greater clarity and if implemented at an early stage could help to mediate any sense of failure or guilt. This is important if parental contact is to be maintained whilst the child is in care.

104. Although some responsible groups within the community point out that there is not necessarily any correlation between culture and colour, others hold the view that substitute care for immigrant children would best be provided by immigrant families. This latter view is based on the feeling that the immigrant or black child growing up in an English home suffers a loss of culture, and when placed on a long term basis, he is eventually faced with identity problems related to his race and colour and to his acquired values and attitudes.

105. Whilst there may be a great deal of validity in this view, in the present situation it is not always practicable to act on it in general terms. Three major factors are important to take into consideration. Firstly, as yet there are insufficient numbers of black families coming forward to provide substitute care for the appreciable number of black children in need of permanent homes. It may well be that practical handicaps related to housing and income are relevant here. In Chapter 18 there is reference to the need for recruitment of foster parents from a wide spectrum of society so that the differing needs of children may be met. Secondly, amongst the available resources of foster parents there are white families who are willing to provide care and emotional security to black children and they may well be able to do this, particularly if supplementary care is provided. As with all offers of care, questions of motivation and suitability must be carefully assessed. Thirdly, the problems which arise for a black child after a period of long term care can be similar to those which

a white child experiences after an equally long period with a family other than his own, even when compounded by difficulties related to race.

106. The need for the provision of substitute care is inevitable in all human societies. For people coming from societies in which alternative forms of child care are provided without statutory intervention, and where this is arranged on a mutually selecting basis between parents and foster parents, a relationship of pseudo-kin develops. In these situations constraints are fewer and the respective role of those involved are more clearly understood. The child is therefore less predisposed to confusion and it is easier for him to retain a sense of identity.

107. The ability to hold on to a true sense of their own identity is needed by all children who experience separation from their parents. For the child of the immigrant family it is particularly difficult to retain a coherent sense of identity. Those who share his care have a special responsibility to provide an environment where a dual culture, like bilingualism, is a positive factor. Such an environment needs a mutual acceptance and respect for differing ways of life. Opportunities have to be created for the child to experience both cultures and not just one to the exclusion of the other. The ways in which this can be achieved will vary from one family to the next but social contact between the foster family and other members of the wider immigrant group would seem to be an essential factor. The agency can seek out members of minority groups who can give helpful information. For example, such people might be immigrant teachers, church leaders, community social groups and immigrant colleagues in the social services.

108. Whatever cultural emphasis prevailed in their childhood, it is clear that many children of immigrant families are evolving their own cultural norms. These differ from those of their parents as external influences, particularly peer group associations but also from the wider society, begin to have an impact on their lives.

109. In summary, the needs of the immigrant child for healthy growth and development are identical to those of other children. There is an additional task, however, for those who undertake to provide substitute care for him. He will need caring adults to help him accept his racial origin and achieve a sense of personal worth. This is particularly so for a black child facing negative attitudes in a predominantly white community. The principles set out in Part II of the Guide are therefore of vital importance in the provision of foster care for children from different cultures.

44

110. The essence of success in sharing the care of a child is in the recognition by all those concerned, both of their interdependence and of the value of the contribution each has to make towards the quality of life experienced by the child. The local authority or voluntary organisation has the responsibility for providing and sustaining the caring team, and it has the ultimate responsibility and accountability to society for its work. This will be discussed more fully in Chapter 18. Whilst the agency can delegate aspects of caring to individuals, it cannot contract out of this overall responsibility and it is the vesting of this responsibility in the agency which must be recognised by all members of the caring team.

111. Although underpinned by statutory procedure, the process of reception into or committal to care basically involves the establishment of relationships between the agency, the social worker, the parents and the child. Out of these will arise certain rights, responsibilities and obligations for each party. It may be helpful to describe these relationships in contractual terms, for an important element in making a contract is in clarifying the terms and in defining the tasks to be undertaken. In this context it may be seen as evaluating what the family and child are seeking and establishing the need for removing the child from his home. It will also mean clarifying the role of the family and this will partly depend on the legal status of the child. Furthermore, the agency will be exploring its services and the alternative type of care which it can provide. Parents must be left in no doubt as to the personal and legal* implications of their child coming into care, remaining in care for any length of time and being placed in a foster home. This is not a once and for all exercise and will need to be regularly reviewed. Within the context of the appropriate legislation, all the parties concerned will need to work as far as possible towards reaching a position of agreement on goals. In fact it may be said that the agency becomes the pivot of a network of contractual relationships between all the parties.

112. How far the contractual terms can and should be formally defined in writing is worth consideration. At the time of reception into, or com-

---

* see especially Section 56 of the Children Act, 1975.

mittal to, care the parents are sometimes required to sign certain forms: for example those authorising the agency to consent on their behalf to any necessary medical treatment, those which give an undertaking to keep in touch with and to notify the agency of a change in their address, or those which give an understanding that the agency may place their child in certain types of placement. Similarly, foster parents are required to sign a formal undertaking, as laid down in the Boarding Out Regulations (Regulation 20 England and Wales) where the period of care for the child is likely to exceed eight weeks. Thought should be given as to how an agency could formally acknowledge its obligations and responsibilities in a reciprocal undertaking, and when this would be appropriate. The agency should clarify its responsibilities towards the foster family, for example with regard to allowances and support to be given. In relation to the parents, the agency should consult and notify them about decisions and changes affecting their child. These factors will be looked at again in Chapters 17 and 18.

113. Defining the process in these terms underlines the fact that planning and decision making for the child in care should be a shared task, in which the agency actively involves the family, the child and those caring for him. At every stage each person involved should have some understanding about what is happening and why. He should understand his role, and what are his responsibilities and obligations. Much of the confusion which frequently occurs in fostering situations seems to develop because of the lack of clarity and definition as to goals and expectations, both at the beginning and subsequently, for the relationships will change over time. This confusion may be exacerbated by the stress factors inherent in the fostering situation. For example, the problem of sharing the parental role and the way in which children attach themselves to those who care for them.

114. The extent to which planning and decision making can be shared will vary according to the circumstances surrounding each reception into or committal to care; to the capacity of the parents and that of the child, depending upon his age and stage of development. Nevertheless, an important principle which should not be lost sight of, is that, however simple and/or limited its application may be in a particular situation, the clarification of goals and expectations has some very fundamental implications for planning and decision making as well as for the outcome of each case. In all situations the functions of the parental role become redistributed amongst the agency, the social worker, the foster parents and residential staff. The balance of responsibility is different in each case and

may change over time, but in every case the overall responsibility for the child and ultimate accountability for the work carried out in relation to him and his family, rests with the agency.

115. The agency however is itself a team which is made up of field-workers, residential workers, day care and domiciliary workers and administrative staff. As in the foster care team, all members of the agency are interdependent on each other and none should 'go it alone'. All members will react to the stress of the situations with which they come into contact. The first part of this Guide has explored some of the considerations on which foster care is based and some of the reactions to separation of society as a whole and of parents, foster parents and children in particular. All these feelings will be reflected in the work of the staff of the agency, and one of the most demanding aspects of social work with children is to remain open to the child's outward or hidden distress.

116. To acknowledge this stress goes against the cultural assumption that children should always be made to feel happy at all costs. But no-one has totally escaped distress in childhood. A child's anxiety in separation will reactivate in many of us painful feelings of distress, anxiety or hostility. If the agency's staff and foster parents can tolerate these feelings both in themselves and in the child, then he will be enabled, sooner or later, to communicate some aspects of what the experience means to him. By sharing his feelings, he may be helped to preserve existing relationships, to form new ones and so to retain his capacity to give love, as well as to receive it. For this reason, if for no other, foster parents and the agency's staff need to be adequately supported in their work with children.

117. The role of the social worker is complex by itself. She must be able to relate to the child, to the parents, to the foster parents, to the wider group of those caring for the child within the community and to the smaller group of staff within her own agency. All of these people will have their individual reactions and anxieties, and will sometimes react towards each other and to the social worker in negative ways which indicate the stress they are experiencing. But if their positive qualities can be harnessed together, then the sum total of their strength is far greater than that of the individuals concerned. At the same time, the social worker must act within the statutory and policy constraints of her agency and work for the 'best interests of the child'. One analogy might be to liken her role to that of the conductor of an orchestra. Normally the conductor does not play an instrument nor does he write the score. He takes the responsibility of acknowledging divers themes and interpretations, but does not permit

their conflict to destroy their harmonious co-existence. The poor conductor is the technician who does not experience the feeling of the music. Similarly, the social worker who performs the technicalities of her job without acknowledging and tolerating the feeling content, will fail in her responsibility to the child. When a concert fails, the conductor is a focal point for criticism. The failure however may be due to a poor orchestra tackling a difficult work or a poor conductor failing to realise the potential resources of his players. The reasons for failure are always complex and so it is in social work. But in social work, the concert season is never-ending and rehearsals via training are limited and often non-existent.

Part II

The social work task

Chapter 8

The prospective foster family

Initial considerations for the foster family

118. The main focus of the social work task in foster care is in meeting the needs of the child. This requires a full assessment of the child so that, in accordance with the requirements of the Boarding Out Regulations, the most suitable home can be found. In practice social workers are usually simultaneously involved in child assessment and in home finding, but for convenience this practice section begins with a consideration of the selection and preparation of foster parents. The aim must be to create a sufficient pool of foster homes so that resources are available to meet the needs of individual children.

119. When foster parents* first offer their services to an agency they will be exploring the possibility of fostering and should participate with the agency in an exercise of information sharing. They should be given the opportunity to discuss the social needs of their area, the services available to meet these needs and the agency's policy concerning families at risk. It will be helpful for them to know how fostering fits in with and complements other community services, to know the number of children in care, the difference between fostering and adoption and the contribution of fostering as a means of care. At this early stage they must be given the opportunity to consider some of the data affecting all fostering situations, to learn about the differing kinds of foster care and to know about the fostering needs of the individual agency. Foster parents should be given as much of this information as possible in writing since this provides a basis for future reference. It also provides a basis for consideration at home with family, friends and other interested people.

120. In considering the possibility of giving foster care, the first stage is focussed on what the job involves and on an exploration of what it might mean to a family to care for a foster child. During this stage all should be given the opportunity to exercise a high degree of self selection or self rejection and many applicants in fact withdraw at this time. Some of the questions and issues which prospective foster families will consider and discuss when deciding if fostering is for them are illustrated in the following diagram.

---

* For ease of reference the term foster parent is used in this chapter to describe all those who are considering taking up this role.

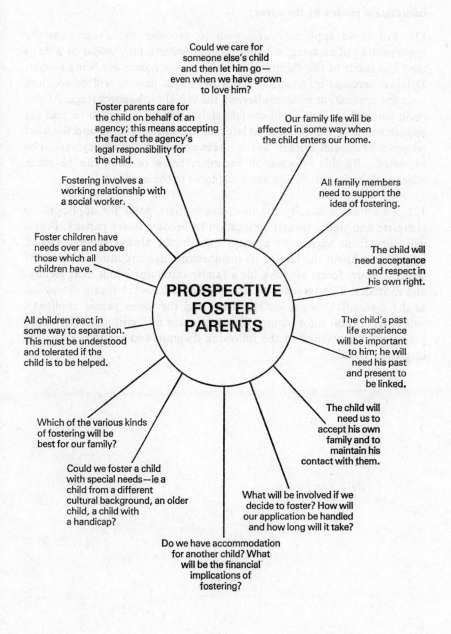

Could we care for
someone else's child
and then let him go—
even when we have grown
to love him?

Foster parents care for
the child on behalf of an
agency; this means accepting
the fact of the agency's
legal responsibility for
the child.

Fostering involves a
working relationship with
a social worker.

Foster children have
needs over and above
those which all
children have.

Our family life will be
affected in some way when
the child enters our home.

All family members
need to support the
idea of fostering.

The child will
need acceptance
and respect in
his own right.

All children react in
some way to separation.
This must be understood
and tolerated if the
child is to be helped.

**PROSPECTIVE
FOSTER
PARENTS**

The child's past
life experience
will be important
to him; he will
need his past
and present to
be linked.

Which of the various kinds
of fostering will be
best for our family?

The child will
need us to
accept his own
family and to
maintain his
contact with them.

Could we foster a child
with special needs—ie a
child from a different
cultural background, an older
child, a child with
a handicap?

What will be involved if we
decide to foster? How will
our application be handled
and how long will it take?

Do we have accommodation
for another child? What
will be the financial
implications of
fostering?

Information needed by the agency

121. For those applicants who wish to proceed, the agency has the responsibility of assessing whether this particular family would be able to meet the needs of the children for whom foster homes are being sought. Detailed personal information about the foster parents will be required once the application proceeds beyond the initial exploratory stage. At this point some discussion about confidentiality will be important so that the applicants know with whom the information will be shared, and for what purpose. The social worker, as the representative of the agency, has to be entrusted with this information in order that a decision can be made which is right for this family and acceptable to the agency.

122. This time is usually the most appropriate point for applicants to complete and sign a formal application to become foster parents. Forms will vary from agency to agency, but should always request factual information about the family, its membership, age structure and circumstances. Many forms also ask for a family statement about their feelings and attitudes. This information can provide a basis for future discussion as the dialogue between social worker and the foster parent applicants will cover factual information, life experiences and attitudes. The major points are summarised in the following diagram and are then discussed in greater detail.

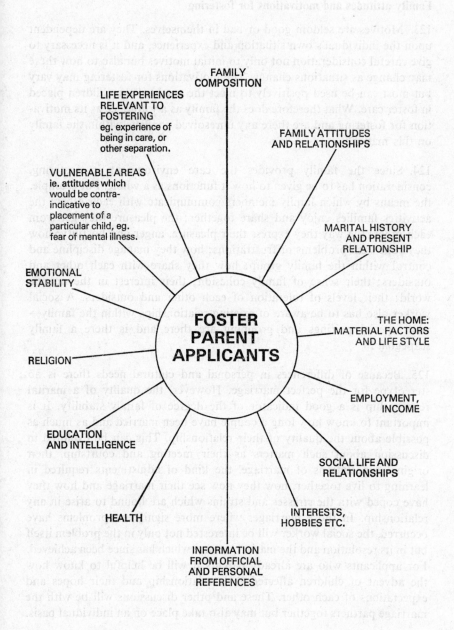

FAMILY
COMPOSITION

LIFE EXPERIENCES
RELEVANT TO
FOSTERING
eg. experience of
being in care, or
other separation.

FAMILY ATTITUDES
AND RELATIONSHIPS

VULNERABLE AREAS
ie. attitudes which
would be contra-
indicative to
placement of a
particular child, eg.
fear of mental illness.

MARITAL HISTORY
AND PRESENT
RELATIONSHIP

EMOTIONAL
STABILITY

FOSTER
PARENT
APPLICANTS

THE HOME:
MATERIAL FACTORS
AND LIFE STYLE

RELIGION

EMPLOYMENT,
INCOME

EDUCATION
AND INTELLIGENCE

SOCIAL LIFE AND
RELATIONSHIPS

HEALTH

INTERESTS,
HOBBIES ETC.

INFORMATION
FROM OFFICIAL
AND PERSONAL
REFERENCES

53

Family attitudes and motivations for fostering

123. Motives are seldom good or bad in themselves. They are dependent upon the individual's own situation and experience, and it is necessary to give careful consideration not only to initial motives but also to how these may change as situations change. The motivations for fostering may vary but most can be used positively to meet the needs of the children placed in foster care. What therefore does the family as a whole see as its motivation for fostering and are there any unresolved conflicts within the family on this matter?

124. Since the family provides the care environment in fostering, consideration has to be given to how it functions as a whole. For example, the means by which family members communicate with each other; the activities families enjoy and share together; the pleasure they get from each other; the way they express their pleasure, anger and hostility; how they cope with problems or frustrations; how they manage discipline and control within the family group; how they share with each other and outsiders; their sense of family cohesion; their interest in the outside world; their levels of toleration of each other and outsiders. A social worker also has to be aware of existing relationships within the family—what special pairings and grouping are there and is there a family scapegoat?

125. Because of differences in personal and cultural needs there is no stereotype for the perfect marriage. However, the quality of a marital relationship is a good indicator of the degree of family stability. It is important to know how long a couple have been married and as much as possible about the quality of their relationship. This can be explored in discussion about such matters as their meeting and courtship, their original expectations of marriage, the kind of adjustments required in learning to live together, how they now see their marriage and how they have coped with the stresses and strains which are bound to arise in any relationship. In those marriages where more significant problems have occurred, the social worker will be interested not only in the problem itself but in its resolution and the marital balance which has since been achieved. For applicants who are already parents it will be helpful to know how the advent of children affected their relationship and their hopes and expectations of each other. These and other discussions will be with the marriage partners together but may also take place on an individual basis.

126. The exploration of past experiences, feelings and attitudes will involve all members of the family. The foster mother, because of her role

as wife and mother, may be the person most motivated to foster and the one who is the prime mover in making the application. It will be helpful to have her view of her own life experiences, about how she perceives herself as a wife, mother and as a person; how she copes with the ordinary and extra-ordinary stresses and strains of her various roles; where and from whom she finds support and assistance. All the considerations basic to fostering should be explored with her in some depth, especially her understanding of children, her expectations of foster parenthood and what she sees as the differences between fostering and ordinary parenthood. She must not feel obliged to give the 'right' answers to questions but should be enabled to express and develop her own views and feelings.

127. The part played by the foster father will be crucial and his role within the family, his views on fostering and the contribution he will make to any fostering situation must not be overlooked or underrated. In the past the parenting role of the foster father has tended to be regarded as less important than that of the mother. Even now he may often be seen mainly as providing a background of emotional and material support, and as someone only to be called on in exceptional circumstances. The father's role should be much more than this. Many men are very actively involved in all aspects of home life and in the total care of their children. How each man sees his role as a father will depend upon the family's social class, its cultural pattern and the age and needs of the children, but the views, feelings and expectations of the foster father must always be carefully considered. Failure to involve the foster father jeopardises the chances of a successful placement. For some children in foster care he is particularly important: for example adolescents who need to identify with a male figure and young children who have been cared for in residential nurseries staffed only by women.

128. Foster parents base their expectations of parenting upon personal experience. The social worker will learn much from observing their children, by talking with the foster parents about their own experiences both as children and parents and by considering with them their present views on child rearing and parental relationships. It will also be helpful to know if they have been separated from their own children for any reason—if so, how did they feel about this and how did they help their child manage the experience? Have they had any experience relating to children going into care? Perhaps they know someone whose children are in care—perhaps their own children have friends who are foster children. Some foster parents may have had first hand experience of children facing special difficulties.

Childless couples

129. Childless couples who apply to foster may need extra help, both through discussion and by practical involvement with children, before they can consider the realities of foster parenthood. The opportunity to meet, visit and talk with residential staff and practising foster parents will be especially valuable for these applicants. Such contacts can bring alive the realities of life with children at a feeling level, as well as on a day to day practical living basis. With these couples it will be necessary to discuss the fact of childlessness. Their feelings and understanding of fertility investigations, treatment and causes will need consideration, as will their ways of coping with the disappointments they may have incurred and the degree to which they have been able to come to terms with the situation. It will be particularly important to explain and discuss the differences between fostering and adoption, since they may be seeking the kind of permanent parental relationship which fostering may not provide.

Single parent families

130. Applications to foster from single parent families merit special consideration, taking into account how their situation may differ from the 'ideal' or 'normal' family which social workers may be seeking and which society approves. In some instances, for particular children, the single parent family may have more to offer than the two parent family; much will depend upon the needs of an individual child and the strengths within the single parent family as well as its outside support systems. Information about family, friends and neighbours is likely to be particularly necessary in relation to this group of foster parents. Their support is not only necessary at times of stress or difficulty, but also in sharing day to day activities and pleasures of parenthood and family life.

Emotional maturity and vulnerability

131. The degree of emotional maturity achieved by foster parents will be of interest to the social worker for many reasons. Foster parents' ability to give without expectation of return is important, since this capacity may be needed to sustain them through long periods without any seeming response from the foster child. They need security in their own identities and self-confidence, as these qualities enable foster parents to provide the continuity and stability which is vital for a child whose own self-concept may be poorly developed. An ability to cope with the stresses and problems of life as well as to learn from their own and other people's experiences will indicate a capacity for personal development and problem solving

which is often essential for successful fostering. It is also useful to explore with foster parents and other family members any particular areas of life experience which may be reactivated by an individual foster child's circumstances or personality. These areas may include attitudes and feelings about sexual behaviour, mental illness, anti-social or criminal behaviour, and prejudices concerning race or religion. The foster family's own awareness of such areas of vulnerability will be most important, not only in making decisions about accepting applications but also when choosing the best foster home to meet the needs of an individual child.

The foster parents' children

132. All members of the household should be known to the social worker and be involved to some degree in the application. This will depend upon their position and status in the household. It will be most important, however, for her to meet the children of the foster family and to have some understanding of their views, feelings and reactions to the idea of foster care. Like their parents the children will need to learn about fostering and to consider how it may affect their daily lives. Children can sometimes be included in the discussions which are taking place between their parents and the social worker and fostering should also be a subject for family conversation in the ordinary course of daily living. The way in which children are involved and learn about fostering will of course be dependent upon their age, but the social worker will always want the opportunity to talk to older children themselves about a proposal to foster and how it is likely to affect them. The principles and methods described in Chapter 10 equally apply in this context. Fostering will require many adjustments from all concerned and especially from the 'host' children who will be called upon to share parents, home and possessions. Their position in the family is bound to be changed by a newcomer and they will inevitably have very ambivalent feelings following the arrival of a foster sibling. This will be so even if beforehand they have been prepared and were in agreement with the plan to foster.

Other family members

133. As well as members of the foster parents' immediate household there may be other people, not necessarily relatives, who are closely involved and who play an important part in family life. The social worker must consider if these people should be involved in the fostering and if so what their expectations are. How do they see the demands and satisfactions which fostering may bring? Do they expect fostering to affect their lives and relationships with the family?

Social relationships

134. A foster family's network of social relationships often throws light on the way a family functions. The kind of friendships that they have, their neighbourhood relationships, their wider community interests and activities and their involvement in life generally are all of interest to the social worker. Social isolation is not usually a good indicator for foster parenthood.

The home

135. Housing and the physical standards of home comfort of each potential foster family must be viewed in relation to the locality of the foster home, the socio-economic group of the foster parents, the foster parents' life style, their cultural background and eventually the needs of any specific child. Adequacy of sleeping and living accommodation is important, as is the opportunity for members of the family to have some space for themselves and some degree of personal privacy. All foster children should have a bed of their own and space for their own possessions. This will be particularly important for older children and adolescents. Standards of nutrition and child care practice are important to ascertain, but again need to be seen in relation to the individual foster family, its location, cultural background and social situation.

Finance and employment

136. A family's financial situation indicates the material security that it can provide and foster home studies should always consider the levels of income and expenditure. Spending patterns, the family's views about money and financial security may indicate values within the family and throw light on the roles of individual family members. Patterns of employment, the actual jobs undertaken and the satisfaction and status that work provides, will also be subject for discussion and consideration. The question of foster mothers going out to work will necessarily involve a discussion on the needs of the family, the role of the other family members, the ages and needs of any foster children and the arrangements that are made for their care in working hours.

Health

137. Fostering can impose considerable physical and emotional strains on both foster parents and their families. It is therefore important, not only for the security of any foster child but also for the welfare of the foster families themselves, that careful consideration is given to their physical

and mental health. The requirement for agencies to enquire into the health of prospective foster parents is laid down by law in the Boarding Out Regulations. Every fostering agency should know of any past or present health factors which could affect a foster family in its capacity to care for a child.

138. Medical enquiries concerning the foster parents alone are not usually adequate since there may be important health factors relating to the foster parents' own children, to members of their extended family and to other members of the household. Full medical reports on the foster parents which include a family medical history as well as up-to-date medical examinations and chest x-rays are very desirable. Foster parents expect and often appreciate a careful medical screening and willingly give their permission for this to take place. The full involvement of their family doctor during the application process can lay the foundations for his future interest in a foster child, for his support to the foster family and for his ongoing co-operation with the fostering agency.

139. Medical reports are of little use unless their contents are understood. If families are willing for their doctor to pass on confidential information to the agency, then the agency must itself use this information in a responsible way. It is important to emphasise that social workers dealing with foster parent applications will need access to general and specialist medical and psychiatric advice in order to ensure that they understand the social implications of any medical conditions or problems which are present in foster parents or their families.

Age

140. Foster parents are recruited within a very wide age range. Whilst there are advantages in children being placed with foster parents who are of an age where they could biologically have been their parents, there are satisfactory placements where the foster parents' age places them in the role of a substitute grandparent. Much will depend upon the age of the child. Of equal importance to age is foster parents' maturity, understanding and ability to adjust to meet children's needs.

Education and intelligence

141. Some idea of the foster parents' education and level of intelligence is necessary, especially when decisions are made later concerning the placement of a specific child. Foster parents need imagination, feeling and understanding for a child. These qualities are not necessarily linked to a

high level of intelligence, for an intellectual understanding of a situation or need does not always ensure an emotional capacity to deal with that situation or to meet that need.

Religion

142. The foster parents' religious beliefs and practices must also be considered. The statutory regulations concerning fostering require that, where possible, a child should be placed with a family of the same religious persuasion or with one which will undertake to bring him up in his own faith. The religion of foster parents may not be of particular interest to the parents of some children in care but in other instances parents will feel strongly about this, and the spiritual climate of the foster home can be important especially in sustaining links with the child's family and his past life experiences.

Personal references

143. A request for personal references is necessary for good practice. Information from such referees is used to supplement that obtained from the applicants themselves, and it can also provide a helpful and interesting view of a family as seen from a different perspective. The value of information provided by personal referees will depend on how well and in what capacity they know the foster family, as well as how much they understand about the demands of fostering. Referees should be people who have some real and personal relationship with would-be foster parents and who are not just remote pillars of society.

144. Before meeting personal referees it is helpful to provide them with some written information about fostering and an indication of the kind of information required by the agency. This should include facts such as how long they have known the family and in what capacity. Opinions are helpful about the foster family as a whole as well as about individual members, and referees may be able to suggest special features which will be of positive value in fostering or which may indicate possible difficulties. Most people feel anxious and diffident when acting as a referee for their friends or relatives and it helps if the social worker recognises and acknowledges these feelings. She should make it clear that the information provided is given in confidence and that their assistance is a valuable but small part of the selection process. A reference from a member of the foster parents' own family is recommended, since it often gives the opportunity for members of the wider family circle to be actively involved in the fostering process at the outset and can provide an additional perspective

60

of the foster family. The contributions of referees are maximised when personal interviews with the social worker are possible and this should always be the aim. If, because of distance, such interviews cannot be arranged by the fostering agency, another agency may sometimes be prepared to undertake this task on their behalf. In this case they must be properly and fully briefed. If personal interviews are quite impossible to arrange, telephone discussions can provide the personal contact which gives an additional dimension to a written reference.

Official enquiries

145. In addition to personal references foster families must also be asked to supply a medical reference and to give their permission for the agency to make official enquiries of the police and local agencies such as the health service, probation service and the housing department. The medical reference provided by the family doctor is discussed in paragraphs 140 and 141. Prospective foster parents must be fully informed about all reference and enquiry procedures and realise that they are necessary in the interests of the children entrusted to the agency's care. They must be assured that all information will be treated in confidence and not passed on to a third party. The official agencies providing information may also need assurance about its use, and this is something which will need to be worked out locally between the agencies concerned. To ensure that official enquiries can be undertaken speedily and accurately, detailed information must be provided to the agencies concerned; full names, dates of birth of all family members, present and previous addresses, as well as maiden names, at least will be necessary.

146. The fostering agency must always give careful consideration to all the information it obtains and confidential medical or police information may come to light which the foster agency will wish to discuss with the applicants. This will require prior discussion with the family doctor or the police to try and resolve the problem. Where police and probation enquiries reveal a record of criminal activity, this must be given special consideration. While this is not of itself a disqualification, the nature and the seriousness of the crime, the age of the person when it occurred and any subsequent convictions will all need to be taken into account, together with the other information available about the family.

Capacity for collaborative working

147. The foundations for the foster parents' future relationship with their placing agency are laid during the application process. This will be the

time when they have their first experience of working with the agency in its statutory duty to seek information about themselves and their family, and in its assessment of their suitability to foster a child. Their capacity to accept the agency role in this situation will often provide a good indication as to their ability for collaborative working if a child is placed in their care. Insensitivity to the feelings and needs of foster parents by agency staff, whether administrative or field workers, will be seen by applicants as an indication of the value and status of fostering in that particular agency. A negative experience at this stage may have a detrimental effect upon future relations or may lead applicants to withdraw at the very outset. Agencies who respond to would-be foster parents as potentially valuable care resources for children will answer letters promptly without being officious, will reply to telephone calls and messages, will follow up applications without undue delay and will at all times keep applicants informed about what is happening.

Chapter 9

The selection process

148. The selection and preparation of foster parents and families is recognised as being a difficult and complex social work task and many social workers approach it with apprehension and uncertainty. Realistic anxiety about decision making and necessary involvement in investigatory procedures can get out of hand if the social worker has unrealistic expectations of finding the perfect family. Whilst not all social workers will be expected to take part in home finding, those who do should be properly equipped for the task. The social worker must have had previous experience of working with children and their families. She should also at some time have been responsible for the supervision of a foster home. She must be well supported professionally by a senior colleague to whom she can turn for consultation, advice, support and supervision throughout the application. This is discussed further in paragraphs 384–387.

149. The social worker's ability to communicate with people is most important. She must be able to explain fostering in a realistic and practical way, to exchange ideas with families and to appreciate what they are able to offer. She will meet potential foster parents from all walks of life, from differing social and cultural backgrounds, and with varying levels of intelligence and educational experience. For some fostering will be a fairly familiar concept, for those coming from other cultures their ideas of fostering may be unlike the social worker's own. Some people are used to dealing with officials and are confident in their ability to talk and express their views and feelings. Others are anxious about making contact with a representative of authority and face difficulties both in vocabulary and in their capacity for communication.

Group discussions—family and individual interviews

150. The methods employed in focussing on fostering and its likely effect upon foster parents and their family will depend upon the needs of the foster parent, the skills of the social worker and agency practice. Personal interviews with individual family members, family discussions and small discussion groups may all be used. At an early stage it is helpful for both social worker and foster family to arrange a programme of interviews giving the time scale of the application process. The first exchange of

information can well take place at group meetings arranged by the agency. Such meetings should provide, in an informal and relaxed atmosphere, an opportunity for prospective foster parents to meet with others who are contemplating fostering. All can then exchange views, explore feelings and ask questions. If practising foster parents are able to join in these meetings there can be an exchange of realistic information about the rewards and problems of fostering. At this stage the prospective foster parent will be considering the issues outlined in the diagram in paragraph 120.

151. Some agencies continue to use group discussions when moving on to consider some of the personal situations of the applicants. It is, however, important to note that not everyone feels able to participate in group activities nor should they be expected to do so. Some of the most sought after applicants, particularly those of differing cultures and nationalities, may not care for a group approach and alternative methods must be available. If group methods are used the social worker must be clear about the purpose of the group. She must also convey this to group members who will need to know what will be expected of them, the degree of confidentiality within the group and how eventually decisions will be made. Much will depend upon the social worker's ability to enable people to be at ease in the group situation, and to ensure their willingness to respond personally to the information and views which are expressed in the group. Consideration will need to be given to how the information relating to individual group members will be kept and recorded in order to meet the agency requirements. It is important that at the end of the group process the social worker and potential foster parents are able to raise any areas of concern which may need further explanation or exploration on an individual basis.

152. The more usual method of considering foster parents for selection is by individual interviews. These take place over a period of time and enable the social worker to talk with foster parents and their families both as individuals and together as a group. These interviews usually take place in the applicant's home but they may also be at the fostering agency. Visiting the foster parents' own home is obviously important for the social worker to obtain an impression of the atmosphere, as well as to see the material conditions of the home and its surrounding environment. Some families are also more relaxed at home. There can be extra strains for the applicants during these visits; they may be coping with feelings of anxiety at the same time as handling the social conventions relating to visitors in their home. Some topics therefore may be more easily discussed at the agency office, but if the value of an office interview is to be maximised

adequate facilities such as comfortable and attractive interviewing rooms must be available. Such facilities are necessary if discussions are to take place in a relaxed, quiet and uninterrupted atmosphere.

153. Interviews with individual family members are as important as the practice of talking with the whole family as a group. The social worker should approach prospective foster parents in an encouraging and relaxed way sharing her views and knowledge with them. She has to enable the family in its turn to share their opinions and experience, to question what she says and seek clarification or explanation where necessary. An approach which enables foster parents to talk about the pleasures of their life and relationships and also to describe their hopes and aspirations, will be more likely to facilitate communication than an approach which emphasises problems and difficulties. From this basis it should be possible for both parties to identify the areas of feeling, opinion or experience which need further clarification. Such an approach can help to avoid the situation of 'game playing' where families merely seek to provide the information they think the worker will want to know and real communication does not take place. In discussion the worker as well as the foster parents may be required to adapt and change on points of view. The social worker there-fore must be prepared to enter into discussions which may expose her own personal views, experiences and, sometimes, prejudices. To do this requires a considerable degree of self-awareness and personal confidence which does not use professional status as a barrier.

154. It should always be borne in mind, however, that some people are unused to discussing their feelings and expressing opinions on rather abstract matters. This does not mean that they are incapable of becoming warm, understanding foster parents for an appropriately placed child. In the selection process, as in continuing work with them, the social worker needs to adapt her approach by using more indirect methods of enabling them to reach a rapport and to demonstrate in less verbal ways their feelings and capabilities. Moreover, some people may be disconcerted if asked to discuss painful areas of their life experience, and social workers should be aware that such reticence can in fact be a healthy reaction which should be respected. On the other hand it may indicate areas of vulner-ability which should be considered in relation to their relevance to the fostering situation.

Decisions

155. There is no optimum period of time for the selection process. However once a family has shown an interest in fostering, there should not

be an undue delay before they become involved in selection activities. At the end of the application process the social worker should produce in writing a comprehensive overview of the prospective foster family and of its membership. This should contain an assessment of their potential as a foster family and of the service they could offer to her particular agency. The production of such a document will enable the social worker to think through each application to the point of making a recommendation, seek further information or professional advice if required, and come to her own personal opinion about the application. This comprehensive assessment should then be submitted to a senior member of staff, or whoever has delegated responsibility for final foster home approval within the agency.

156. Fostering agencies will wish to ensure that decisions about applications to become foster parents are made with care. They should take into account the needs of children in care and the motivation and resources of the prospective foster family. Some agencies hold group discussions amongst their social workers before coming to a decision. Some delegate these decisions to a specially selected panel. Others place this responsibility on to a senior worker. Whatever method is employed, however, the decision should never be taken by the social worker on her own. Some families in fact take a decision themselves not to proceed. Although attracted to the idea of fostering a child, they later decide that it might be best for their own family not to do so. They may find that there are better ways of helping with the care of children in the community. For example daily minding or club work could give them the opportunity they seek.

Refusing applications

157. Not everyone who wishes to foster will be able to evaluate their own capabilities for the task and reach an appropriate decision, and it is the agency which holds this final responsibility. Telling prospective foster parents that their offer of service has not been accepted is a very difficult task. Some departments have definite policies about not giving their reasons to refused applicants. Sometimes the reasons given are evasive, do not ring true and result in families pursuing their applications with other departments, only to be faced with a series of further disappointments. When this happens applicants often become angry and resentful and social workers are left feeling that they have acted dishonestly and unhelpfully. A definite refusal, though unpleasant, is more helpful than evasion and delay.

158. Identifying and explaining the areas of disqualification can give some foster families the opportunity for reconsideration and perhaps change. Sometimes, however, it is not possible for social workers and families to agree about the disqualifying areas. In these instances the social worker will need to explain her views in terms of her own professional judgement and the agency's overall responsibility for individual children. Foster parents may also need to be given the opportunity to explain their viewpoint to another representative of the fostering agency. An appropriate person would either be the supervising senior or the senior with responsibility for fostering services. The difficulties of explaining decisions based upon confidential information are referred to in paragraph 146 but these can sometimes be overcome. With some families social workers may feel that to identify certain 'problem areas' would be too damaging to family defences and functioning. In these situations they are faced with trying to refuse the family's request to foster whilst not rejecting them as people. A criterion for the social worker in this situation is that she should not leave the family in a more disturbed state than that which existed before their application to foster a child. The question of helping those people who, although they present to the department as prospective foster parents, have such problems that they need help in their own right, is very difficult. Social workers may be faced with either changing the entire focus of their work with such applicants or referring them, perhaps more appropriately, to another colleague for assistance.

The role of the senior social worker

159. Social workers dealing with fostering applications need professional support, advice and supervision from a senior colleague throughout the process. The senior can act as a sounding board for the social worker in her consideration of the implications of information available about the foster family. She can help the social worker identify those important features of the application which may have been overlooked or which need additional consideration. In some cases the social worker may become over-identified with a foster family, in others she may fail to establish a working relationship; when this occurs the senior will need to assist her in looking at her own contribution to the situation, as sometimes personal experiences and feelings can cloud judgements. In some circumstances it can be helpful for all concerned if the senior meets the applicants; such a meeting can be of use if for some reason communication between the family and the worker seems to have broken down or become difficult. In extreme situations the senior may even decide that another social worker should take over. The senior will also be involved in monitoring the progress of all applications and ensuring that unnecessary delays are

avoided. When delays occur she will wish to know the cause. This may be pressure of other work, but delay may also indicate that the application has reached a point which poses problems. It is important to remember that fostering and work with children can bring to the surface feelings which are painful to all concerned, including the social worker. She may need special help and advice from her senior if she is to maintain a professional balance between her own feelings, the expectations of the foster family and the function of the agency she represents. This is discussed further in paragraphs 386 and 387.

Keeping records

160. The need for accurate and carefully prepared records concerning work with prospective foster parents cannot be over-emphasised. These records should show clearly the facts, feelings, opinions and professional judgements which go into the final decisions concerning individual families. They should indicate when and by whom the decision was made, and state who was informed of the decision together with details of the date and means of transmitting this information.

161. When negative decisions have been reached, the reasons for such decisions must be clearly recorded for further reference. When applicants are accepted, the information gathered during the application process will be the beginning of the foster home file which will contain basic information about the foster family provided by themselves, their doctor, official and personal referees (see chart, paragraph 122). It will also include the social worker's record of the application process, the important facts and features of the application as they emerged from interviews, discussions and home visits. The social worker must be disciplined in her case recording and aim at producing a concise record of events. The record should be in a form from which information can be easily extracted and which distinguishes clearly between facts and opinions. The foster parents' application file will form the basis of the foster home record, and as such will be an important tool for the social worker and the administrative staff of the agency in meeting their responsibilities for any child subsequently placed.

Meeting differing needs

162. So far emphasis has been on consideration of the suitability of foster parents in the abstract sense. In practice however, foster parents are not considered in a blanket form to undertake any or all types of fostering. As foster care is used to help children with a wide range of individual needs and in a variety of differing circumstances, thought must be given to the most

68

appropriate kind of care which each foster family is able to offer. This will be a matter for discussion and exploration throughout the preparation and selection procedure. Some foster families have a special ability to meet the needs of more than one child, in which case they will be a particularly valuable resource for sibling groups which enables families to be kept together. Some may have a special feeling for children in stressful situations and an ability to work closely with their families. In which case they may be specially effective as short stay foster parents. Some may have particular affinity with adolescents in which case they will be much needed since this group of young people have special needs.

163. The practice of expecting all foster parents to begin with short stay placements is not recommended. Some foster parents may benefit from this experience of learning on the job, others may not. It is important that social workers face up to the different emphasis, demands and skills of the various kinds of fostering activities, if they are to make most effective use of fostering resources and to ensure that the foster placement arranged at least tries to meet the needs of all involved. The use of foster care in more specialised circumstances, such as for severely handicapped children, children on remand or subject to interim care orders, will require special consideration during the selection and preparation process. It will require additional information and practical opportunities for foster parents to learn about the children's special needs. It will also call for the careful investigation of local resources such as special schools and medical facilities.

Awaiting a child

164. In some situations where the approval process has been successfully completed there will be a delay in placing a child. This is sometimes inevitable as the whole object of foster care is that the home should be appropriate to meet the needs of a particular child. Careful preliminary selection must therefore be followed by careful matching. This waiting period can be very frustrating for foster parents, particularly if they are not fully aware of the reason for it. The agency has an obligation to keep in contact with them, to explain the reason for delay and to assure them of its continued interest in their offer of service. This may be the task of the social worker already well known to them or of a fostering liaison officer whose function includes an oversight of available foster homes. The waiting period can be used positively as an opportunity for further preliminary training and, in particular, the support of belonging to a foster parent group may be helpful. Where the waiting period is prolonged, circumstances in the foster family may change and the social worker will have to assess what reappraisal of the application is necessary before introducing a child to the home.

Chapter 10
Communicating with children

165. It is not an easy matter to share the care of a child. Perhaps it is even more difficult to share with the child and to work, not only for him, but also with him. The practice of foster care would be easier if it were just a matter of negotiation and arrangement between the adults involved in the situation, but one of the dangers of working under pressure is that fostering practice can become arrangement dominated rather than child orientated. It is possible for the adults to strive to give the child the kind of care that they themselves would have chosen if they had been in his situation. They identify not with the child but with their own childhood.

166. A child separated from his family, or from those on whom he has come to depend for his sense of security, is a child who is at risk of losing his sense of identity. It is a frightening experience for him if the adults in his world begin to move him around like a pawn in a game. The rules of life are changed but no one has explained. Part of himself is no longer known or valued in this new world and this part of himself is in danger of withering away. It is not an exaggeration to say that the aim of communicating with children is to keep them alive. By this is meant helping them to maintain a sense of their own identity and of their worth in relation to other people, and helping them to know about their own feelings in regard to what is happening to them, particularly in times of change. Every child in care will need help too in answering questions such as—Who am I? Why am I here? What is going to happen to me?

167. All children who come the way of the social worker have been through periods of anxiety and stress which may have been overwhelming. This experience can lead some children to clamp down on feelings and to 'forget' so that the adults responsible can be seriously misled about the true state of affairs. Other children may become angry and hostile because this is more tolerable than feeling lost and isolated. Communicating with children in such circumstances is not easy and the social worker will need to seek contact with the suffering part of each child, because locked up in the suffering is each one's potential for living and for relating to the world. To help children to put painful feelings into words imposes a strain on social workers, for it arouses painful memories of distress that each has

70

experienced and that belong to living. If they are not careful they can find themselves avoiding this essential aspect of their work.

168. In communicating with children social workers have long ago learnt that the question and answer method simply does not work. Courage is needed to take risks, and to put into words what we know from our experience is likely to be the way that children are thinking and feeling in a given situation and at a given moment. The social worker may be wrong, but at least the child will give her credit for reaching out and trying to understand. If the social worker is right, it is likely that the child will show no immediate reaction and may appear not to have heard what has been said. Here again the social worker must not be deceived, but must watch for the signs of relief which may be evident in small ways later on; signs such as a child letting a foster mother help him off with his coat, instead of reacting negatively by turning away from her. A great deal of communication between social workers and children takes place on a non-verbal level. On the whole children are quicker to size up situations than are adults. They are sensitive to attitude, tone of voice, and general approach and demeanour, and they draw their own conclusions.

169. Their direct approach to reality sometimes comes as a shock to the adults concerned. A foster child will need to experience his social worker as a real person and doing things together may help. A child getting to know his social worker is likely to want to establish what sort of a person she is by asking questions about her, direct and indirect. Are you married? Do you have children? Do you visit other children? He may be seeing the social worker as all powerful for his good or for his removal. Will the social worker herself adopt or foster him if it does not work out here in this foster home? He will expect straightforward answers to these questions and he will begin to assess whether he can trust her to keep her word or whether she makes promises which she later fails to keep. In spite of his direct approach to reality many of his reactions will, however, be influenced by his fantasies. Children are curious about the content of written records kept by the agency and a child can be disturbed by a social worker making any written notes in his presence.

170. Communication can only be established within a relationship of trust and for this to develop it is essential for a foster child to get to know his social worker. This will involve the social worker explaining who she is and what her job involves clearly, accurately and appropriately for that particular child. For one eight year old foster child a descriptive answer to his question 'What do social workers do?', enabled him to make swift and full use of the social worker by asking a series of direct questions

about why he was in care, where his mother was and whether he could meet her. Talk has to be backed up with appropriate action. As well as children needing to know what social workers do, and that means do in relation to them, they also need to know how often they can expect to see their social worker and when she will next be visiting the foster home. A social worker who dropped in on a teenage girl in foster care was told off for not having said when she was coming and was told 'I'll only remember afterwards what it was that I wanted to say to you'. Visits to foster children may appear to the social worker to be a routine matter, but to the child it may be a vital opportunity for him to talk to someone who has been closely involved with his past: someone to whom he can turn when things are going wrong, who has the skills of perception, empathy and communication and yet at the same time is able to keep the whole situation in perspective.

171. The development of a positive professional relationship with children is not unique to social work. A good experience with a teacher, a doctor or dentist enables a child to meet another teacher, doctor or dentist with more positive expectations. His first expectations are then firstly of the professional service and only then of the person. Because the relationship between the social worker and the foster child is a professional relationship, then the expectations on both sides should be developed accordingly. The social worker must be clear about her role in relation to the child—the social worker who is just 'auntie' or 'uncle' or who is 'the lady from the council who comes to see Mrs. X' is in neither case rendering a service to the foster child.

172. If a child is to benefit from the love and care of a foster home, then he needs to be aware of the agency's function in relation to himself. It may be more important for him to feel, understand and use the support of the agency than it is for him to develop a close personal attachment to the social worker. The skill of the social worker will be in personalising the support of the agency in a warm but essentially professional relationship with the child, and for this reason changes of social worker should be kept to the absolute minimum. A good relationship, however, is one which if necessary can be transferred to another social worker and which notwithstanding can increase a child's confidence in the supportive strength of the agency itself. Most adults have a protective caring instinct towards children and it is not always easy to relate to a child in a professional sense. This is especially true in relation to very young children in distress. Also in a professional relationship it may be necessary to tolerate a child's negative and rejecting behaviour.

173. Part of the service to the child is to protect him from physical and mental harm. Harm may come to him as the result of external forces such as the frustration, anger and aggression of the adults in his world. Such aggression may have its roots outside the situation of the child and he may be the unwitting objective of its expression. Harm may also come to him if his own behaviour becomes too destructive and provocative to the point of being beyond the tolerance of his caring adults. Children caught up in such situations need the support of communication with someone outside the negative pattern of relationships. This is clearly a responsibility of the social worker who must be alert to both the spoken and unspoken signals that all is not well.

174. It cannot be too strongly stressed that social workers must train themselves in the discipline of observing and understanding the meaning of what they both hear and see. To do this they must spend time with the child. They must not miss unspoken messages or fail to pick up distress signals. The state of a child's mind can often be seen in his facial expression. For example, the face can reveal confidence and trust, or anxiety, suspicion, uncertainty and longing. The way in which a child moves and uses his body can tell something about his general state of wellbeing or otherwise. There may be restless hyper-activity with accident proneness, or lethargy which can indicate a degree of physical or mental ill health. These signs must not be missed and, moreover, looks can reveal a great deal not only about the child himself, but about the quality of care that he is receiving. A child's attitude towards food, towards bedtime and sleep are matters that need consideration, because they indicate something about the general state of affairs that exists. Perhaps nothing can indicate more to the social worker about a child's ability to be at ease with himself and others, than his capacity to play. Patterns of play will be dependant on the age of the child. If he can be absorbed in constructive play by himself and can also play co-operatively with others, this is a favourable sign that he is coping with life. On the other hand, if he is continuously destructive and disruptive of the play of others, and if this state of affairs persists, it indicates that special attention and help is needed.

175. With most pre-adolescent children play will form an important medium of communication and it is useful to distinguish three aspects of this. Firstly, play as a shared social activity where the child and the social worker do things together. It is in this way that a child really has a chance of getting to know his social worker as a person and until he is sure about this he may well not be able to ask any questions or tolerate hearing any answers about his personal situation. Secondly, there is play set up by

children to engage social workers in communication when the child selects an object or activity as his medium of communication. This may be quite simply something sticking out of his pocket, or the badge he is wearing, or the hint or direct invitation to play a particular game together, or a sharing in a teenager's choice of records, or discussion of the posters on his wall. Again skill is needed in learning to distinguish between something set up deliberately by the child in the hopes that it will be taken up, and a talk about general matters which he may not particularly wish to enlarge upon. Thirdly, play as a substitute for language which might either be deliberately initiated by the social worker or sometimes initiated by the child who will draw the worker into his game.

176. Whether communication is through play or more formally verbal and direct, there is one theme that will be ever present. This is that of the child's ambivalence, and however much the social worker is forewarned about this he will be constantly puzzled and bewildered at every new manifestation. How does she react when an eight year old makes the statement 'Mum's left me, she's bad' and immediately dissolves into wild and helpless laughter? An adult reaction of flight into reassurances that all is well will not help a child. He knows that this is not true. But 'Tell me about it' may well help a child who is struggling with the difficulty of understanding and accepting what is happening to him.

177. The ways and means of communicating with children are many and various and social workers may wish to consider not only working directly with the foster child but also with a group of foster children in similar situations. To the social worker who is new to work in the child care field it presents a challenge and with it a need to adapt to new methods of communication. In the nature and form of communication, a child's chronological age is probably of less significance than is the stage of his emotional development. With older children who are incorporating a number of earlier stages, communication may be on many levels at different times, sometimes with the more adult part and sometimes with the more babyish. In any one day she may reassure a young baby on his transfer by arranging for him to be held comfortably in a car rather than being left on his own in a carry cot on the back seat; she may seek out an appropriate coffee bar for a talk with an adolescent; she may talk with a twenty year old who had returned to the agency to go over his life as a child and to reassure himself about his identity before embarking on marriage and having children of his own; she may spend some time on a kitchen floor playing at 'hospitals' with a three year old who is in temporary care due to the illness of his mother. Children sometimes need an oppor-

tunity to talk about themselves and their situation in a non-direct way. They need to test out their thoughts in adult company. Often a car journey gives them an opportunity to talk when they are not the primary focus of attention but where they feel secure enough to communicate their thoughts.

178. A child in a foster home, like any adult experiencing a new situation, will wonder 'Is this really me?' The social worker and the foster parents can help him in his confusion by holding on to the other part of him which existed before his placement. The need to communicate his past to the child can be met in many ways. For example, for one foster child it was the time around his father's death that seemed appropriate for the social worker to take him back to as many as possible of the people and the places that he had had connections with in the past, demonstrating what had happened to him and who he was in a very concrete way. Another method might be either in working with a child to prepare a tape recording or scrap book about his life, or making use of a scrap book prepared by the foster parents or recently added to by them. A child being given a copy of his birth certificate for the first time may need to question or requestion the implications of its content. In this sort of situation it is never sufficient that a once and for all explanation is given; constant repetition is needed, and at different stages of development a child or young person may need to go through familiar ground many times before he can accept the position.

179. The skill of communicating with children in the context of their being separated from their parents and in the care of an agency, is a skill which has to be learned. It can never be perfected and can always be improved. It is vital to the successful care of children and its nurture should be a major aim for training programmes, both in qualifying courses and in the later inservice provisions within all social work agencies.

Chapter 11
Assessing the needs of a child

180. Assessment in child care, as in all social work must be an ongoing process. As the basis of all effective planning and decision making, it calls for skills both in the assembly of relevant data and in its subsequent interpretation. The first assessment will be concerned with decisions as to whether or not a child is to be received into care, and quickly interwoven into this consideration will be the assessment as to the best kind of care which can be offered to this particular child. Later will come the reassessment of the validity of retaining the child in care alongside ongoing reviews as to the effectiveness of the care being given. Each assessment interacts with the one preceeding it and none can be seen in isolation from another.

181. Discussion about the provision and use of preventive resources is outside the scope of this Guide, but the removal of a child from home should only occur if it is in his interest and only after all other alternatives have been considered and pursued. The use of foster care in situations where the best interests of the child really lie within his family is an admission of failure; a failure of social policy and of the social services to deal with the problem at source. The implications of separation have been discussed in an earlier chapter, and it is evident that an awareness of the consequences of separating children from their families argues strongly for maximum attention being given to preventive measures.

182. However if a child has to leave his own family, then assessment of his possible need for foster care may take place either at the point of reception or committal to care or later when the child is already living in a children's home or nursery. Either way the assessment should, as far as possible, be a collaborative effort at every stage, actively involving the social worker, the family, the child, the caregivers and other agency and and allied staff.

183. Whatever the immediate purpose of the assessment, the material to be taken into consideration will be the interaction of facts and relationships which go to make up a picture of the child and his environment. This can be expressed diagramatically as follows:—

76

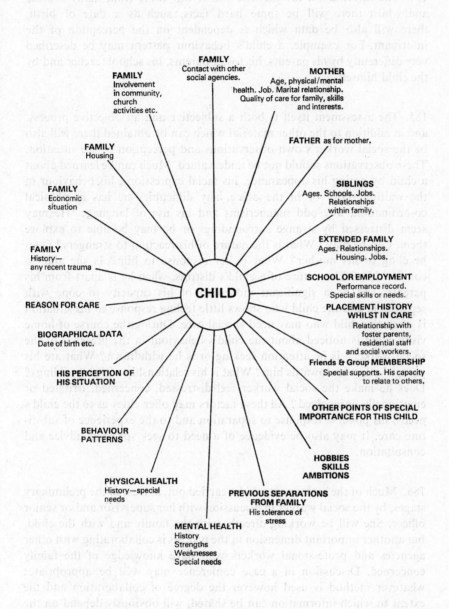

FAMILY
Contact with other
social agencies.

MOTHER
Age, physical/mental
health. Job. Marital relationship.
Quality of care for family, skills
and interests.

FAMILY
Involvement
in community,
church
activities etc.

FAMILY
Housing

FATHER as for mother.

FAMILY
Economic
situation

SIBLINGS
Ages. Schools. Jobs.
Relationships
within family.

FAMILY
History—
any recent trauma

EXTENDED FAMILY
Ages. Relationships.
Housing. Jobs.

CHILD

SCHOOL OR EMPLOYMENT
Performance record.
Special skills or needs.

REASON FOR CARE

**PLACEMENT HISTORY
WHILST IN CARE**
Relationship with
foster parents,
residential staff
and social workers.

BIOGRAPHICAL DATA
Date of birth etc.

Friends & Group MEMBERSHIP
Special supports. His capacity
to relate to others.

**HIS PERCEPTION OF
HIS SITUATION**

**OTHER POINTS OF SPECIAL
IMPORTANCE FOR THIS CHILD**

**BEHAVIOUR
PATTERNS**

**HOBBIES
SKILLS
AMBITIONS**

PHYSICAL HEALTH
History—special
needs

**PREVIOUS SEPARATIONS
FROM FAMILY**
His tolerance of
stress

MENTAL HEALTH
History
Strengths
Weaknesses
Special needs

77

184. The information for the assessment will come from many sources and whilst there will be some hard facts, such as a date of birth, there will also be data which is dependent on the perception of the informant. For example, a child's behaviour pattern may be described very differently by his parents, his foster parents, his school teacher and by the child himself.

185. The assessment itself is both a subjective and an objective process, and in addition to the other material which can be obtained there will also be the social worker's own observations and perception of the situation. These observations should not be undervalued. Much can be learned about a child by noting his appearance, his facial expressions, his behaviour in the waiting room or in the office, any difficulties he has in physical co-ordination, any odd mannerisms and his use of language. He may seem distressed by strange surroundings or he may be able to explore them. Can he play? What is the nature of his reaction to strangers? Does he cling to his mother? What is her response to him? Is she able to comfort him? The nature of a child's distress, when he is apart from his parents, will be a significant indication of his capacity to cope with separation, and the child who shows little feeling response to his situation is often the child who may need special care. During the course of home visits, what is noticed about the child's behaviour in the presence of the social worker—is he attention seeking or is he withdrawn? What are his parents' attitudes towards him? What is his relationship with any siblings? Does he make the social worker feel distressed, concerned, irritated or emotionally uninvolved? All these factors may offer clues as to the child's needs, his possible response to separation and to the experience of substitute care. It may also be evidence of a need to seek specialist advice and consultation.

186. Much of the assessment will be carried out, at least in the preliminary stages, by the social worker in discussion with her supervisor and/or senior officer. She will be working directly with the family and with the child, but another important dimension in the process is collaborating with other agencies and professional workers who have knowledge of the family concerned. Discussion in a case conference may well be appropriate; whatever method is used however the degree of collaboration and the extent to which information can be shared, will obviously depend on the quality of relationships and degree of co-operation between different workers at field level. Of particular importance are contacts with the health visitor, the general practitioner and with the staff of the school.

187. With young children the health visitor is an essential contact. She may know the family well and may be able to provide detailed information about the health and development of the pre-school child together with any significant history since his birth. For example, she may know of any history of failure to thrive as a baby and this may be indicative of difficulties which are either present now or which could emerge later. Knowledge of the child's birth history and of the mother's health both during and after pregnancy will also be of value, as are details about immunisation or other treatment currently required. If contact with the health visitor has been avoided by the family or if she has failed to gain access to the house, this may in itself be an important fact.

188. Parents may be willing for an approach to be made to their family doctor. If he knows the family well, then he also may be a source of valuable information about relevant health problems within the family. If some special assessment of the child's health and development is felt to be necessary, in addition to the medical examination required prior to boarding out, then it may be very appropriate for the doctor who already knows the child and his family to arrange for this to be carried out. Furthermore, for the child the examination may not be a threatening procedure if carried out by a person whom he can trust.

189. Paediatric, psychiatric and psychological facilities vary a great deal in different areas throughout the country, as does the practice of local agencies in making special arrangements for using consultants. In this respect it is essential to contact the area specialist in community medicine (child health) who may well have relevant knowledge of the health of the child and this may be information which is not available elsewhere. As a general rule whenever there appears to be some concern about a particular child's health, growth and development, or where there are very real signs of behaviour problems, then it is most important that the social worker consults the family doctor so that a referral to an appropriate specialist for consultation may be made at an early stage. Similarly, if the child suffers from a known handicap or disease, then it is necessary to seek advice about its management and on the timing of reviews. This will have particular implications for the placement of the child in knowing what kind of care and handling he needs, and what demands will be made of those who undertake his care. Where a parent suffers from any kind of serious condition, particularly mental illness, then it is equally important that the social worker should seek advice as to the implications of this for the child and the family as a whole. This may be vital in terms of assessing a parent's capacity for resuming care of the child or maintaining contact with him.

190. A child spends much of his time in school and information about his educational progress, behaviour, relationships and attendance record will be important in the light of any difficulties at home. Similarly, problems in learning may indicate emotional disturbance or even some kind of organic problem. The parents' attitudes, whether the child arrives perpetually late and whether he seems tired or hungry, may all be factors indicative of the home situation.

191. The social worker has a vital role to play in making as full an assessment as possible of the total family situation surrounding a child's entry into care. Clearly, however, it is impossible to cover all areas in depth in the initial stages. But assessment is an on-going process and this chapter is intended as a guide to the kind of issues which should be explored as the relationship between the social worker and family develops. The study of this material will lead to an assessment of the child's needs and of the likelihood of his being helped by placement in a foster home.

192. It is never possible to meet all human needs, but it is possible to try to assess those to which priority should be given. Each child will present a different constellation of needs but some of the varying needs of a child in care can be expressed as in the diagram opposite.

To be seen as an individual
with his own special needs

To have
hobbies

Experience of
good parenting

An environment in which
to develop any special
skills

To be loved
and to be able
to love

To maintain contact
with his own
culture

Experience of
family life

To practice his
own religion

Knowledge of
his identity

To experience a
caring discipline

**A
CHILD
NEEDS**

Opportunities to test
out adult values

Knowledge of and
contact with his
family of origin

Knowledge that he has the
support of a social worker
who knows him personally

Opportunities
for mixing with
his peer group

Not to be subjected to
demands he cannot at
that time meet

To have friends

To experience the
satisfaction of
success in some
area of life

Access to hospital
or clinic if
special
treatment is
needed

To attend a
specific
type of
school

193. The decision to seek a foster home for a child in care should only be made after a careful assessment of his needs, and after a prognostic consideration of the effect that such a placement might have on himself and on his relationships within and outside his family. If the child is being assessed at the point of reception into care, much of this data will have to be acquired within a short space of time. If the child is already in care it is essential that the assessment is made on up to date material and that incorrect assumptions about the child's background are not translated into 'known facts'.

194. The time scale is an important factor, and this may pose a dilemma for the social worker who wishes to make a very thorough study in order to select the most appropriate form of care for the child. Time is particularly important for the young child, whose capacity to tolerate breaches in the continuity of his relationships is limited according to his age and stage of development. If for assessment purposes he is kept 'in limbo', as it were, in a temporary placement, then it might well prejudice his future capacity for making relationships. Time is also important in terms of working with his parents. If they too are left 'in limbo', they may suffer similar effects of separation from the child and may begin to disengage from the situation altogether so that attempts at rehabilitation may prove to be difficult. There is a real danger of the child losing his links with his family unless they are continuously involved and helped whilst the child is in care. Their participation in a formal assessment procedure can help them to share the agency's concern for their child, and this can lay the foundation for future collaboration. This highlights the importance of devoting social work resources to the building of a collaborative relationship from the start.

195. The value of assessing the child in his own home and within his own family cannot be over-emphasised. In some circumstances, however, a child may need to be in a more neutral environment where he is apart from the pressure of negative family relationships. This may be in a residential establishment or in a short stay foster home, and it is important to remember that in this situation separation itself will have affected the child.

196. It is not a helpful practice to label children as being suitable or not suitable for fostering. Children who come into care have an infinite variety of physical, emotional, ethnic and cultural backgrounds and their earlier life experiences are compounded and intensified by the effects of separation itself. If a child is to grow up into a healthy and mature person, the

period in care should give him some form of compensatory experience. His need for stimuli to develop socially and intellectually is best met in the context of continuous and secure relationships with caring and dependable adults with whom he can feel wanted and valued. A fostering placement will not always be the most appropriate method of providing every child with such an experience and a residential placement, on an interim or longer term basis, may facilitate his development and meet his needs in a different way. Ideally any placement should be related to what the child can use, adapt to and accept at each and every stage of his development. A formal assessment procedure can help to determine what might be best for a child at a particular point in time.

197. Whatever his age, care in a family setting as provided by a foster home imposes emotional demands on the child in terms of subjecting him to close relationships. His capacity for making, sustaining and responding to such relationships is therefore important and it will be affected by the quality of his earlier experience. The assessment should reveal if a child has suffered much early deprivation, as this may later affect the chances of a successful fostering placement, or at best demand exceptional understanding, love and patience on the part of the foster parents. The child has to learn new ways of relating to himself and to other people. In the process he may constantly test out the ability of his foster parents to control and contain him within their care. Chapter 3 emphasised the importance of a continuity of experience for all children and particularly during the first three years. A foster home placement can provide the optimum conditions for continuity of care, as it is easier to adapt to individual routines, habits, likes and dislikes within a family group. A foster home therefore should always be considered as the first choice of placement for a pre-school child. There is nothing magical in a family as such. It is the quality of personal interaction provided that determines whether or not it is an invaluable caring environment for a young child.

Children with special needs

198. Some children who are received into care have special needs over and above their need for substitute care. These are the children who suffer from a physical, emotional, mental or intellectual handicap. They and their families may have had to live with this handicap from the time of the child's birth, or it may have occurred as the result of illness or accident in later years. These children make special demands on those who care for them and on society as a whole. In recent years considerable emphasis has been placed on the vital necessity to assess the total needs of each such

child and of those who care for him. Such assessment must be made on a multi-disciplinary basis and the involvement of the parent and the child is of prime importance. When a handicapped child is received into care the factor of handicap should not be a barrier to placement in a foster home. But before this is planned an acknowledgment of his special needs as a handicapped child must be included in his overall assessment.

199. It is not easy to assess the degree of disturbance in a child who has had a negative experience of parenting in his own home. Defining this experience merely in terms of good or bad, all or nothing, is too simplistic. It may be more helpful, and may lead to a more optimistic and constructive evaluation, to consider whether the care has been 'good enough' to enable development to take place. Also it is important to take into account that each increment of some continuity will enhance a child's capacity for making and trusting relationships. A child may have had little in the way of consistent caring from his mother, but nevertheless had spasmodic periods of good experience from her, as well as from other members of the immediate or extended family, such as father or an older sibling or grand-parent. In the case of an older child, a neighbour, teacher or residential worker may have become a significant caring adult in his life. A child's needs may often appear overwhelming, and there is sometimes a temptation to fall back on stereotypes and to concentrate on his weaknesses rather than on his strengths. Emphasis on the positive side of a child's personality may well balance out some of his more negative qualities and problems.

Involving the child
200. At the time of assessment it is not only important for the social worker to begin to establish a relationship with the parents, but also for her to relate to and communicate with the child. He will no doubt have views about his needs. The social worker has a special role in relation to him whilst he is in care, because she must demonstrate by her action the parental responsibility assumed by the agency. Ideally if the social worker can first get to know the child in his own home, then this in itself may represent some continuity of experience, reduce the distress and offer some security to him in the process of actual separation. Furthermore, it is in the context of this developing relationship that the social worker can begin to help him understand what is happening and to share the pain which separation brings. The extent to which this is possible obviously depends on the child's age, development and emotional needs. But even with a very young child the social worker should communicate in simple terms who she is, why she is there and what is going to happen. She must be able to

understand his spoken and silent communications and in turn be able to demonstrate to him the care and concern which is embodied in the practice of the agency. This capacity to communicate with a child is an essential quality in a social worker, for if such communication fails at the point of assessment then the future care of that child will be at risk of failure.

201. A former foster child writing to the Working Party said:—

> I do not know how it was decided I should be fostered in the first place. I suppose I was too young to be told. When I went to the first foster home, before the second fostering, I was called to the Matron's office and asked if I preferred being in a private family or in a home with lots of boys and girls. I cannot remember what I said. I was very shy. I don't think I fully understood what I was being asked. I remember asking why my own brother could not be with me, and not getting an answer. The next thing I was told I was going on holiday by the sea with a nice family that had a dog. I was quite excited. I was not told that I was a foster child, and did not know that it was to be a permanent home, but thought that it was just a holiday. After about a month I was told that I was staying for good. I remember feeling upset as I had not got any personal belongings with me (toys etc.), nor had I said goodbye to all my friends at the home where I had been living.

Emergency situations

202. Assessment in this context is an essential procedure. The first step is to decide what constitutes an emergency and whether the actual situation in question necessitates separating the child from his family. It must also be examined in the light of whether it is a temporary failure in a family's ability to cope or whether it is indicative of a more fundamental breakdown. Agencies should avoid creating emergency situations by their failure to investigate and to deal with a referral until the last minute. For instance where it is known that a parent has to go into hospital in the near future and where there are no other probable alternatives to reception into care, then the arrangements for placement should not be left until the point at which the parent is due to be admitted. Delaying the assessment of need until care is imminent will seldom lead to the provision of the care best suited to the individual child.

203. There will always be some situations in which there is little time available for assessment. It may be a matter of days or possibly only hours. The questions for the social worker are then how to make best use of the time available in order to make some assessment of the child's needs, how these can be met, and the preparation of those who will care for him. Firstly, it is important to obtain as many factual details as possible, particularly name, address, date of birth, doctor, and school if relevant. Even in a crisis a parent is often able to provide useful details about feeding, daily

routines, handling, favourite possessions, etc., which are so important for minimising the distress of separation for a child. Sometimes relatives or neighbours providing temporary care can be helpful in this way too. The social worker's initial observations of a child's behaviour in the office or in his home, are also important: as is information from a health visitor, family doctor or school. Secondly, some thought needs to be given to the actual management of separation in a situation where there may be little or no time for prior familiarisation, preparation and introduction. This is considered further in paragraphs 232 and 242. In fact much of the assessment may have to be carried out during the actual process of separation. The essential factor is that in the rush to cope with an emergency the discipline of assessment should not be overlooked.

204. The assessment of children in care will be made in many contrasting situations. It may take place in the rush of an emergency admission or committal by a court, or it may be achieved in the relative calm of a case conference held in a reception home or in the area office. But whatever the situation, there are some vital ingredients to good practice which should always be present. The first of these is that the assessment should be based on the fullest information it is possible to obtain; the second is that the assessment should be the result of a shared consultation which involves the social workers, the foster parents, other associated professionals, the parents and the child. The third essential is that any decisions reached should be recorded together with the reasons for the decision being made; the fourth is that the child and his parents should be aware of the assessment which has been made and of its implications for his future care.

205. An assessment of a child should lead to a working hypothesis as to the kind of care and environment which will best meet his needs and it should set a target for the future work of the caring agency. It must be emphasised that the long term effects of separation will be influenced by the long term experiences which follow. The actual care, however, will always have to depend on the resources available and it may not be possible to achieve the ideal for each and every child. But time spent on an assessment is time well used, for it will enable an agency to achieve the best possible match between resources and need.

Chapter 12
Choosing a home for a child

206. When a child has been assessed as being one whose needs will be best met in a foster home, then the process of choosing a home begins. On one hand there is an outline of the kind of home which might meet his needs. Ideals now have to be tempered by reality as the best possible match is sought for the individual child. It should be the aim of every agency which provides a foster care service to build up a pool of potential foster parents. The selection of foster parents for such a pool is considered in Chapter 18 but at the time of choosing a home for a child, the emphasis should be on matching the needs of a specific child with the assessed qualities and expectations of an approved foster home.

207. The tug of love situation can exist at the time of placement as well as later on. Whether his placement in a foster home is being considered straight from the child's own home, from a children's home or from another foster home the move will involve him in ambivalent feelings. The dilemma for a child can be that if his decision is made the main criterion for action then he has to take on the burden of rejecting one home in order to go elsewhere. He may not be able to tolerate this. Often children may not be able to verbalise their feelings and the social worker has a particular responsibility to be aware of the unspoken wishes of the child. A child's participation in decision making therefore may be limited because he can be immobilised by a conflict of loyalties. At the same time opportunity should be given for older children to have some control over their future and they should perhaps be allowed to take risks. If mistakes are made, the young person should be helped to put the experience to positive use. Whatever the age group a skill in communicating with children is essential. This need is discussed in Chapter 10.

208. It is not always easy to predict just how an individual child will respond to a new environment, and in generalising about the likely effects of separation it is important to remember that children are individual and overtly react in different ways. Some may react immediately with anger and protest, even with very destructive or aggressive behaviour. Others may be very withdrawn, almost unable to respond outwardly to the care given at all. Some children may appear to settle into a new environment

with apparently no difficulty of any kind, and only when they feel safe and trusting do they begin to test out the security of the placement. The stresses, strains and demands on an individual child will pose different problems for individual foster families. Some will be able to manage and tolerate behaviour of one kind and not another. During the selection process the particular strengths and weaknesses of a foster home have been assessed and possible areas of vulnerability recognised. In the process of matching a child with a prospective placement, it is crucial to try and anticipate areas of possible stress and difficulty. Preparing a foster family beforehand and helping them to understand the child's behaviour and attitudes is important, for it is sometimes easier to cope with difficulties when they are expected. This recognition of potential problems will also indicate any additional social work or other specialist support which should be provided. Fostering is altogether a difficult task and foster parents should never be asked to undertake the care of a child whose needs are clearly outside their capacity to meet.

209. A foster family's expectation of their role will have been considered at the selection stage. The needs and expectations of a prospective foster family matter in each and every placement; these should be considered in relation to the needs of a particular child. Similarly both the social worker and the foster family need to be aware of the possible impact of a particular child on the family as a whole. He is likely to have an effect on family organisation and life style. In addition, the placement involves the family in a whole new network of relationships; with the agency, the social worker, the child's family, whether absent or in contact, and possibly other agencies and specialists if the child requires treatment of any kind.

210. Fostering is not in itself inappropriate for children suffering from any form of handicap, but their condition calls for special care and understanding. The foster parents of handicapped children have to be able to distinguish between normal disturbances caused by the stress of separation and those related to the handicap. They have to be aware of the dangers of over-protection which may create or reinforce inappropriate dependency in the child. They have to be able to apply concerned and consistent discipline rather than be prey to a deep reluctance to control in case they cause further harm to the child. The choice of a home which is unable to meet these needs will not help the child.

211. Tensions in fostering relationships are often related to difficulties over control and punishment. For this reason the issue of discipline should be

carefully discussed at each stage of every placement, but particularly during selection. It will be important to discover what is usual in the family and what adults can accept. All control should be exercised from within a caring relationship. The overall combination of care and control needed by any particular child will depend upon his age and developmental need. Within a consistent pattern of care there may be times when additional disciplinary measures are necessary in response to a particular incident. Whatever sanction is applied, it must never violate the child as a person, must be felt by him as appropriate to the misdemeanour and must take into account his previous experience. For example, a child who has previously suffered physical abuse may be especially vulnerable to what might in other circumstances be seen as a normal chastisement. Similarly, a child who has undergone mental suffering will have particular vulnerabilities. As with most issues in fostering, this is one which requires general attention at the selection stage, renewed discussion in the context of a particular child's needs when a foster home is being chosen, and specific focus in the event of subsequent behavioural difficulties.

212. One of the most crucial questions in selecting a placement is the length of time the child is likely to be in care, as this will be a factor in determining the task to be undertaken by the foster family and their role in relation to the child which must be made clear from the start. Underlying this whole issue is the relationship of the child to his parents, whether they are likely to resume care of the child eventually, and if not whether they are able to maintain some kind of contact or none at all. This is discussed in more detail in Chapter 15. If the aim is eventual rehabilitation, then the placement must be planned, prepared for and committed to this from the start. Foster family, child, parent and social worker need to share the task of keeping the child's attachment to his family alive and together work towards his return home. In this respect continuity in terms of maintaining a child's environment is important in mitigating the adverse effects of separation and keeping in touch with his family. A foster home geographically close to the child's own home and neighbourhood will maximise opportunities for retaining links with his family, school, friends, playgroup, etc.

213. Where, however, the child requires a substitute family situation in which he can make his primary attachments, the role demanded of the foster family will be very different. In this situation consideration needs to be given as to how a child's sense of identity can be maintained, whether his own family are able to remain in contact or whether they are partially or totally absent from his life, and to the extent to which the foster family can meet his particular needs in this respect. Inevitably there are situations

the outcome of which it is not possible to assess or to predict accurately at the outset, or which change over time; for instance short term situations become long term or indeterminate. However, what needs to be stressed is that such changes should not just happen without formal recognition and acknowledgement. The role of the foster family must always be clarified and redefined. Consideration should be given to whether or not the placement remains an appropriate one from the child's, the family's and foster family's point of view.

214. The parents' attitude toward the selection of a fostering placement is important. Parents may be actively seeking or requesting foster care or at least be co-operating over this. On the other hand, the suggestion of a foster home may be seen as the final sanction of society that they are unfit parents, and may reinforce their feelings of deprivation and stigma already compounded by the loss of their child. However, if they have been helped from the start to feel that they have a valuable and essential contribution to make in planning for their child, then perhaps they can come to understand the reasoning for the choice of such a placement in relation to his needs. Without such involvement, the placement may be less successful, and this can be so whether the parents abdicate altogether or are disruptive in their attitude.

215. Where parents cannot accept the idea of fostering, this raises the difficult issue of whether the agency should over-ride their wishes. The child's needs should be paramount in the selection of a placement but this is not always as straight forward as it sounds. It must not be overlooked that part of the child's needs may well be a continued harmonious relationship with his parents, and the possible gains of foster care must be assessed against the possibility of losing his parents or facing the fact that unhelpful and stressful conflict may be generated through prolonged and determined opposition. In certain cases, particularly with school age children, it may be necessary to consider whether a residential placement is a positive form of care for the child with which parents are more able to co-operate. Indeed the child, if old enough, may prefer this as a more successful way of maintaining family ties. If however it is decided to place a child in a foster home against parental wishes, the placement must be adequately prepared and given particularly skilled social work support. Otherwise it is at the risk of breakdown and may lead to a state of conflict and divided loyalties for the child. In these circumstances the agency will wish to consider the adequacy of the existing legal status of the child and his parents.

The needs of siblings

216. Parents will usually have firm views about keeping their children together in one home, and the issue of planning and selecting placements for siblings poses a number of dilemmas. The overriding commitment may be to keep them together and it makes sense that this possibility should always be considered first. In this consideration thought must be given to any difficulty in meeting the needs of an individual child, or perhaps of two children, within the family group. In some families children may have little experience of growing up together and of establishing close relationships with one another. There may be very destructive rivalry between them. On the other hand for some children the attachment to siblings or with a particular sibling may be of extreme importance. This may be especially true in the absence of other family relationships, for instance where parents have totally disappeared or are dead, but is equally true in other circumstances in terms of continuity of experience. The presence of a loved sibling can be a crucial factor in easing and managing the stress of separation from parents and home. Nevertheless decisions and plans can only be made on the basis of an assessment of the individual needs of a child and the quality and meaning of relationships and interaction between them or within the group. It can be very difficult to find a foster home placement which will accept several children. Time has to be given to such a search otherwise siblings may remain in residential care for no other reason than that they can all be together.

217. Separate placements, or perhaps placements of two children together, may have to be arranged through lack of resources. On the other hand they may offer more in terms of meeting individual needs. Either way it should not mean loss of contact between siblings, for where the size of the family precludes fostering the children together, then family ties may be kept by fostering children with near neighbours or with families which are related to one another. The requirement is the selection of foster families who can accept the commitment of either working together or with a residential establishment in order to keep the children in touch with each other. Such a situation, however, puts additional demands on the foster parents and this should not be underestimated. When families are divided in this way, the pairing or grouping of the children is of great importance. The obvious pairings may not in fact be the best, and this is an area where often it is the children themselves who can offer the best suggestions as to who goes with whom.

218. When all the children are placed together, attention must be paid to the foster family's ability to meet the needs of more than one young child with all the investment of time and energy and possible stress which this may involve. This is particularly so when the children are under five years of age. In such a situation, the offer of additional services and support, for example a home help or financial provision, can enable the foster mother to have assistance with the heavy domestic chores involved.

Life style of the family

219. The stress of separation from his family can be lessened if the child can go to a foster home which has a life style similar to that of his own family. The social worker will need to know about various practical aspects of family life: how daily routines such as meals and bedtime are organised and the importance placed upon them; the way leisure time is spent; the kind of activities in which a foster child would be expected to share. Children can tolerate and thrive in a vastly differing environment to their own home, but such differences can create problems and conflict of identity. They should be the exception rather than the rule.

220. For some families religion is an important factor in their lives. In the assessment of the child, it will have been ascertained how important religion is in the family life generally and what meaning it holds for the child. Where religious practices are strictly observed, for example the observance of religious festivals, dietry requirements, rituals, then clearly this will have implications for the kind of life style to which the child has been accustomed, possibly for his diet, and for child-rearing practices and cultural values generally. Special consideration will need to be given to the placement of such a child so that his sense of identity and continuity of experience can be preserved. There may also be implications for maintaining his links with his own community and neighbourhood.

221. In cases where religion is clearly of significance, efforts must be made to find an appropriate placement in order that as much continuity as possible can be preserved for the child. Being deprived of his distinctive religious identity, which may also have specific cultural implications, adds to the trauma of separation. It also prevents a child from identifying with his family or community.

222. With the best will in the world, however, it may not always be possible to place a child with a foster family of the same religious persuasion, particularly if the child is also from a minority ethnic group. In such a situation the foster home must be selected with particular care. To foster

a child from a distinctive religious background will demand from the foster parents a greater flexibility and a recognition and tolerance of differences between themselves and the child, as well as the ability to cope with practical demands such as taking him to a place of worship or preparing a special diet. Furthermore, it will involve helping the child to avoid possible confusion of identity and loyalty. He may have feelings of being different because of his religion as well as not being a natural child of the family. He may also be geographically separated from other members of his religious community. This will make demands of the foster family over and above those normally made in caring for a child separated from his family and usual environment. Before a placement is made it is vital that the foster family is fully aware of such demands and expectations, and that they have agreed willingly to carry them out and have taken into account the possible affect on their own children and life style. Some indication of the kind of help and support which they can call upon and expect in dealing with this situation should be made clear beforehand, for example advice about particular religious observance, special dietry laws and contact with relevant community groups.

223. Some children who come into care will be from immigrant communities. Their situation has been discussed earlier in Chapter 6. Some responsible groups hold the view that substitute care for immigrant children is best provided by families of like origin. This view is based on a recognition of the importance of cultural factors in identity formation and of the psychological and social problems which can result from cultural damage and confusion. This may be especially relevant to long term care, but it has implications too for short stay placements, particularly when the child is not old enough to comprehend the facts of the separation. As with religious aspects, this is an aspect of continuity of experience which can help to reduce separation trauma and which should not be overlooked in selecting a foster home.

224. The needs of each child and family will vary, but even when the needs of the child indicate that a foster home culturally similar to his own home is required, realistically it may not be possible to provide this because of an imbalance between demand and the availability of such homes. The fact that the placement selected does not offer a similar cultural environment should not mean that cultural factors are ignored. The foster family must have a positive attitude towards the child's cultural background and be willing and able to understand and accept certain aspects of that culture which are relevant to fostering. For example, the foster parents' ability to give help with the care of skin and hair of a

black child is crucial to the child's self image. Similarly, both parents and foster parents must have an understanding of each others family culture. Some immigrant groups do not favour permissive behaviour in their children. They traditionally use a more controlling framework of discipline than that which is found in many families in the host community. If misunderstandings arise they will only cause more hurt and confusion to the child.

Predictive factors

225. The choice of a foster home for a child inevitably brings with it a large element of prediction. Prediction is difficult in social work but a few studies have attempted to look at the success and failure of long term foster home placements and their possible predictive factors. This is a difficult field for research studies and there is a lack both of ongoing work and of studies which have been replicated on a national basis. In addition studies vary in their focus, some looking at the rate of breakdown, others considering current adjustment of foster children, or the adult adjustment of former foster children.

226. Comparisons of and general conclusions from various studies should be treated with caution, and evidence on specific or clusters of factors predicting success and failure is conflicting and complex. Nevertheless attention is drawn to the following areas which seem to emerge as significant in several studies, and it may be pertinent to take account of their relevance both in selecting a placement for a child and in assessing the social work task in each particular situation.

    i. The very high risk of breakdown in long term fostering, particularly during the first year, to a lesser extent during the second year of placement, and during adolescence, is a consistent finding in all the research. This should serve to underline the importance of social work support and supervision during these critical periods.

    ii. The child's age at placement is an important but complex factor. Generally the younger the child when placed, the greater the chances of successful placement, particularly if he is placed before twelve months and up to two years. Children placed over the age of five tend to be less successful. However research findings also indicate the higher degree of disturbance in children who come into care before the age of five and points to the vulnerability of the age group two to four.

94

iii. In addition to his age the child's previous experience of substitute care also appears to be significant. In relation to residential care, some studies suggest that children who spend time during their first three years in residential care are more likely to fail in a foster home. However, it is the length of time which seems to be the critical factor, and a short period in residential care may sometimes be conducive to success, particularly where it is used for careful assessment and planning for placement.

iv. As far as previous experience of foster care is concerned, in general changes appear to point to a greater possibility of poor adjustment, if not breakdown, in subsequent placement. Nevertheless, studies show that a second placement may be successful where the first was short term and did not terminate by reason of failure or breakdown. Obviously, this must also be considered in the context of the age of the child.

v. Contact with the natural family is another important area for consideration. There is evidence to suggest that children are less disturbed and the placement more successful where they are in touch with their natural family, particularly if the contact is consistent and frequent. This also links with the children's understanding of their situation, both in relation to the foster family and the agency.

vi. A number of factors relating to the foster family too, are seen to be significant in several studies, for instance the age of the foster mother. Some evidence suggests that those over thirty are less likely to fail than those under twenty-five, and the children placed with such foster mothers are less disturbed. However, age in itself may be less important than its implications in terms of maturity and experience, and the greater possibility that their own children, if any, are not near in age to the foster child(ren).

vii. Certainly some studies show that experienced foster mothers, that is experienced in terms of the length of time they have been fostering or the number of placements which they have undertaken, are associated with a low incidence of breakdown and disturbance.

viii. Furthermore there is some evidence which suggests that social class is an important factor. Several research studies have indicated that placements within lower social class families tend to be more successful, but other studies are inconclusive.

ix. Both the presence and absence of natural children of the foster parents is shown to be significant in terms of success. Possibly, contrary to expectations, placements with childless couples are particularly successful. This may be due to the absence of rivalry, but perhaps more important is the foster parents' attitude towards their own childlessness and their understanding of the fostering role. This understanding may depend on the quality of work done during the assessment and selection stage. Where there are natural children, the effect on the outcome of the placement, successful or otherwise, depends on their age in relation to the foster child. Evidence suggests that if they are under five, younger than the foster child, or within three to five years of the age of the foster child, then there is a higher risk of failure or breakdown. Again, however, much will depend on the recognition and understanding of the potential risks by both foster parents and social worker and the positive efforts made to minimise them.

227. It should be emphasised that reference to the various studies will not provide absolute proof for or against a particular foster placement or confirm that the placement of a specific child is desirable. It may nevertheless, be a useful way of testing individual assessments. Furthermore, it may help to point out some of the risks involved and indicate where and at what stage social work time and possibly specialist support should be given to the placements. It is not always possible to await or rely on formal studies in order to evaluate the reliability of practice. However, a careful and honest assessment of each decision in the light of subsequent developments is a form of reality testing readily available to every social worker and supervisor.

Decision making to be shared

228. The selection of the kind of placement and the choice of one in particular should never be the responsibility of the social worker alone. Decision making at this stage should again include some kind of team approach. How this is arranged will obviously depend on each agency's organisational framework. What is important in the context of any organisation, is that the reasons underlying the choice should be clearly recorded, as should a definition of the aims of the placement and expectations of the roles of all the parties involved. These factors should be the basis for the contractual relationship for each individual placement and will be important in terms of continuing assessment and future reviews. The relevance of this for the organisation of the agency is referred to in Chapter 19.

Chapter 13
Placing a child in a foster home

229. Once the decision to foster a child has been made then a great deal of careful thought must go into the preparation for the placement and into the act of placement itself. Whatever happens at this stage will have a profound influence on the ultimate effectiveness of fostering as a means of care for this particular child. It is essential that at this time the social worker has opportunities for professional consultation and for supervision within her employing agency.

Who is involved?

230. Up to this time the discussions with the foster parents, the parents and the child will have explored the possibility of foster care. But now the situation alters and generalisations about the nature of fostering change to specific factors relating to this child and to this particular foster home. Concepts previously explored in an abstract sense are now related to a real situation. The social worker has to move from an abstract consideration of need to actually enabling needs to be met, and she will have to work simultaneously with the child and those directly involved in his care. These people will include the foster family, residential social work staff and the child's own family. It may also include short stay foster parents or the staff of a hospital where the child may be living at the time. All these parties will have their own needs and reactions to the placing of the child in this particular foster home. In practice of course, individuals are not held in discrete parts but are involved in a dynamic process reacting to and affecting each other. The skill of the social worker will be in meeting their separate needs as far as is possible. But at the same time she must focus her work on the primary person in the situation, and that is the child.

Sharing information with the child

231. Any change in a child's life may reactivate former problems and former questions. One such question for a child relates to why he is in care. When a child is being placed in a foster home he may have been in care for a long period of time. He may have spent some years in a foster home or residential placement, on the other hand he may have had many moves

97

between differing forms of care. Other children will be coming straight from their own homes. The variations are considerable and were discussed in Chapter 1 of this Guide. However, in all situations the individual child will have the need to know the answer to his question 'why am I in care?' The principle of shared and maximum involvement stressed in earlier chapters requires this. This may seem a statement of the obvious, but it is all too easy to assume that because the grown-ups know why a situation has occurred, the child will too. Of course, the child's ability to understand will vary but even quite young children should be talked with and helped to grasp what is happening to them. The mere imparting of facts is not enough; communication with the child needs to be at the level of his feelings about the situation.

232. When the child comes into foster care direct from his home, he needs help in order to grasp and to accept as far as possible the reasons why he is leaving his family. This work will have been started before he is separated from his family, but in emergency admissions this kind of discussion will have to be carried on in a very concentrated period of time, or even while the move is under way, or sometimes even in retrospect. In any event it is not a once and for all exercise, and it cannot be too strongly emphasised that adults must remain sensitive to the child's needs for subsequent discussion. However, helping the child to face and integrate the separation experience must begin at the earliest possible moment so that bewilderment and pain do not lead to his blocking out what is happening to him, or to his concluding that the reasons must be related to his own badness. Facing up to this is unlikely to be easy either for the child or for the adults in his world, but collusion with the child to avoid inherent stresses must be avoided. Once a child is placed in a foster home his social worker will be his link with the agency responsible for his care. If the child and the social worker have not shared, and do not continue to share, with each other their perception as to why he is in care, then she cannot fulfil the responsibilities of her job.

233. For the child being transferred from a residential establishment, this kind of work should have been undertaken at the point of coming into care, but a further move may reactivate feelings associated with old partings, even right back to the primary separation from mother. It is necessary to be mindful of this so that the current move to a foster home is set within the total context of the child's life, past and future.

234. Preparing the child for his first meeting with possible foster parents will be part of the social work task. It is usually best if the social worker

is relaxed and honest about the purpose of the meeting, since children are quick to sense if they are not taken into the confidence of adults. Any false position tends to increase feelings of insecurity and makes it difficult for them to give expression to doubts and fears.

235. During the process of placing a child in a foster home a social worker has to answer many questions from all involved. Part of her work is to consider also the questions which have not been asked, and to make sure that all the relevant information is made available and not just that which is requested. No two situations are alike and the dependance on a check list of relevant questions is not to be recommended. Lists however can be helpful, if they are regarded as being the starting point for flexing the imagination and for considering the unique needs in each individual case. What kind of question then can arise at the time of placement in a foster home? The following chart is a starting point from which the practitioner can continue in relation to a particular child. In practice the list of questions will be longer and will include the detail of sleeping, feeding, toileting and all the personal data unique to each child. The social worker will need to be sensitive and imaginative to make sure that she recognises and communicates all these facts.

236. Some questions for the social worker when arranging the placement of a child in a foster home

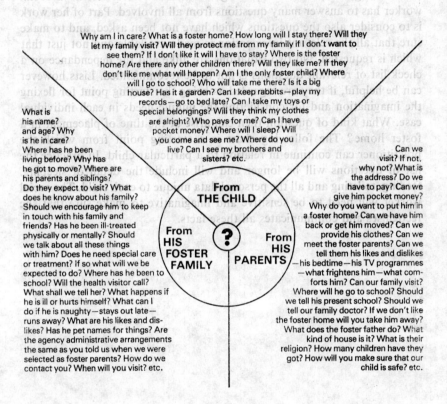

From THE CHILD

Why am I in care? What is a foster home? How long will I stay there? Will they let my family visit? Will they protect me from my family if I don't want to see them? If I don't like it will I have to stay? Where is the foster home? Are there any other children there? Will they like me? If they don't like me what will happen? Am I the only foster child? Where will I go to school? Who will take me there? Is it a big house? Has it a garden? Can I keep rabbits—play my records—go to bed late? Can I take my toys or special belongings? Will they think my clothes are alright? Who pays for me? Can I have pocket money? Where will I sleep? Will you come and see me? Where do you live? Can I see my brothers and sisters? etc.

From HIS FOSTER FAMILY

What is his name? and age? Why is he in care? Where has he been living before? Why has he got to move? Where are his parents and siblings? Do they expect to visit? What does he know about his family? Should we encourage him to keep in touch with his family and friends? Has he been ill-treated physically or mentally? Should we talk about all these things with him? Does he need special care or treatment? If so what will we be expected to do? Where has he been to school? Will the health visitor call? What shall we tell her? What happens if he is ill or hurts himself? What can I do if he is naughty—stays out late—runs away? What are his likes and dislikes? Has he pet names for things? Are the agency administrative arrangements the same as you told us when we were selected as foster parents? How do we contact you? When will you visit? etc.

From HIS PARENTS

Can we visit? If not, why not? What is the address? Do we have to pay? Can we give him pocket money? Why do you want to put him in a foster home? Can we have him back or get him moved? Can we provide his clothes? Can we meet the foster parents? Can we tell them his likes and dislikes —his bedtime—his TV programmes —what frightens him—what comforts him? Can our family visit? Where will he go to school? Should we tell his present school? Should we tell our family doctor? If we don't like the foster home will you take him away? What does the foster father do? What kind of house is it? What is their religion? How many children have they got? How will you make sure that our child is safe? etc.

Although this diagram has divided the questions between the participants many will be shared. The crucial thing is that the right questions are asked and that communication flows freely between all concerned.

The problem of giving answers

237. A question once put either directly or indirectly is not necessarily dealt with by one answer alone. Few people can remember everything that is said to them and each will have his or her own perception of both question and answer. In foster care an important factor is that as far as possible the basic information needed by each party should be made available to them, and where gaps exist this fact should be acknowledged. For example, a child may not know that his father is in prison or that his mother has a terminal illness. It is not enough for the foster parents to know the facts. They must also know what the child has been told and, if there is a gap in his knowledge, what if anything they should do about this. If a child has been removed from parents who have ill-treated him then the foster parents must be told. They will also need to know the form of ill-treatment so that they do not inadvertently cause further fear in the child. A social worker may spend many years answering and re-answering some of the questions raised in the chart, but in foster care practice it is essential that at the time of placement she formulates the questions relevant for this child, this foster family and these parents. At this time she must make sure that the information basis of the placement is as well laid as is that of the personal relationships concerned.

238. The need of foster parents is to have relevant information about a particular child, in addition to their general understanding of children. Social workers may face a dilemma here. Much of the information that should be given is confidential, but if foster parents are to be adequately prepared a great deal of this must be shared with them. If the placement later fails, or the child is in fact never placed, the social worker cannot retrieve the information which has been given. Nevertheless, it is not right to expect foster parents to respond skilfully to an individual child without proper preparation. It is important, therefore, in sharing confidential information about the child and his family to consider what facts actually need to be passed on, and what the foster parents themselves need to know as opposed to what the wider foster family should be told. Much information may be restricted to those in 'parenting' roles.

The time scale for the child

239. Choosing a home for a child runs parallel with preparing him for placement, and perhaps the first essential in this preparation will be an exploration of his capacity to take part in the decisions about the time factors involved. Over preparation can raise anxiety, but what can be discussed with a child and what can be imparted by non-verbal communication will depend on his stage of development. His stage of

development will also determine his ability to handle the concept of time, and in working with deprived children this factor may relate much more to the developmental rather than to the actual age. If we accept that stress can activate regression, there comes the implication that it decreases the time span within which a child can project, consider and retain an idea. This time factor must have implications for involving the child in decision making and in preparing him for placement. Many children are enthusiastic about a project but later, after much adult work has brought it to reality, the child says 'But I don't want it now'. The time scale of an adult may tolerate a delay between the decision to foster and the arrival of a foster child. But the parent or the child himself, when regressing under stress, cannot tolerate such a gap between decision and action. In the fostering situation the time scale for the child must be within his comprehension but there is a danger that our adult time scales for preparation and placement relate to adult needs. This time scale will be a vital consideration in working with the child—it will affect not only decision making but also how much he can be expected to participate in the preliminary exploration of potential foster homes.

Pre-placement contact

240. There should be an introduction between child and foster family in advance of the actual placement, although obviously the length and nature of this will vary according to the situation and to the age of the child. The opportunity to know more about the foster family through meeting them beforehand is an essential way of easing the moment of placement itself.

241. When the child comes into foster care directly from his home, it is helpful if the foster mother can visit the family to meet parents and child before the fostering starts. It is even better if this can be followed up by the mother, or another adult of similar significance to the child, taking him on an introductory visit to the foster home. The advantage of the mother doing this, especially but not exclusively in the case of a young child, is that it can reassure the child that mother actually knows where the foster home is and, therefore, by implication, where he will be. This can help the child to avoid feeling irretrievably lost and abandoned by his parents. There are advantages for the parents too. Such a visit should give them a more realistic view of the people who will be caring for their child, where he will live and how he will be looked after.

242. Prior meetings between child/foster parents and parent/foster parents allow for direct discussion about the child's particular needs and idiosyn-

crasies. Through this, and through direct handling of the child, the foster parents begin to get to know him and in turn become familiar figures to the child. In this way child and foster parents have the best possible start together. This contact, together with the continuity of as much of his former life as possible, makes a link in the mind of the child between parents and foster parents. This can ensure that the transition from home to foster home, and back again, will be as smooth as possible. In short stay cases it is all too easy to neglect this preliminary work just because the period of care required is so short. This fails to recognise the child's limited ability to comprehend time and to hold constant for himself the familiar routines and experiences which provide security and comfort. Additionally, it is sometimes thought that this kind of prior familiarisation is not possible in emergency placements. Quite apart from the fact that the number of emergency placements could probably be reduced through an acceptance of the importance of preparation, this overlooks what can be achieved in a limited amount of time. Even as little as an hour or so together before leaving his home can give the child and foster mother a better start than if there had been no period of familiarisation at all.

243. So far as a planned longer term placement is concerned, the length of the introduction will depend upon many factors. The most important will be the child's age and stage of development. Visits will need to be fairly close together and, again, the small child's shorter span of memory must be appreciated. However, it may also be important for an older child that introductory visiting is fairly concentrated, so that the situation does not drift into uncertainty and go 'off the boil'. It is not possible to lay down an ideal time. Some children may need many months of getting to know the foster family; others a much shorter period of time. The wishes of the foster family must always be considered in this respect but must be discussed with them in relation to the needs of the child. When the foster family has made up its mind that it wants to have the child, this is clearly an important factor in making the situation work. But they must not rush the child and the social worker into missing several important steps. The temptation may be considerable but must be resisted. The social worker must always accept responsibility for the final decision, taking into account the child's wishes both overtly and indirectly expressed.

244. The first meeting between child and foster parents should, whenever possible, be in a place familiar to the child. This can help him to feel less anxious and to behave more naturally. In planned long term foster care the child is usually moving from a residential establishment, in which case his social worker should be present at this first meeting. The child's key

residential worker must also be closely involved at this stage. This involvement of the residential worker will help the child and make it easier for him to talk about the proposed fostering in between visits. Thought will need to be given as to whether any members of the foster parents' family should be present at the first meeting. However it should not be just a day out for the family; each person must be there for a purpose and too many people might overwhelm the child.

245. After the first meeting a usual pattern is for further short visits to be made. It may be helpful if the foster parents call for the child and take him on an outing to a neutral environment, such as a local place of interest, or for a meal. If the foster parents alone have taken part in the first visit this would then be a chance to bring in other members of their family. Further contact can then be arranged, including visits to the foster home. In the case of the 'long stay' child it is more likely that the social worker or residential worker, rather than his parent, will take part in any visit to the foster home. Such visits should be as informal as possible with little fuss, for example not too elaborate a welcome or too formal a meal. Then overnight or weekend visits can be planned, depending on the age of the child. Again too much excitement or artificiality should be avoided, as the child needs to get to know the family as they usually are, and they him.

246. So far the focus has been on the child but this pre-placement work involves and makes considerable demands on the foster family. Whilst the determining factor must be the child's interests, the foster family must be able to contribute to decision-making at this stage; if they feel uncomfortable about plans made this will intrude in their beginning relationship with the child. The placement of a foster child makes demands on each member of the family. The number of interpersonal relationships are increased within the family and patterns of living, including family activity, have to be adjusted to accommodate to the needs of the foster child. Visiting relatives, taking trips, playing games, routines about mealtimes, bath time, etc. all may be altered by the presence of another child. The foster parents' own children need to be involved again here. For example, they may be prepared to share toys with a child who is staying for a short time but would feel differently if he is going to be there for a long time. These issues will have been considered during the selection process, but they can usefully be rediscussed in light of the reality of placement.

When the decision is made

247. If all goes well during the preparatory period and the placement is finally decided upon, then the child must know in advance the date of the

proposed move. It he is old enough he can be involved in fixing this as part of his central involvement in the planning period. If the stay is for more than a few weeks, and if it includes a change of school and neighbourhood, then he must have an opportunity to say farewell to his teachers and friends and to tell them where he is going to live. When transferring from residential care he must be able to say proper goodbyes to the staff and to other important people connected with the home. He will need to be reassured that he will be welcome back on a visit if he so wishes. If his parents are still in contact with him, or are important to him, he must know that they are aware of the date of his move and the address of where he is going. In these instances it will help the child to know that his parents are being kept fully informed or are involved in the discussions about his placement. When there is active parental involvement it would normally be appropriate for the parents and foster parents to meet during the introductory stage. Finally, the child must know who will be taking him to the foster home on the actual date of transfer.

The time of transfer

248. When children go to foster care from their own homes it is highly desirable that the parents and foster parents help with the actual transfer of the child. This can be regarded as essential for young children, as the direct handover avoids yet another potentially bewildering or even frightening experience of unfamiliar handling by a third person. However the situation is managed, the child should always have the opportunity to say goodbye to those he leaves behind. Farewells are always stressful but children need the security of saying goodbye. The adult who slips away so as not to upset the child does in fact cause distress but is not there to see its manifestation. For children already in care on a longer term basis it may be important that the social worker who is known to the child takes him to the foster home. The journey will provide an opportunity to talk over any last minute uncertainties which might quite naturally arise.

249. Whether going to a short or a long term placement the child may want to rediscuss certain crucial issues at this time, for example about the position of his own family in relation to himself and how much contact they will expect to have with his foster parents. Clearly, in relation to short term care, this is an area for reassurance because if the stay in the foster home is accepted by everyone as temporary, it is designed to help both parents and child through a particular period of difficulty. In indefinite situations, particularly where the child has been in care for some time and is being moved from residential care, the situation may not be so clear cut.

However, where parents matter to the child, every effort should be made to minimise his conflict so that he does not experience avoidable guilt about relationships with either his own or the foster family.

250. The foster parents will be required to complete the statutory agreement to foster this particular child. Although this will have been discussed with them in general terms at the point when they were considering becoming foster parents, they will now need to see the agreement in the light of a specific individual undertaking.

251. The point of transfer is the time when the social worker should ensure that the full resources of her agency are involved in giving practical support to the foster family. This involves re-checking and making sure that the necessary information and material aids have been given to the family. Information which must be given to the foster parents at this time will include:—

Name, address and telephone number of social worker.

Name, address and telephone number of senior social worker or fostering liaison officer.

Information about out of office hours arrangements.

       ,,   ,,   agency policies, especially delegated decisions for individual children.

       ,,   ,,   boarding out allowance—amounts and arrangements.

       ,,   ,,   provision of clothing for children.

       ,,   ,,   equipment available to foster families.

       ,,   ,,   other special services available for foster children and families.

Much of this kind of general information and procedure can usefully be set out in a departmental handbook for foster parents. It is also important to see that the child has adequate clothing and his personal possessions on arrival and that the foster home has the equipment necessary to give proper care to the child, for example cot, nappies, feeding bottle, and so on.

252. The foster parents should know exactly when the child will be arriving, or is to be collected by them, and who else will be, or should be, present. For example, if in preparation for placement the child had

developed a special contact with a child of the foster family, it may be helpful if he or she is in the home when the child arrives. The foster parents should know when they may next expect to see the social worker; this should be at least within a week after the placement. They should be reassured that if necessary they are expected to make contact in advance of this visit, and if they are on the telephone the social worker should make a point of telephoning the day after placement to ask how things are going.

Immediate post-placement

253. For the first few days after placement the foster family will be wise to keep life as normal as possible with no emphasis on treats or excursions beyond those which the family would usually have. It will be important to allow the child to show any distress and to stand by him through this period and not to attempt to jolly him out of it. It will be a time of many new experiences, for example going to a new school is always something of an ordeal. An introductory visit would probably be helpful, and the foster mother would be expected to take the child to school on the first day as a mother would her own child. Another new experience may be meeting the family doctor and it may be necessary to introduce the child to a new doctor fairly speedily. The point has been made that the foster parents need full information to enable them to answer questions. For a child currently receiving medication the social worker should make sure that contact is made with the new family doctor giving him the name and address of the child's former doctor.

The child's contact with his social worker

254. Change reactivates old memories and the child's contact with the social worker may be a focal point for talking about himself and his past. As he needs to know when he will see his parents after placement, so too the child needs to know when his social worker will next visit him. The child who is old enough to understand should be given an absolutely definite time which must be adhered to at all costs. It has already been suggested that the social worker's next visit should be within a week of placement. For children of all ages, placement is a move from the known to the unknown and a happening of major significance. If the social worker stands by him and sees him through all that is involved, then the chi'd is aware of a reliable, sensitive, available person who bridges past and present; someone with whom he can talk over what is happening and how he is feeling in order that he can make some sense of it all. This is how the child needs to perceive the social worker. Without first hand

contact and real communication with the child it will be almost impossible for the social worker to monitor his reactions. She needs to be confident that what is happening to him is in his best interests, also that everything possible is being done to minimise any unavoidable trauma.

The parents and the social worker

255. The fullest possible involvement of the parents throughout the assessment and placement process has been emphasised as being important for the child, for the parents themselves and for establishing the pattern of future working relationships. After placement too the parents will need early attention from the social worker. For example, news as to how the child is, as well as an opportunity to share their reactions to the changed situation.

The residential social worker and foster care

156. In the chapters on assessment and on choosing a home for the child reference has been made to the residential social worker, and at this point of discussing the placement of a child in a foster home it may be helpful to summarise the points made in relation to the collaborative and co-operative work of the field and residential social worker.

257. When fostering is being mooted for a child who is already in care and who is in a residential establishment, the involvement of the key people in the establishment will be essential. The job of the residential social worker should always include contributing to decisions about the children whose lives she shares. Her active presence at case conferences and in other discussions is necessary. Of all the 'officials' involved she is likely to be the one who knows the child best and she should take part both in the general decision to foster the child and in the selection of a particular placement. Once the decision to seek foster care has been made, the residential worker must be given all necessary information to enable her to play a full part in preparing the child for placement. It may be that the residential social worker is the person who initiates with the child a discussion about fostering. The choice of person would need to be discussed and decided between the relevant agency staff, but daily contact will make it almost inevitable that she is drawn into the fostering plans by the child himself and he will want to talk of his foster home with residential staff as well as with the field social worker.

258. It has been suggested that children in residential care should first meet the prospective foster parents on their own territory. This can make

it easy to involve the residential worker at the initial meeting. The field worker will be present but the residential worker will be the one who eventually effects the introduction. Similarly, it may be helpful for the residential worker to accompany the child and social worker on introductory visits to the foster home. Clearly prospective foster parent-residential worker contact is essential. In these instances the residential worker will be fulfilling the role undertaken by parents when children are placed directly from home. The intimate information which they have to give about the child can be helpfully shared with the prospective fosterers to aid the familiarisation process. To this end it may be possible for some foster parents to spend a weekend in the children's home with the child.

259. When a child is ready to leave a residential home for foster care there will be repercussions in the group being left behind. Groups of all kinds are affected by arrivals and departures and perhaps never more so than a group sharing the experience of day to day living. The residential worker is part of the group in that context and to her will fall the responsibility for seeing that the change is discussed in the group, and with individual children as necessary. In this way many problems may be avoided. For instance, this will make it easier for the misunderstandings and anxieties of other children to be brought into the open. In one residential establishment it was the custom to refer to contact with a prospective foster home as 'going on holiday'. If the proposed placement broke down, or equally if the prospective foster child permanently disappeared from the scene, the word 'holiday' might come to have ominous connotations for the children left behind. These could be very different from the usual pleasurable ones experienced by children living at home. It is advisable that the child is enabled to go back to see the group at least on one occasion. This is essential not only for the sake of his own sense of continuity but also for the sake of the children in the home. This can reassure the group that the fostered child is still safe and well. No matter how well it is explained, fostering can remain mysterious and even frightening to children.

260. If the preparation period is successful and the move agreed, the residential worker will then also have the major responsibility for preparing the child's clothes, toys and other possessions. She will do this in conjunction with child if he is old enough. The most necessary thing here is to make sure that nothing of importance is left behind. Throughout the child's stay in care, the child, field worker and residential worker will have been building up for him a record of significant happenings and photographs of friends, family, home, etc. This album—his picture memory—must go with him and this will be the time to see that he has any photographs he wants of the friends and staff he is leaving behind.

261. When the moment comes for the child to go, the residential worker must be there to say goodbye to the child and to reassure him that he will be welcome back on visits. She should also see that other staff for whom the child has special feelings are also able to say proper goodbyes—for example, the cook, domestic or voluntary helper. In some instances, it may be desirable for the residential worker to accompany the child and social worker to the foster home. This highlights the need for the social worker to make plans in advance and to keep to them. The duty rota in a children's home is made ahead and if this has to be accommodated to meet the needs of the child, time must be allowed for proper arrangements to be made.

262. All this illustrates the team work required in fostering children from residential establishments. The relationship between residential worker, field worker and senior social worker needs to be one of trust and frankness. The residential worker may need to recognise her ambivalence about the proposed fostering because of losing a child of whom she has grown fond. Or it may be that the residential worker is unhappy about the way things are going. In which case she should know which senior social worker to approach and feel able to discuss the situation with her. At all times the residential worker should be as much involved as the field worker in monitoring and assessing the preparation for placement.

The need for skilled social work at the time of placement

263. This chapter has emphasised that placing the child in a foster home calls for skilled management by the social worker. She has to work with the child, the parents, the foster parents and her residential social work colleagues. The essence of the social work task is to make sure that the needs of all these people are considered and met as far as possible so to do. Foster homes are a valuable and vital resource in the family and child care services but this resource can be wasted if care is not taken in the placement of foster children. The work at the time of placement lays the foundation for the ongoing care of the child.

Chapter 14

Care in a foster home

264. Once a child has arrived in a foster home the social worker becomes the focal point for ensuring that the agency maintains a complete and comprehensive overview of the welfare of the child. The child will now be the centre of a network of people who have concern for his care. The social worker must support and maintain this network and make sure that the full use is made of the resources of the agency and the community. She will be involved in the continuous reassessment of the needs of the child and in the monitoring of his growth and personal development. She will also have to develop and maintain a professional relationship with him so that he sees her as a person whom he can trust.

265. In all this work the social worker will personify the agency, and is the primary means by which it can fulfil its continuing responsibilities for the child. The statutory powers of the agency cannot be overlooked and will need to be the subject of frank discussion between foster parents and the social worker. These responsibilities are defined by statute in the legislation relating to children (see Appendix III) and those specifically relating to foster children are to be found in the Boarding-Out Regulations. The responsibilities of the social worker are not only concerned with promoting the development and general welfare of the child, but also with actually protecting him from any situation which could cause him harm. In extreme situations she may need to take the initiative in removing the child from the foster home.

266. The means by which the social worker will carry out this work will include making regular visits to the foster home, where she will see not only the foster family but also the child on his own. The frequency of these visits should be determined by need and should never be allowed to lapse on the grounds that a child has settled and therefore 'no visit is required'. The Boarding-Out Regulations make regular visiting a statutory requirement and ensure that contact is maintained with the child. All visits must be recorded and the child's situation reviewed at regular intervals.

The social worker as a co-ordinator

267. In order to carry out her task the social worker must have a comprehensive knowledge of the constellation of people and agencies who are and have been concerned with the child. A partial knowledge of this group will indicate a partial knowledge of the child. Good practice demands that the child is seen as a whole person, and the following chart is an indicator as to the potentially important people in his life.

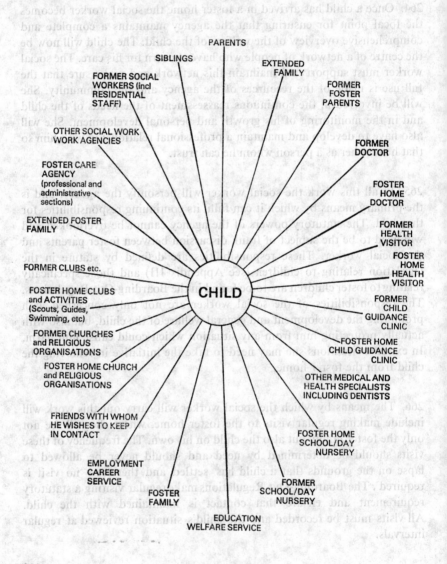

268. A child who arrives in a foster home brings with him his past. This past has to be welded into his new life and information has to flow between his past and present environment. Children in care, because of their past life experiences and special situation, have extraordinary needs. The importance therefore of the total range of professions and services being available to these children cannot be over-emphasised. Despite the special needs of such children, there is a danger that they will be the very children who may fail to receive the benefit and support of the services which are available to all children. Their lives are often subject to disruption, and sometimes constant movement and change, and it takes extra vigilance to ensure that they are not also deprived of the services available to other children in the community. It is vital that the positives of their past are carried forward to the present, whether by maintaining important relationships or by carrying forward information essential to the maintenance of their personal identity. This will often involve former foster parents and residential staff keeping in touch with a child for many months or years after he leaves their care.

Involvement of specialist services in the community

269. A social worker must have the ability to work in collaboration with other professionals and with the agencies which offer community and specialist services. She must understand not only the contribution that such people can make towards the welfare of all children, but also their particular contribution to children in care, whether they are in residential or foster care. At the same time, other professionals have to appreciate the task and the functions of agencies providing child care and foster care services. Failure to establish good working relationships between those people concerned with the needs of children can be very serious and even fatal, and definite efforts have to be made to establish such relationships. The problems of collaborative work are often linked with misunderstandings and with failures and delays in communications. Whilst communication is a two-way process, the social worker should be particularly aware of the part she must play in facilitating effective communication between the various individuals and agencies concerned with children who are at risk.

270. She must understand the contribution of the health visitor in assisting foster mothers, particularly with the developmental care of young foster children. The health visitor will be able to answer general questions about a child's feeding and development and can be a great support to a foster mother. The social worker will need to know about

the health visitor's role in the developmental screening of children, and should refer to her the children who have been identified as requiring special medical follow-up. These, for example, might be babies with poor birth experiences. The family doctor, too, will be able to offer an important service to the foster child and to the foster family as a whole. His involvement and knowledge of the family may have been over a long period of time. He will also be the person who will be able to help with any medical queries that the social worker or the foster mother may have concerning the foster child, and be able to make any necessary referrals for specialist medical help.

271. Children who have special educational, emotional or health needs must have access to psychologists, child psychiatrists and paediatricians. Sometimes such specialists will have been involved in former assessment of the child. Sometimes too they will be actively involved in his ongoing treatment. Agencies providing services for children need to have access to such consultation, not only to advise on general arrangements for medical and psychiatric help, but also to provide direct help to the social workers responsible for the supervision of the child.

272. When offering support and assistance to children in foster care, considerable emphasis is appropriately placed on the child's emotional development and on the exceptional aspects of childhood resulting from being in care. The social worker should not, however, overlook the more ordinary aspects of childhood and child development and she will be watching the child's physical, intellectual and social development. This is particularly important for the young child in care and Appendix II gives detailed guidance on this point. Regular medical examinations are required by law for boarded out children and these provide useful and essential information for the social worker. But in addition she will also need to observe such things as the child's rate of physical growth and his general appearance, she must know and record any illnesses and accidents, whether they are ordinary childhood ailments or more serious conditions. If the child has any particular medical or physical need, his social worker should ensure that the appropriate treatment is sought and obtained.

273. As far as the child's educational and intellectual development are concerned, the social worker will make regular visits to his school and will see the annual school reports. These are of importance to the social work agency as it acts as any good parent who is concerned about the welfare and development of children in care. In order to have a complete picture of the child and to plan for his future, he should be considered in his

school setting as well as in his foster home. Some children present themselves very differently in school than they do in their foster homes, and the teacher's knowledge and understanding of the individual child must not be overlooked. The contribution and involvement of the staff of the school will be helpful in meeting not only the child's educational needs but also many of his social needs.

274. Even if careful collaborative work has been achieved, it is necessary when a child moves from one place to another for many people to be informed about the exact details of such a move, when it took place, where the child came from, where the child moved to, how long such a move is likely to last and any special features relating to the individual child relevant to their work with him. Professional and official records often have to be transferred from one place to another and the transfer of such documents can be a complex and lengthy business. The agency responsible for arranging and making the move should therefore employ swift and effective procedures in passing on all relevant information. The social worker is a key person in such communication and she should set in motion the procedures to transfer information between the agencies concerned. She also has to ensure that all necessary documents actually travel with the child.

The social worker and the child

275. So far only the services for the child have been considered, but there is also the vital and essential contact with the child himself. However much external assessment is made of the child's progress and happiness, only the child himself can really know what it is like to be a child in care and what it is like to be a foster child in a specific home. His relationship with his social worker must be such that he can pass on his feelings about his home. An earlier chapter stressed the need for social workers to develop their skills in communicating with children. Some social workers may have had little experience with children and consequently may be self-conscious when approaching them in a professional capacity. But lack of skill must never be an excuse for social workers failing to try to establish direct contact with the child. From talking and playing with the child and seeing his pictures, hearing stories about his activities, seeing him with friends and hearing about his friendships and visits to other children for tea, etc., the social worker will gain a helpful overall picture of the child's intellectual and social development which will be vital to her task of promoting each child's individual welfare.

E*

276. In all work with children social workers must know the child as an individual, and be able to build up a relationship based on trust in which she can demonstrate care and concern for him in his own right. For the child in foster care the social worker is particularly important as she may have shared with him experiences such as his departure from his own family. She may have known him in his own family setting and as such be the embodiment of his past. She may know other adults or children in his past, and may still be in touch with his family or be the person who makes sure that his contacts with his own family are maintained. The social worker may have seen the person who has first told him about fostering and introduced him to his foster parents. She should be the person whom the child sees as the bridge between his past and his present situation and who can act as a mediator between the two. She should also represent the authority of the agency in whose care the child is, and in this role she should be seen as a comfort and support rather than as all powerful and threatening. She will in any case be an adult and will be viewed by the child in the light of his previous good or bad experiences with adults. The skill of the social worker in communicating with children is a vital element in understanding a child's reactions. For example one foster child became very distressed when the social worker arrived to give his foster mother a lift to a foster parents' meeting. But he was eventually able to explain to her that, as social workers were able to remove foster children from foster homes and not return them, he thought that there was the probability that they might also remove foster mothers and not return them. He did not want this to happen to his foster mother.

277. Whilst for any child in care a good relationship with the social worker is important, for the child in long term care it is essential. It is she who must ensure that his life does not become a disconnected series of relationships, experiences and events and that his current situation is relevant to his present and long term needs. For the child needing short term care it will be in many instances the active, persistent and positive involvement of his social worker that will ensure that he returns to his family without undue delay or avoidable emotional damage. It has already been stressed that an ability to communicate and work directly with children is an essential tool of the social worker. She must be able to respond to and understand children's non-verbal as well as verbal ways of communication. An imaginative approach to children involving play, drawings, pictures, photographs, life-story books and shared activities as well as just talk can enable the social worker to share the child's feelings, fears, pleasures, fantasies and life experiences. A social worker must also

116

allow children to talk about and sometimes to demonstrate their distress. The worker's approach to the individual child will depend upon his age, his use of language, his social and cultural background, his intelligence as well as his emotional wellbeing.

The child in short term care

278. Children in foster care on a short term basis, and especially young children with a limited concept of time, will need regular reassurance about their return home. They need constant help to keep alive the image of their parents, family and home. News of events and happenings within the family, letters, cards, telephone calls, visits to and from home, all help a child to cope with some of his feelings of separation anxiety and make the period away from home more manageable. Everyone concerned with the child must be involved in this process: his own family and friends, foster parents, the school and particularly the social worker whose task it is to co-ordinate activities, to make sure that communication and information flows freely between all those concerned in helping the child and to offer practical help with arrangements when necessary.

The child in indeterminate care

279. Children in foster care for indeterminate periods of time have special needs. Their future may be uncertain and their family situation unclear, complex and ever-changing. Older children may be able to understand such situations intellectually but will have great difficulty in living with uncertainties, frustrations and the anger which they may feel as a result. This anger and frustration may be expressed in ways that make the task of caring for them in the foster home or at school particularly difficult. Social workers must recognise the stress such children face. The child may be feeling that he is to blame for his predicament. He may be frightened of his own resulting behaviour and feelings. Providing support and help without false reassurance is an important social work task. Children need to be able to rely upon and trust their social workers and foster parents; they need to be kept informed of changes in plans and new developments as soon as they occur. They must be free to ask questions themselves about their situations as well as to express their feelings without fear of rejection. How a child will cope with this situation will again depend upon his age and stage of development, but all children will be under considerable stress and have difficulty in coping with uncertain situations. Links with their past, their family and their home environment will be important, and for older children the need to maintain contact with friends and school-mates is essential and should not be overlooked.

117

The child in long term care

280. The social worker must be particularly sensitive to the special needs of children in long term foster care, and understand that these needs will differ and will be expressed differently at each developmental stage. She should be clear how her role in respect of the child fits in with that of the foster mother. She must provide information for the child about himself and his past, either directly or through the foster parents. She will perhaps be the most appropriate person to help him consider and talk about some of the more painful experiences from his past and how they affect his present situation but it will be important that she does this in consultation with the foster parents. Many children in long term foster care do, however, have helpful and regular contacts with their own families and foster care has been chosen for them as the most positive way of ensuring that this is maintained. Much will depend on the child's age when he was admitted to care, the reasons for his admission, the agency plan for his future, the parents and the foster parents and their ability to understand the needs of the child and to work together. The quality, quantity and consistency of the social work effort will also be of vital importance if children in care for long periods of time are to keep in contact with their own families.

281. Long term foster care can provide a positive means of care for some children. Examples of situations where such care might be planned are, a motherless child where the father is unable to provide a home, a child who does not wish to be adopted, a child with one or both parents who are mentally or physically ill or handicapped and unable to give adequate care to him. Furthermore there are some children who become available for adoption, but are already securely settled in foster homes where the foster parents are not ready or able to take this step.

282. In addition to the children for whom long term care is planned, some have drifted into long term care through lack of planning. Unplanned long term care is an indictment of practice. The children concerned are in a difficult and uncertain position. They most often lose direct contact with their own parents and families or maintain only infrequent tenuous links. Whilst having lost their place in their own families, as foster children they do not have the legal security of adoption*. These children may be subject to all kinds of feelings of conflict and divided loyalty concerning their parents and their foster families. Their sense of identity may be impaired because important information about themselves and their family of origin may have been lost over the years. For these children the

* When the Children Act 1975 is implemented custodianship would be an alternative.

fostering agency carries a heavy responsibility in planning, updating plans, keeping information for the child to use and have access to and in making sure that the child's legal situation and status meets his needs and is understood by him. Managing this type of changed circumstance is discussed further in Chapter 17.

The social worker and the foster parent

283. The foster parents' relationship with the individual social worker may begin at the time when they first apply to foster, at the pre-placement or placement planning stage or when a child has already been in the foster home for some time. Unfortunately in some agencies there is a high turnover of staff, and foster parents have to develop skills in relating to what can be an ever-changing flow of social workers. In turn this puts an extra responsibility on each social worker to maintain a continuity of approach. To achieve such a working relationship each has to understand the agreed aims and objectives for the individual child, and each must know what is expected of themselves and of other people in working to meet those ends. These responsibilities will be determined by agency policy and statutory responsibility. Their means of fulfilment will be decided by taking into account the needs of the child and the specific nature and skills of the individual foster family, as well as the professional judgement of the social worker. If foster parents are to be effective and helpful they must also understand the policies, working methods and statutory responsibilities of their placing agency. They must also know which decisions have been delegated to them in respect of the child's day to day care and to whom they need to turn in other situations. For example, foster parents do not have the authority to sanction the child's discharge from care. The parents are required to make such arrangements with the care agency. Ensuring that foster parents are knowledgeable about these factors is an essential part of the social work task.

284. Foster parents are entrusted by the agency with personal information concerning the child and his family. This will be necessary if they are to give effective care and co-operate in the agency plan for the child. The failure of agencies to provide foster parents with basic factual and personal information not only minimises the effectiveness of fostering as a form of care, but it can also lead to fostering failures which are detrimental to both children and foster parents. Chapter 13 has looked at the information which foster parents need about children and their families. It also discussed some of the implications for agencies of sharing such information. Foster parents must also be kept advised of changes in family

119

situations and circumstances because original information can soon become out of date and inaccurate. In some fostering situations it may in any case be the foster parents who first know about significant developments affecting the child and his family and the sharing of this information becomes very much a two-way process. Where there are several changes of social worker it can soon be the foster parents who have the most information about the child.

285. The social worker will recognise that foster parents, by providing direct care for the child in the intimate setting of their home, will have the opportunity to form a close relationship with him which differs from that of the social worker who is removed from day to day family living. The foster parents' role will be in meeting the practical and emotional demands of the child, but at the same time they have to take into account the effect of this work on the rest of their family. They have to meet the problems of the child's own parents, also the expectations of the social worker and of the placing agency. The social worker needs to be appreciative of the demands this task makes both in terms of personal feeling as well as physical stress. An example of such a situation occurred when a twelve year old boy recently fostered was rejecting all the friendly attempts on the part of the foster father to involve him in a hobby they both shared. The foster father was feeling hurt by these rebuffs and left out of the family circle, while he watched a warm relationship building up between his wife and a younger foster child. It was essential that the foster father's feelings were recognised and accepted, as well as those of the foster child, if their mutual desire to make the placement work was to survive.

286. A relationship between a social worker and the foster family which accepts the ordinary stresses of family life, as well as considering the additional stresses and strains imposed by fostering situations, will be a healthy one for them and their foster child. This will need to involve for instance the acknowledgement that a foster child appears unsettled by his social worker's visits which may re-activate past distress, that the foster parents may fear that the social worker's intervention may challenge and upset the family equilibrium, or that the social worker is in danger of being seen as competing with the foster parents for the child. At the same time each family will have its own Achilles' heel and each will have its own methods of problem solving. The social worker's intervention will be largely concentrated on issues affecting the welfare of the child.

287. Some agencies are able to arrange additional support and help for foster families by providing opportunities for group discussions, not only

for foster parents but also for foster children. Not all families wish to participate in group activities, but those who were involved in groups during the selection and preparation process will probably welcome the opportunity for further discussions based upon their actual fostering experiences. Some foster parents may belong to foster parent associations which can help those who feel isolated in their fostering role. Much benefit to the families and children in their care can result from discussions in groups, since the support obtained by sharing experiences and views with other foster parents provides an additional dimension to foster care. Discussion groups often concentrate on the basic essentials and characteristics of the fostering task and draw upon the different and combined experiences of the group membership. It is not essential that the foster families own social worker should be involved in the running of their group, for groups are often more beneficial if they do not concentrate on the specific situations of their members. Social workers less involved with the participants as individuals and who have skills in group work may be best employed for this task, as long as they are in close communication with their colleagues.

288. As fostering essentially provides care and treatment in a family setting, it will be important that the social worker knows the foster family as a whole and not just some of its individual members. The way the family perceive her function, their communication and relationships with each other, the degree of family cohesiveness, the family's approach and contribution to fostering will all be important factors in providing a good environment for the child. She will, therefore, need to have the opportunity from time to time of meeting and communicating with the total family group, for example, visits during the evening when everyone is at home can provide the opportunity for involvement and discussions with the whole family. Taking advantage of family occasions which already exist may be more effective than setting up formal family meetings, but the social worker must develop an acute sensitivity in distinguishing between professional contact and an unjustifiable intrusion into family life.

289. As in all her work, the social worker's effectiveness will depend upon her relationship with individual members as well as with the family as a whole. She should be alert to any possible areas of misunderstanding and remember that sometimes it is the unstated feelings and anxieties which prevent communication and may damage relationships. For example, in times of special difficulty the social worker may be anxious that the foster parents will ask for the child's removal, the foster parents on their part may be concerned that the social worker intends to remove the child from

their care. The reality of the situation is likely to be that everyone wishes the child to remain where he is and given a chance would like to find ways of working together to this end.

290. The social worker will also be concerned about the practical aspects of foster family life including matters such as finance and domestic arrangements. Sometimes the agency's procedures concerning foster parents' allowances can actively make difficulties for foster families. This is especially so where there is a delay and payment is made in arrears. Social workers need to be alert to the practical pressures on foster families and ensure that financial and other arrangements are reviewed and adapted to meet individual need. Fostering can impose physical as well as emotional strains upon families who foster. The possibility of help and practical assistance with such things as domestic chores or additional washing and perhaps special agency support from community resources, for example, a place in a playgroup, are all part of the support which might be provided.

Sharing responsibilities with other social work colleagues

291. So far it has been assumed that only one social worker will be concerned with the child, his family and the foster parents. In some cases, however, the parents of children in care are separated, divorced or in any case not living together in the same home. Some are homeless or without firm links with any one place, or local authority area. As a result situations arise where the parents live outside the administrative boundaries of the care authority. Brothers and sisters may then be in the care of different agencies or boarded out in a separate area of the same agency. This fragmentation of families and inter-agency work results in social workers' being involved in a series of relationships with other social work colleagues. There are situations when the work with the parents of the child in care is undertaken by another agency and the child's social worker may not know or even have met them. Working with colleagues from other sections of the same department can present difficulties, but inter-agency work can be even more hazardous as fostering policies and practice may differ. In these circumstances there is more opportunity for conflict situations which arise to become polarised, for communications between the concerned professionals to be poor or even non-existent and for links between the child and his parents to breakdown. Social workers involved in inter-agency work should meet together from time to time to review and agree on the plan for such children. Particularly when children are in long-term care, plans should be carefully considered and agreed. All the workers involved will then have a commitment to their respective roles and responsibilities for the child and his family.

292. The joint use and sharing of foster homes either between area teams in one agency or between different agencies also requires careful practice. There are inherent dangers in such arrangements. These include the possibility that no one agency or area team takes responsibility for the support and nurture of the foster home. There is more chance of over-use and over-crowding of such foster homes, and there is also the possibility that the placement of children from a second agency may disturb and disrupt the progress of children already living in the home. When foster homes are shared one agency should hold the responsibility for the foster home as a resource, support the foster family and monitor the overall effectiveness of the care provided.

293. The social work task when a child is placed in a foster home will therefore involve four distinct types of work. These are with the child, with the foster family, with the parents and with the agencies and services in the locality where the child is living. All four areas of work will be interlinked and will often make heavy demands on the time of the social worker. In maintaining a balance between the sometimes conflicting demands of her clients and colleagues the social worker must have the support of supervision by a senior in the agency. This is considered in Chapter 19. Such support is particularly essential in agencies where there is a high mobility of social work staff. Ideally one social worker should maintain a continuous responsibility for a child, but if changes of personnel have to occur it is vital that at least a consistent approach is maintained.

Chapter 15

Parents, foster parents and the child

294. The nature of the contact between parents, foster parents and the child is of central importance throughout the fostering process and must be planned in relation to the needs of the child. The very essence of this process is that his care is shared and his parents have a very important part to play. Although there are some who are unable or unwilling to meet their child's needs, and some whose contact with their child must be limited or prohibited by the agency, for the majority of those in care the maintenance of links between a child and his family must be an essential part of the social work task. This chapter considers the place of parental contact and the practice implications.

Why is it important?

295. As shown in Chapter 2, the concept of a 'fresh start' for a child admitted to care has now lost credence in child care theory. The importance of involving the family as a whole and, where possible, actively maintaining relationships has been increasingly accepted and appreciated. Firstly, where rehabilitation is the aim, it is vital that the child maintains a continuing link with his family to maximise the opportunity for and facilitate his eventual return home. Secondly, with or without this aim in view, it is essential for the child's emotional well being and sense of identity that he comes to know the reality of his own background and family and understands why he is in care. While this is not to say that physical contact with parents is a prerequisite for the establishment of personal identity, self-knowledge is, and this is usually enhanced and made easier by actual contact.

296. Furthermore, recent research findings have highlighted the importance of this area. Parental contact, a child's knowledge of his natural background and his understanding of the fostering situation generally are features which have been shown to be associated with successful placement. Success in this context means not only less likelihood of foster home breakdown, but also a child's better emotional adjustment and fewer problems.

297. Earlier in the Guide it has been seen that fostering embraces many different kinds of substitute care along a continuum from the quasi-adoptive situation to the provision of short term care in an emergency. Another differentiation has emerged in a number of studies and has led to the identification of two distinct concepts of fostering, inclusive and exclusive. (It should be emphasised that the original use of these terms was in the context of a particular American agency specialising in short term care. Here, they have been applied more broadly and within themselves cover a range of situations). The inclusive model describes the kind of situation which embraces not only the child but also his family, and promotes the sharing of his care with his family and the agency. It recognises the importance of the child's background and actively attempts to keep this alive and meaningful for him, as well as facilitating contact and rehabilitation with his family where possible. The exclusive model, on the other hand, describes the situation which tends to exclude the child's family and knowledge of his origins, possibly denying the reality of fostering altogether and sometimes the role of the agency. This approach is often rationalised as being the only way to provide a child with security and continuity.

298. While it would seem that the former would tend towards the more successful type of placement, and the latter would seem akin to the 'fresh start' concept, this simplistic presentation needs to be treated with caution. Placements of both types may in fact have much to offer a child, but in different ways. This raises the question of what is appropriate in meeting a particular child's needs. There is no easy answer to this, but comparing the attributes of these two models may be a useful way in which a social worker can consider the nature of a particular placement. She needs to consider what is actually happening and why; whether this is the outcome of positive planning in the interests of the child and his family, or whether the situation has evolved over a period of time; whether it is a satisfactory placement in which the child's needs are being met, or whether it requires some fundamental reappraisal. Whether or not actual contact is possible and beneficial the issues at stake are the nature and degree of sharing in the child's care. This is important whether the situation is one in which attempts are being made to maintain fully the attachment of a child in short term care to his parent by regular contact, or whether, at the other end of a continuum of fostering situations, it is one where knowledge and information about his family background is maintained and imparted to the child at appropriate stages even although he may have no memories whatsoever of his family as such.

Why is it difficult?

299. The dilemma is how a child's security and continuity of experience can be promoted within the context of his care being shared between his parents, his foster parents and the agency. Earlier reference has been made to the child's need to establish a sense of identity, and understanding how this is accomplished points up a number of difficulties. This sense comes partly through knowledge of his family of origin as well as of the fostering situation itself: in essence that is knowing who he is, why he is here and what will happen to him. The other essential factor is his continuity of experience which, as has been discussed in Chapter 3, is dependent on his making and maintaining attachments. Where in relation to his stage of development the separation is too long for him to maintain attachment to his parents, then he needs to be able to establish an attachment to a substitute. The speed with which a very young child will establish his attachment to whoever is caring for him obviously has implications in this context.

300. This demands a very great deal from foster parents, and their feelings expressed in their own words in Chapter 5 provide graphic illustrations of the stress involved. They are asked to give a degree of emotional commitment which a child requires for satisfactory development, but at the same time not to regard themselves as his parents. It is inevitable that the longer that they care for the child and the more that they invest of themselves, the stronger will become the bond with the child. Indeed, this is the very kind of involvement he needs to give him a sense of belonging, particularly where his attachment to his parents cannot be maintained or where one never existed. Some of the difficulties around contact are irritations arising from practical uncertainties or inconveniences, which may intrude upon personal plans. Others however, stem from more emotional factors such as the wish to protect or possess the child. Nevertheless it is necessary to distinguish between the kind of possessiveness which perhaps arises out of a desire to deny the reality of foster care and which may imply a failure at the selection stage, and that which may realistically develop with a long period of caring for and emotional investment in the child.

301. There can also be particular difficulties for parents in maintaining contact with their child in foster care. The concept of filial deprivation discussed earlier in Chapter 4 is helpful in highlighting these and in developing an understanding of some of the problems and prejudices which face the parents of children in care generally. Of particular significance is the process of disengagement which takes place with prolonged

separation. In any event, it can be extraordinarily difficult for even confident parents to know how to behave towards their child when he is being cared for by others. It is not hard to appreciate how this may be intensified when parents, who already feel sensitive through having relinquished their child, then see him being adequately cared for by others. It can only serve to reinforce their feelings of depression, guilt and inadequacy which are often at the root of disruptive behaviour or which lead them to withdraw from the situation altogether. Much understanding and active support is required from the social worker to avoid disengagement and/or unhelpful contact often characterised by unkept promises or lavish gifts. It is also very hard for parents, already feeling inadequate and perhaps seeing themselves as having failed in their parental role, to be confronted by an indifferent or resentful response from their child, or possibly to be ignored and rejected altogether.

302. For the child too the fostering situation is not an easy one, and it is made more difficult for him if the adults are in a state of conflict and tension. It is this which is likely to exacerbate divided loyalties for him rather than the fact of separation in itself or being cared for by someone other than his own parents. The importance of communicating with the child himself, both directly and indirectly, is considered in Chapter 10 and this is very relevant here. It may be difficult for him to express openly his real feelings and confusions about his family and foster parents, or to ask questions about his background of which he may have no memories. Children resort to all kinds of strategies to justify to themselves the situation which they are in, and to protect the adults and themselves from their fearful, angry and hostile feelings. It is important, therefore, to offer him the opportunity where he can feel free and safe enough to express his feelings and ask questions. Observations of behaviour and non-verbal cues are particularly relevant in this context. Upset and disturbance following parental contact is frequently difficult to cope with and painful to observe, and it is often hard for the adults not to want to protect the child from such distress by discouraging further visits or any discussion about the experience. In fact such reaction in the child may in itself be a healthy response and be part of the process within him of acknowledging the reality of his situation and coming to terms with it. The adults have a vital role in enabling and supporting him to face the pain and the stress which this involves, which will in the long run promote his emotional health and his capacity for making relationships, rather than colluding with the avoidance of such feelings. Sharing the care of a child is an ideal that is difficult to achieve and must take into consideration the feelings of all concerned if it is to have a chance of success.

How should social workers proceed?

303. The important point is to recognise that once a placement has been chosen the social worker's responsibility is not only to the child, parents and foster parents individually but also in respect of the relationship between them. Her task in forging and maintaining links between them is not always easy. We have already referred to the range of different kinds of foster care. This has implications for the role expected of foster parents, as the extent of contact between child and parent may vary in quality and quantity depending upon the particular aims of foster care. Of course no human situation can be absolutely predictable over all time and changing circumstances may call for a revision of plans. Nevertheless, in every instance a pattern of contact should be agreed upon clearly from the start and commitment given to fulfilling the arrangements made. All types of placement demand the same close attention to detail. Any plan must take into account the attitudes and wishes of those concerned and this requires effective communication with and between all parties. Upon the social worker falls the particular responsibility for ensuring that differing attitudes are correctly perceived. It is all too easy to ascribe to others that which they do not feel or want because it fits in with one's own viewpoint, or presents the easiest solution. Through thorough discussion it is often possible for a regular pattern of visiting to be agreed upon which provides an opportunity for the child and parents to share activities and interests so as to further their relationship with each other. These visits may include brothers and sisters and members of the extended family, or, in some cases, be with them alone.

304. At an early stage, preferably during preparation for placement, some definite arrangements about contact between the child and his parents should be made. Elsewhere we have stressed the importance of establishing a working relationship with parents at the outset, and this particular aspect requires to be dealt with at this point. It is essential that the social worker is involved in establishing an acceptable and meaningful relationship with and between all parties. All too often it seems that this is left for the parents and foster parents to work out alone, but this is an unsatisfactory practice which can lead to problems. Not least is it difficult to break into an established, unplanned pattern of visiting once foster care is under way. It is the responsibility of the agency through the social worker to set limits and boundaries which all can tolerate. Parents, foster parents and the child all need to know the answers to such questions as: When may parents and other family members see him? Where will visits take place? What about taking him on outings, for overnight stays etc.? What

128

about writing? Is there a telephone in the foster home and may it be used to talk to the child and the foster parents? For the parents it will often be helpful to have a containing framework, within which they know what is expected of them and how they should behave in a situation where, although they have the status of parents, they are not performing the usual parental role. For the foster parents too, clearly defined arrangements and expectations about visits will be reassuring.

305. In particular thought needs to be given to the setting in which visiting takes place. For practical reasons it often takes place at weekends and in the foster home without the social worker being present. Again the potential and actual stresses are well illustrated by the foster parents' own comments (Chapter 5), and serve to remind social workers that they must think carefully about how such visits are arranged and how important is preliminary discussion and agreement between parents and foster parents. However the foster home is not always the best place for a child to meet his parents. It may be better for visits to take place on neutral ground, perhaps at the office, or in a less formal setting such as a cafe or the local park. The desirability or otherwise of using the office should be influenced by the kind of accommodation offered. The constraints of some office settings would weigh against their use for this purpose, for example gloomy buildings or cramped space. On the other hand cheerful, comfortable surroundings where parent and child can be together without feeling overlooked and which provide, for instance, refreshment and play facilities, may be very appropriate.

306. The possibility of the child visiting the family home must also be assessed and acted upon if suitable. Sometimes, because of special circumstances, visits have to be arranged to hospitals, hostels or prisons. Such visits may be helpful to children in terms of maintaining relationships but they must be arranged and managed with special care, including support for the child, parents and foster parents. The social worker can often take an enabling role when the child meets his family; if not actually present throughout she may need to be available if required. However, it seems best that the social worker should only be present when the child's welfare requires this. In these instances attitudes are crucial. Visits which take place under the constant watchful eye of the social worker or foster parent are hardly conducive to maintaining natural, spontaneous relationships. There may be parents who are likely to be so damaging to their children that they cannot be allowed to see them alone, but these will be a minority. It must not be forgotten too that in order to maintain constructive contact parents may need practical help, such as financial assistance towards their fares, or being accompanied on the journey.

129

307. Poor arrangements and insensitivity to the needs and feelings of everyone involved is likely to result in deterioration in the relationship between the important people in the child's life, to his detriment. For example, foster parents may become resistant to parental contact or parents may withdraw from continuing contact. Within the context of an understanding, accepting relationship the social worker can help child, parents and foster parents to express their feelings and reactions following visits, especially if these have become a focus for conflict or have occurred at some crisis point for the child or his family. Difficulties cannot always be eliminated but if they are accepted and understood they are likely to be more manageable, although this is not a once and for all exercise.

308. In a short stay placement there may be no difficulty in reaching agreement, since as much contact as possible will help the child maintain links with his family to whom he will return. Face to face contact is the ideal, but if it is not possible or is infrequent then the use of the telephone and/or written contact assume extra significance. It is easy to overlook, for example, the importance of the absent parent telephoning or writing to the child, and for news of him similarly to be conveyed to the parent, possibly directly by the child himself if he is old enough. Likewise, photographs or other personal mementos will help to maintain vital links for both parent and child.

309. Contact can also make an essential contribution towards the well-being of the child in longer term foster care, whether or not there are plans for rehabilitation. However, the social worker must be mindful of the processes, described earlier, which are likely to develop in situations of prolonged separation. Merely paying lip service to the principle of contact without actively working with and positively encouraging the parents to maintain consistent links with their child, will not lead to a meaningful relationship or indeed any kind of continuing relationship with him at all. As has been said elsewhere, the problems facing parents in this situation are considerable. Feelings of depression, guilt and inadequacy often make it impossible for them to take the initiative and keep in contact without much support and encouragement from the social worker. If they are to remain involved with their child, they must feel that they are able to share in concern for him and that their participation is valued and useful. At the minimum plans should be discussed with them and they should be helped to understand the reasoning behind them. The agency must be clear about the parents' rights and responsibilities and make them aware of these as well as taking these into consideration when reviewing the needs of the child.

130

310. A difficult but not uncommon situation is where parents visit in an inconsistent fashion, sometimes making unrealistic promises about future visits or making a home for the child to return to, which are then never fulfilled. It is not easy to decide whether some contact is better than none, and research findings about the value or otherwise of irregular contact are inconclusive. Possibly the only way to approach this is to examine the meaning of contact for all concerned. Sometimes it is possible to work towards helping foster parents to understand and accept the feelings of parents which underlie their difficult behaviour, and to help parents understand the child's need for reliability and consistency. For the child, some contact may enable him to have a more realistic view of his parents' qualities and may avoid his idealisation of them or seeing them as bad. The kind of fantasy relationship with absent parents is often seen in children who have no contact, and the 'hidden parent' continues to influence his feelings and behaviour. At the minimum, no child should be left alone with unspoken thoughts and questions about his family or to bear the guilt of causing the breakdown in the first place. However, good practice demands that the social worker must take the initiative in enabling such feelings to be discussed. A passive attitude or waiting until the questions are raised by parents, foster parents or the child is tantamount to dis-couragement. In some instances a child may refuse to see his parents and when this happens this needs to be explored, taking into account the facts and feelings involved.

311. A more difficult situation is perhaps where parents have been lost or have drifted away long before the present social worker takes over the case. Sometimes a conspiracy of silence surrounds the whole question of the child's family and the fact that he is fostered at all, and the social worker may be excluded, or perceived as a friend, rather than as a representative of an agency. It is essential to understand how this situation arose: could it be poor social work practice that has not continued to involve the parents, coupled with frequent turnover of staff and high caseloads? Or could it be that the foster parents wanted to avoid contact altogether? Nevertheless, it may be that such a placement has much to offer in terms of the very kind of security and continuity of experience which the child needs. In these situations very sensitive work by the social worker will be necessary to achieve an acceptance of reality essential for the child's well-being.

312. Whether or not parents should be brought back physically into contact after a long period is a difficult decision. It can be tempting to let sleeping dogs lie, although the needs of the child indicate that there should

be contact, or at least that he should understand how and why he came into care and who he really is. It is easy for social workers and foster parents to collude in a view that all is well in such a situation, but in fact the child's and his parents' view might be otherwise if this were sought. They might enjoy and value contact even if there is no intention of the child returning home. On the other hand, neither may want it and this may not just be a denial of the 'in care' situation.

313. When it is necessary for the social worker to initiate discussion around the reality of what is happening this is not to be undertaken lightly with the exception that it can be completed in one or two interviews, or with long intervals in between, or when the social worker may be on the point of leaving. Active intervention of this kind must be done on an intensive basis, possibly within a short period. It will undoubtedly bring out strong, conflicting and painful feelings for all concerned, and they need to feel contained and supported. For the social worker herself this is not an easy task, as it is usually uncomfortable to be at the centre of such ambivalence, and it is essential that she has access to adequate supervision and consultation. Where contact is not possible but where foster care is assessed as being in the best interests of the child, then the social worker has an important role in keeping in touch with the family so that they are not denied the right of knowing what is happening to their child. Equally, from the child's point of view it is essential that information about his family is obtained, preserved and made available to him at appropriate stages.

314. Undoubtedly, any arrangements concerning contact must be reviewed at regular intervals to ensure that they are of positive value. Monitoring the effects of such visits must be part of the ongoing social work activity. In certain situations unpredictable and inconsistent contact may prove to be harmful and destructive, and some parents' behaviour so disruptive as to be intolerable for the child and the foster parents. It may be both necessary and appropriate in such cases to consider the existing legal situation. The proper use of legislation is an important aspect and may go a long way towards promoting the child's security and continuity of experience, as well as acknowledging and clarifying the reality of the existing situation. The use of adoption* or the assumption of parental rights, thereby securing the placement, may in fact free the parties from feeling too threatened to allow discussion of the child's background or contact with his family. Any such action must of course, be based on an

---

* When the Children Act 1975 is implemented custodianship would be an alternative.

objective assessment of the child's needs and not undertaken primarily to meet those of the adults concerned. For some parents this may come rather as a relief than be experienced as a loss of control, for they too can feel equally insecure in an indeterminate type of situation where their role as parents is so unclear and uncertain as to be virtually meaningless. However, the agency must ensure that every effort is made to involve parents. They should at least be informed of actions to be taken and helped to understand why, as well as be made aware of their rights to object and to appeal.

315. The inherent difficulties for the social worker in managing these relationships should not be minimised. There is the discomfort of being at the centre of conflict and inevitable ambivalence. There is also often the experience of the pain which may result from being in touch with the deprivations and longings of others. At times this can be intolerable. Adopting strategies which attempt to avoid facing the feelings and tensions involved will only lead to disastrous consequences for the child. Often there is agreement between all parties about the best way to help the child and an ability and willingness to work towards this end. In such instances the role of the social worker will be to ensure that the necessary communication takes place and to co-ordinate joint effort, perhaps sorting out relatively minor misunderstandings and difficulties. In other instances it is not possible to reach agreement about how the child's needs can best be met. The interests of the people concerned may be in conflict and sometimes adults are not able to subjugate their own needs to those of the child. In all instances the primary professional responsibility of the social worker is towards the child. She must try to sort out the emotional and practical difficulties which occur, get agreement to compromise, act as conciliator and mediator and generally help the individuals concerned to work together in the interests of the child. This is a complex task. It means avoiding the line of least resistance and not allowing subjective, personal bias to dictate the course of events. Sometimes it will mean making difficult and unpalatable decisions and being prepared to carry them through.

316. In summary:

i. It cannot be too strongly emphasised that discussion and agreement about visiting should take place at the earliest possible moment, preferably when the placement is being planned. What is decided then is likely to determine the future contact between parents and child in foster care.

ii. There should be careful attention to detail, for example, frequency of contact, where this should take place, who should be present—as well as to other ways of maintaining links between the child and his family.

iii. There should be continued opportunities for all concerned to give their views and to talk about their reactions.

iv. There should be regular evaluation of the pattern of contact, and if necessary a redefinition of the legal framework, to ensure that the needs of the child are being met in the best possible way.

317. In this area of work, as in others, open discussion and planning at the beginning lays the foundation for continuing work throughout the period of care in a foster home.

Chapter 16
Relatives as foster parents

318. Few children grow up without the experience of their family having to face some of the inevitable problems of life such as illness, moving home, or caring for elderly relatives. When such crises arise, the family usually calls on the resources of its extended family and the children may find that grandparents or an aunt and uncle take over their immediate care. However, with the current factors of economic stress, of geographical mobility and with many families living in inadequate housing, it is sometimes not possible for families to turn inwards for help with the care of their children. Instead they may turn for assistance to social services departments or to voluntary organisations. Help may be needed in contacting other members of the family or, in many instances, the help required will be financial assistance in paying for the care of the child.

319. When parents first seek help with the care of their child and it becomes clear in the course of discussion that there are no means which can be introduced to enable him to remain in his own home, the possibility of relatives already known to him being willing to look after him will normally be explored with the parents by the social worker. In other situations, after a child has come into care, those concerned with assessing his needs and choosing the best placement for him will explore whether it is practicable and desirable for him to be placed with relatives. To remain with or return to familiar adults will obviously lessen the natural unhappiness which most children will feel on being separated from their parents. Boarding out with relatives is one way in which a child may be cared for without removing him completely from his own family.

320. However, when the relatives become official foster parents, they become part of the network of those who care for the child. This is a new dimension to their lives and one which calls for many adjustments, not the least being the acceptance of an outsider into their family affairs. They will share many of the feelings and experiences of other foster parents and, as with any other foster family, their own strength and stability will be the foundation for their success. But the stresses of fostering by relatives are considerable and are sometimes underestimated, both by the family and by the social work agency involved. At its best the child has the love and

135

security of familiar care; at its worse he may become a vehicle for bitter jealousies and disputes and the object of a tug of love where neither side can win. In the latter situation the child is exposed to much conflict and thus to the greater possibility of serious emotional damage.

321. Whether the social work agency approaches relatives with a view to their becoming foster parents or whether relatives offer themselves as foster parents, it is essential that early in discussion the social worker should explain to them the full implications of fostering. In particular, the role of the agency in approving and supervising the placement and the agency's power of removing the child.

322. In addition the social worker should talk with the child and his parents about the full implications of such a placement. Unlike other fostering situations the adults concerned, and in some cases the child too, will bring to the arrangement a history of subtle inter-personal relationships of which the social worker has no direct knowledge. Tensions and jealousies between a child's parents and substitute parents are almost inevitable at times in any fostering situation. They may well be stronger and more deep-seated if the persons concerned are members of the same family. If the parents are actively opposed to the placement, it is unlikely to be successful and, where they are separated, there may be a greater tendency for the extended family to take sides with either the father or the mother. This can make it difficult for the child to keep or to develop positive feelings towards both his parents. The social worker's part in the caring process will be to try to gauge the extent to which these tensions are likely to be aggravated and to assess the extent to which they can be contained.

323. The relatives' motives in offering the child a home may be complex and not easily discernible. A child's development, however, may be seriously hampered if his foster parents are motivated by a sense of shame or guilt that a relative of theirs is in care. The child may feel unwanted if he senses that he has been offered a home primarily from a sense of duty. If he is in care because he has been ill-treated or neglected by his parents, then the relatives may be more judgemental in their attitudes towards the parents than if they were not members of the same family. They may make fewer allowances for the parents when considering the events leading up to the situation which resulted in the child coming into care. This in turn may lead to problems of identity for the child in later years.

324. A number of children boarded out with relatives by local authorities are already living in the relatives' household when they are given the status

of a foster child. No information is available on a national basis as to why and how the local authority has become involved, but it is reasonable to suppose that in the majority of cases the relatives approach the authority mainly, if not wholly, because of the need for financial assistance. Reception into care is offered and the child boarded out. Thus foster parent status is gained only as a means to a financial end. Some relatives who have cared for a child for a long time hope for greater security vis-a-vis the parents if the child becomes officially a foster child. They may be slow to accept that this is not so, and may subsequently blame the social worker as a representative of the local authority when they come to appreciate the true position.*

325. When a child living with relatives is received into care, there may be a temptation for the social worker to give little thought to the question of whether or not it is really in the child's best interest for him to remain with these relations. She will be influenced by the knowledge that, if at all possible, it is best for a child to remain within his family, but other important factors have to be taken into account, such as the length of time he has been with these relatives, the degree of his attachment to them and the availability of alternative provision better suited to his needs. A deeper analysis of his total situation may lead to the conclusion that placement elsewhere is more likely to be in his long-term interests.

326. People who foster a relative's child not unnaturally see themselves as the child's relatives first, and as his foster parents only second. This is especially so if the child was living with them before he was received into care. Unlike many others who offer their services as foster parents, they may not be seeking primarily to fulfil the conscious or unconscious emotional need to care for a child. Unlike other foster parents, they do not become involved in an assessment of the kind of child who would best fit into their family. Perhaps more important still, they know more about the child they are to foster and about his family than does the social worker. Her investigations may well be resented and this may particularly be the case when the discussion, although centred on the child, has caused members of the family to express their feelings about each other for the first time. This kind of situation calls for great sensitivity to the feelings of both the adults and the child. Both may have considerable ambivalence towards the sharing of care with a third party who comes from outside the family network.

---

* An application for custodianship under the Children Act 1975 may be appropriate.

327. As already indicated, related foster parents' feelings towards the child's parents may be more intense and confused than those of unrelated foster parents. The potential for breakdown, therefore, is always there and there is a greater risk of collusion on the part of relatives to withhold certain information from the child, for example his illegitimacy. But in these areas of conflict the social worker's share in the stress may well support the foster parents in their work of caring for the child.

328. The child who is boarded out with relatives may have more need than has the child boarded out with non-relatives, to talk with his social worker about his parents and the reasons for their not being able to care for him. The relatives' sensitivity in these areas may make for difficult communication with the child, and the social worker may appear to threaten their position by her seeming intrusion into their family affairs. Skilful sharing of the care in this situation can be of great benefit to the child, but it is a situation which calls for considerable professional skill in the social worker concerned. When the placement is successful it provides an ideal placement for the child. Failure in such a placement is, however, often hard to detect. It is sometimes very difficult for any foster parents to ask for a child to be removed from their care. If he is a relative they may find it impossible to reveal the true situation. Here the agency must take its full responsibility for sharing in the caring process. It is essential that children who are boarded out with relatives should receive as much attention in supervision and review procedures as should any other child in care.

Chapter 17

Reviewing progress and managing change

Reviewing progress

329. The responsibility of care agencies to make and carry out individual plans which meet the needs of children entrusted to their care cannot be over-emphasised. Failure to do so may have disastrous long term effects, not only in terms of the personal suffering caused for the children themselves as they grow up into adulthood, but also for the health of the community at large.

330. The statutory minimum frequency for reviewing children in foster care is set out in the Boarding Out Regulations for England and Wales. It is in the first instance within three months of placement and subsequently on a six monthly basis. Most agencies arrange their formal review systems to meet statutory requirements, while recognising at the same time that good practice requires that reviewing is a continuous process and cannot take place only at set intervals. There is, however, general agreement that formal reviewing is essential for good case management and that procedures for this need to be established and maintained.

331. The responsibility for the maintenance of regular and effective review systems is vested in senior members of the agency staff, and if reviews are to serve a useful purpose both the senior staff and the social worker must recognise their value. In addition good administrative and clerical support will be necessary, not only to provide timetables and reminder systems, but also to ensure that reports are typed and that other information is collated and available for all concerned.

332. The initial review which is held following a foster home placement is most important. For all children and foster families the first weeks and months of placement are crucial in making initial adjustments and in learning about the realities of living together. For children placed directly in foster homes for either temporary or indefinite periods, the work undertaken with them and their families during the early weeks of care will affect the chances of the child's return home. At the review the family situation, the appropriateness of the current placement and plan and the

139

efficacy of the social work input will all need to be evaluated. For the child placed on a long-term basis, an early review helps to identify any unexpected developments. This initial review often needs to be held in advance of the statutory three months.

333. At this and all subsequent review sessions consideration is given to the child, his circumstances and his needs in the widest sense. The review will include a survey of his physical, emotional, intellectual and social development and an assessment of the present situation, including changes relating to his family, his foster family and any other important people in his life.

334. The child's legal situation will be reviewed to ensure that it continues to be appropriate to his present need. Any changes such as the revocation of the order committing the child to care or the assumption or rescinding of a parental rights resolution should be considered. In some cases it is appropriate to discuss the desirability of an application being made for an adoption order*. The statutory responsibilities of all parties will be identified. These will include: the agency in terms of its responsibility for foster home visits and case recording, medical and educational reports; the foster family in terms of their undertaking to the agency; and the parents in terms of their responsibility for such things as financial contributions and keeping the agency informed of their whereabouts. Agency practices, both administrative and professional, should be re-examined to ensure that they continue to meet the needs of individuals. Parental contributions and other financial considerations, including boarding out allowances, and their method of collection or payment may require adjustment.

335. Thought should be given to details of the arrangements for and management of review sessions, for example: where is the most appropriate place for the review to take place, what information needs to be available at the review and in what form, who need to be present at the review, how will the decisions made at the review be recorded and communicated to other people concerned, who will need to know about the decisions that are taken? Sometimes reviews will be held in a social worker's office; on other occasions it may be more appropriate or convenient for them to be held in the foster home, the residential children's home or even on occasions in a school or clinic.

---

* An application for custodianship under the Children Act 1975 may be appropriate.

336. A team or case conference approach to reviewing has much to recommend it, although it may appear to be expensive in terms of manpower. The membership of a case conference might include parents, foster parents, the child, residential staff, teachers and medical and nursing personnel. In the long run this may be more economical since it can prevent confusion, provide a better basis for planning and facilitate good working relationships and communication. The composition of the review team will vary according to the needs of each child. In some situations it is not appropriate to include parents or foster parents in such a group discussion. It is essential that, wherever practicable, they should then have an opportunity prior to the review, of discussing their circumstances and views about the child's progress and future with the social worker. These views should be taken into account in reaching a decision about the child's welfare. Similarly, where the child is not included he should, according to his age and capabilities, be given a specific opportunity of expressing his opinion prior to the review. The aim of all case reviews will be to agree a plan tailored to meet the needs of each individual child and his circumstances.

337. In many agencies special forms are used to record the information for reviewing. These forms provide details and summaries of the progress, developments and changes which have occurred during the period under review, and will indicate how far previous decisions and plans have been or can be implemented. Whilst information about the past is important, reviewers need to be alerted to the dangers of spending too much time looking back instead of planning for the future. Information for a review must include a realistic appraisal of the present situation together with its implications for the future.

338. Review reports are usually produced by the social worker, based primarily upon her involvement with the case. They may also incorporate other reports relating to the child, including medical reports, school reports, specialist reports, reports from residential workers or foster parents. In some agencies residential workers and foster parents produce their own written reports which can be of great assistance and add a very important further dimension to the review and case record. If reviews are to be effective, written reports need to be available and time must be allowed in advance for their preparation and reading. The senior member of staff responsible for the review will require to see the review form in conjunction with the complete and up-to-date case file for the child and the foster family.

141

339. To ensure that the plan formulated at the review is executed, additional decisions will need to be made concerning the action required, the methods to be adopted and the individuals responsible for action. Unless reviews decide 'what, how and who', plans tend to remain written hopes on case records. All those who have participated in the review, either at the case conference or separately in discussion with the social worker, must be made aware of the review plans and of the part that it is envisaged they will play in carrying them out. This applies particularly, of course, to the child, foster parents and parents.

Managing change

340. As well as planning for change the social worker must be able to react positively to unplanned change. Some of the changes which occur in fostering are subtle and develop gradually without comment or recognition, others are quite obvious and overtly demand attention. She will have to be particularly sensitive to gradual changes which grow into major developments, since these can require radical adaptations in plans for the child. For example, intended short stay placements which become prolonged require special recognition since when a child stays on a more long term basis the roles, responsibilities and relationships of all concerned need to be re-defined, clearly understood and accepted. Other examples are when long term fostering moves into the possibility of adoption* or when the child's legal status is altered by the assumption or rescinding of a parental rights resolution. In these instances the rights and status of some or all of the people concerned will change and their relationships are bound to be affected as a result. If the agreed decision is that the child would benefit from adoption, parents should be fully involved in discussions about the selection of the adoptive family. They should be able, if they wish, to meet the prospective adopters on neutral ground, provided that this is mutually agreeable and that the experience can be used constructively by all the parties concerned. This will involve the social worker in careful explanations and discussions of objectives and alternatives with the child, his family and the foster family.

341. Definite changes in the composition of the foster family such as pregnancy or the birth of another child, illness, or the death of a close family member, are all easily recognised, but their implications for the family and for its fostering responsibilities will need to be assessed and balanced. When the same foster home is used for long stay and short stay

---

* When the Children Act 1975 is implemented custodianship would also be a possibility.

children, the arrival and departure of other foster children, as well as the additional demands they make during their stay, will need to be carefully considered and balanced.

342. Unfortunately many agencies are faced with a high level of staff mobility and this brings complications in terms of providing fostering and childrens' services generally. It is always essential that foster families have an identification with the care agency which is not solely based upon their relationships with an individual worker. This is particularly so where there is a high turnover of staff. In foster care continuity of staff is important and unnecessary change should be avoided wherever possible. When it is necessary to transfer the supervision of foster families from one worker to another careful consideration must be given to its planning and management. Whenever possible the worker will wish to meet her new colleague to discuss the total situation and make introductions. Whether this is possible or not, a clear summary of the total situation should be on the record. This should include decisions and plans for the child, the factors and relationships which affect the situation and all those involved, also any information which will be relevant to the new social worker and her task. The new social worker will be involved in taking over an established situation and will enter a series of already existing relationships. In some instances she will benefit from previous good practice and relationships, at other times she may discover strong feelings of discontent or even personal animosity. These will need to be carefully assessed and handled. The timing of staff changes needs to be taken into account, since it is unwise for a social worker to embark upon a new development in a fostering situation if she is unable to see it through.

343. Fostering situations come to an end for a variety of reasons which can include: the child returning to his own family at the end of a short or long period in foster care; the child moving from the foster home to another care situation such as from a short stay foster home to adoption or from an assessment in a foster home to a residential home; a young adult going out of care after reaching the age of majority; and a child leaving a foster placement that has broken down. Most of these moves should be the result of careful planning and preparation. Some, however, may be hurried and unplanned, occuring at times of special difficulty and stress.

344. The same kind of considerations apply at the end of fostering situations as at their beginnings. These include: an understanding of the effects of separation; the need to make the move as easy as possible for

the child by minimising the disruption of daily life and routine; the need to link the past with the present and to try and ensure that the child understands what is happening and why; and the need to make sure that all those involved know about the move and why it is happening. Children who have been in care for long periods will need preparation and support of a similar nature to children who are being placed into entirely new family situations. Their parents too will be learning to live with a new situation, whether their child has returned to their care or whether he has moved on to another foster home or community home.

345. For foster children going out of care because of age, the aim during the preceeding years and months will have been to help them to become as financially, socially and personally independent as possible and to prepare them for adult life. Some of these young people will have made a permanent and secure home with their foster families. They may remain there until they marry and set up home themselves. Others may be planning to establish themselves independently, and in this respect will be similar to their friends and peers who are not in care. Some may be continuing in full time education. This will mean that the agency is likely to continue to provide financial support for them during this period. Some young people may not have been able to establish themselves and may have difficulties and problems which continue to need the help and assistance of the agency. Their experiences of care and their relationships with the agency and its social workers, will probably affect how young people feel about becoming legally independent and whether they will see the agency as a place they would turn to for future help and assistance. Throughout the time a child is in care the agency will have been concerned that he has information about himself, his family and life experiences. In the time before he goes out of care it will be important to confirm and rediscuss this personal information, perhaps confirming some important details in writing as well as making sure that personal documents and photographs, which may have been kept on the agency file are given to their rightful owner. At the actual point of leaving care, social workers will need to make clear the agency's continuing interest and concern in such a way that young people will know that future contact would be welcomed and acceptable. There is statutory provision for financial help to be made in certain circumstances.

346. Foster parents will have special needs when a child leaves their care. They may have feelings about losing the child, particularly if he has been with them for a long time and if their emotional investment in him has been great. They may need a period to recover as a family both emotionally

144

and physically. The position of short stay foster families is important in this context, as their work may be both exhausting and intensive and there can be a danger of not realising the extent of their involvement with the foster children. A failure to appreciate this may lead social workers to overuse and overtax the capacities of foster families who take children for short periods.

Foster placement breakdowns

347. The social worker's task in relation to unsuccessful fostering situations is a difficult one. It may involve decisions which will directly bring about the end of a placement. In extreme cases, such as where a child has been subjected to ill-treatment, the decision will be made without delay. In most instances, however, the decision to move a child is more difficult to take, for many reasons. The care alternatives available for the child may be poor, and there is a tendency often to prefer maintaining the unsatisfactory present rather than risk the unknown future. In these situations social workers must be aware of the signs of stress in both the child and the foster family. The child's behaviour within the foster home or outside at school, work, playgroup or with friends may reflect stress and anxiety. The state of his physical development and general health may be an indicator of inadequate care, as may be the general health of the foster family. The child's perception and opinions will need to be sought where possible in addition to those of the foster parents. A distinction will need to be made between the child who, when angry with his foster parents, says 'I shall ask my social worker to find me a new home' but would be horrified to be taken seriously, and the child who is really giving the message, verbally or non-verbally, that the situation has become unbearable. In the latter situation timing is all important if this highly painful experience is to make sense to the child, and the social worker will have to consult with colleagues in other professions and agencies as well as discussing the situation with senior staff of her own agency. Failure to recognise and face up to difficulties may lead to an emergency breakdown which is likely to be damaging to all concerned.

348. When failures occur it will be necessary to consider how best to manage them, taking into account the feelings and needs of those most involved. For the child the failure will raise anxieties about his future; it may well reactivate previous experience of separation or rejection; and it will constitute a threat to his security as well as giving rise to feelings of guilt, blame and depression. Foster families may also feel guilty about the failure and there may be disagreements and recriminations within the

foster family as well as feelings of anger and shame. They may be enormously relieved to have lost the burden of a difficult child, and may be very uncertain as to whether or not to continue as foster parents to another child. The effects upon foster parents' own children will need to be understood and recognised. They may need some help in their own right, especially as this may be a time when their parents may have lost confidence in themselves.

349. At the end of all fostering placements the social worker should give time to the foster parents who have relinquished the child's care, and to the child and his subsequent caregivers who may be his family or residential staff, new foster parents, or adopters. The work should focus on helping everyone to cope with the effects of the change as well as to live with the new situation. Social workers will not be immune to the feelings of guilt, failure and frustration which surround foster placement breakdowns. Such feelings may be particularly strong if the worker was responsible for making the placement or has invested much of herself in terms of time, effort or feeling into maintaining it. She will be the person in personal contact with the child and the foster family and will see and experience the pain involved for them at first hand. She must be able to manage her own feelings, since she will need to help provide emotional support for the other participants as well as organising the practical arrangements involved.

350. The senior social worker or supervisor will be particularly important at this time, in providing personal support for the social worker and professional assistance in reaching and carrying out realistic decisions. The need to evaluate each placement at its termination is important, not only as a way of monitoring the care provided for the individual child, but also as a means of the social worker checking the effectiveness of her own work. A careful review at this time will ensure that the knowledge gained about the child can be used to full advantage, that the most suitable use is made of the foster home on other occasions and that the practice knowledge gained is identified for future use.

351. The selection of the child's next placement after a breakdown must be carefully made. It should obviously depend upon the needs of the child but these may be difficult to determine in the immediate situation of stress. It will also inevitably depend upon the available alternatives which may include residential provision, special assessment and observation facilities or even another foster home. In many instances children need to have the opportunity of keeping in touch with former foster families. Some

children derive much benefit from an on-going contact with their foster family either by letter, telephone or visits. For other children one return visit to the foster home may be all that is required, but this may be especially important to reassure a child who left during a time of crisis. Where actual links are not or cannot be maintained, then both foster families and children often wish to have news of each other and in many instances the social worker is in a position to provide this.

352. In summary, the forms of change are many and various: a foster home failure, a return home to parents, illness in a foster home, the death of a grandparent, going to a new school, getting a new job; all these will have their ripple effects on the life of the child, his family and foster family. The way in which change is managed by an individual is an indication of his security and capacity to make positive adjustments to new situations. Whatever the nature of the change the social worker should carefully record the facts of the situation, and the implications of all change should be the subject of discussion with the senior social worker in the agency.

Part III
Resources for a foster care service

148

Chapter 18
Foster homes

353. Previous chapters have been based on the assumption that agencies have available a source of potential foster parents and that their existing foster parents are given adequate personal, financial and material support. It is easy to make these assumptions, but in reality recruitment and support demand a great deal from the agency in terms of staff time as well as finance. To be cheese-paring in these respects is false economy. In making the best use of its resources, moreover, the agency should consider fully the potential of some foster parents in offering extra services beyond those traditionally associated with the fostering role. Making full use of foster homes as part of the resources available for the promotion of good child care is the subject of this chapter.

Finding foster homes

354. Fostering is essentially a community activity and its success depends to a considerable extent on public attitudes. The general public, however, is often confused about the rights and responsibilities of foster parents and foster children, of parents and of the organisations which act in loco parentis. Agencies should accept more responsibility for enabling the community to have a better understanding of the situation. National and local campaigns are needed to educate the general public about the needs of children who are separated from their parents, and which could also give a wider knowledge of the reasons why children come into care. Against a backcloth of informed and sympathetic public opinion, local and regional campaigns to recruit foster parents could then be geared to local circumstances.

355. Traditionally foster parents have been seen as the best source of recruitment of others, through gaining the interest of their friends and acquaintances. Foster parents' own thinking about this aspect of their role has developed with the growth of foster parent groups, and many now see recruitment as an integral part of their task. This commitment can be very valuable and their participation in meetings held for prospective foster parents can be beneficial, particularly in assisting with the process of self-selection. No-one can understand better what it means to be a foster

149

parent than someone actively engaged in providing a home for a child, and an honest description of the difficulties as well as the joys of fostering can bring a greater sense of reality into the discussion. Some experienced foster parents may be willing to allow their names to be made known through citizen's advice bureaux, health centres, etc., to people who would like an informal discussion about fostering, but who are not yet ready to make an approach to a social work organisation.

356. Children in care have a multiplicity of needs and if fostering is to meet even some of them, a flexible and responsive approach is essential. Foster parents of varying ages and backgrounds are required, and sometimes specific campaigns are necessary, for instance to recruit people from ethnic minority groups. Whilst the content of the information to be conveyed in advertising and other forms of publicity must be provided by the social workers, its presentation may require skills which are not to be found in the social work organisation. It may be helpful to use expertise gained in the commercial world. Whatever method of presentation is used, fostering should be shown honestly, unsentimentally and with 'warts and all'. It must be remembered all the time that publicity will be seen by parents and children in care as well as prospective foster parents, and has the potential of prejudicing them against fostering as well as demonstrating its value.

357. In finding new foster homes more extensive use could be made of local radio and television stations. These media can present the need for foster homes against the background of local conditions. A variety of presentation is possible, for example 'straight' publicity about the general or particular need for homes, 'phone in' programmes or features involving existing foster parents. The direct participation of children in care is a controversial matter and this method of recruitment is not acceptable to everyone. It is however argued by some that provided children are carefully selected and supported, their involvement is justified if it results in their placement in a foster home. The safeguarding of the children from damage is of vital importance, and for this reason their involvement with the advertising media should be carefully supervised by the social work agencies concerned.

358. Many social work organisations have found the local press to be helpful in publicising the need for foster homes, and well written and accurate articles can achieve desirable results. Small advertisements asking for homes for specific children have long been a method employed by social work agencies, though often criticised as being ineffective and

wasteful of resources. There is also some reservation about specific advertisements when these lead too quickly to a concentration on the needs of a particular child before the applicants have fully considered the implications of fostering generally. Nevertheless, the fact is that many children have been placed in foster homes as a result of this form of advertising. It is, of course, courteous as well as sound practice that an agency advertising for foster parents outside its own geographical area should notify the agency covering that area of its action.

359. As part of an on-going recruitment drive, mobile exhibitions are a useful means of keeping fostering needs before the public eye. An essential accompaniment is the provision of information in the form of handout material which provides enough facts to enable enquirers to decide about their next step. These handouts should cover such matters as the agency requirements regarding age, status, family composition, accommodation, allowances and the supports available. Co-operation with neighbourhood organisations (schools, churches, community relations councils, health centres, parent-teacher associations, women's groups, trade unions, etc.) can be a useful contribution to on-going publicity of the need for foster homes. Here again the participation of foster parents alongside social workers can be an advantage and good handout material is essential.

360. The results of each recruitment drive or advertisement for an individual child are a valuable source of information for future practice. Such feed-back can indicate the characteristics of people in a particular locality who are interested in fostering and therefore what resources might be available. Neighbouring agencies and authorities with similar conditions can benefit from sharing knowledge of this kind.

Supporting foster families

361. The professional support that social workers should provide for foster families has been described in detail throughout the Guide. This relationship between foster parents and the individual social worker is a key one in promoting the welfare of each individual child in foster care. To fulfil this function each party must understand its own and other people's role. Social workers should be clear about their role as a representative of their employing agency. They must ensure that foster parents understand the aims and functions of the agency and that they are clear about its statutory responsibilities for the children in care. The social

worker should also inform foster parents about the administrative provisions which are designed to support all those engaged in the foster care service.

362. Foster parents have an important relationship with the fostering agency over and above this child-centred relationship with their social worker. Agencies should recognise and promote this. The development of large multi-functioned social services departments with complex organisations and high staff mobility, has made the task of foster parents more difficult. In many instances foster parents do not know to whom they can turn for help or how to approach the social services department in times of need. They are left with a feeling of confusion, isolation and lack of support which can adversely affect the children in foster care, alienate existing foster parents, hinder recruitment of new foster parents and cause the loss of valuable human resources.

363. The need to provide a continuing and consistent link between foster parents and the agency, to nurture foster parents as a valued departmental resource and to promote foster care by providing special training for foster parents, has led some departments to appoint special fostering liaison workers. Depending on individual agency structures, these workers may be based centrally or in the area teams. Some specialise in fostering only, and where such appointments have been made they seem to have been widely appreciated by foster parents. An administrative officer who is concerned with overall fostering matters can be an important link between social services departments and foster parents, and also of invaluable assistance to social workers. As social workers cannot be readily available at all times, there is a case for a clerical member of an area team to be named as the telephone link-person for foster parents. Such a worker would be able to take responsibility for passing messages to social workers, would have the advantage of being much more readily available and may well be able to deal with some of the practical queries with greater speed and sometimes without even needing to involve social workers.

364. The value of information handbooks for foster parents has become increasingly and widely recognised. These books give foster parents information about their rights and responsibilities, the legal requirements placed upon the department, administrative procedures, details of staff within the department especially in their local area, information about boarding out rates and additional allowances, details about procedures in the event of illness or consent to medical treatments, information on the individual child in their care and the telephone numbers for use out of office hours and in emergencies.

152

365. The development of foster care associations, often including departmental representation on their committees, is encouraging as one of the means of promoting communication between departments and foster parents. Foster parent discussion groups can enable foster parents to meet each other, help to overcome isolation and frustration and provide mutual support in coping with problems as well as offering opportunities for more formal training.

366. It is important to recognise, however, that not all foster parents are interested in joining groups or participating in any form of training. Many regard their task as an individual contract between themselves and the agency, and their relationship with the social worker through the stages of selection, placement and supervision meets their need for support. Some find it difficult to talk about their feelings and it would be counterproductive for them to discuss problems in a group situation. These foster parents provide an equally valuable service. Indeed one of the main ingredients of fostering is the spontaneity of those undertaking the task as part of the ordinary community.

Using the expertise of foster parents

367. Where foster parents do wish to enlarge their role, local associations can provide a valuable means of using their individual and collective expertise in improving fostering practice and in the planning of foster care services. The contribution of foster parents in recruitment has already been mentioned. In addition skilled foster parents can help in the training of recently approved foster parents and social workers who are new to the fostering task. Their support to less skilled or confident foster parents when faced with problems that they themselves have tackled successfully in the past, can reinforce the support given by social workers. Sometimes foster parents have special knowledge of caring for a particular type of child, for instance a child with an unusual handicap, and can give helpful advice to social workers and foster parents coping with a similar situation. Some local authorities are appreciating the value of having foster parents co-opted on to their Social Services Committees. In all agencies it is sensible to include the views of foster parents in reviewing fostering allowances. All these illustrations demonstrate the versatility of the fostering resource in providing services outside the traditional role.

368. The knowledge of foster parents about their own individual fostering situations should, in addition, be used to the full. Many foster parents

could usefully keep records about the progress of and developments concerning their foster children which could form part of these children's departmental records. As already mentioned, the participation of foster parents in reviews can give an added dimension. Generally any opportunity of incorporating their knowledge into departmental discussion and recording can only be to the advantage of all concerned.

369. Foster homes are increasingly being used for the placement of children with special needs, for example physically and mentally handicapped children and older children with very disturbed backgrounds, or for the assessment of children when they first come into care or are remanded by a court. These situations demand a high degree of skill in foster parents, which may be developed by structured training courses, as well as by individual discussion and a considerable amount of support from social workers. The foster parents involved are often people who already have appropriate experience, such as married women who were formerly teachers, nurses and social workers now wishing to resume work, who choose this type of work in their own home situation. In other cases both foster parents are employed full time in specialised foster care and there is a full employer/employee relationship with the local authority. This type of care offers a more individualised approach to children's needs than is often possible in a residential establishment. The cost of these two forms of care will be comparable, because such foster parents need full material support as well as personal support and adequate remuneration; this is likely to involve, for instance, domestic help and the provision of relief assistance so that they may enjoy their own leisure time pursuits.

Fostering allowances

370. Fostering is an onerous and responsible task, providing a valuable service to the community as part of the spectrum of facilities available to children in care. This should be recognised fully in financial terms, as the value an agency puts upon its foster parents will be reflected in the level of payments and the way in which they are made. Whatever the method of fixing levels of payment, there can be no doubt that boarding out allowances should adequately cover the cost of looking after a child. It is the essence of fostering that a foster child should participate in the life of the foster family in the same way and to the same extent as a natural child of that family. The allowances payable to foster parents should be adequate in range and amount to allow such participation to take place without financial loss to the foster parents or a reduction in the opportunities available to foster parents' own children. Fostering without adequate allowances often means sacrifices by the foster family.

371. The cost of living index can make available a general baseline for a realistic assessment of the cost of caring for a child, but it should be remembered that local circumstances vary. In addition rates need to be reviewed at regular intervals to keep pace with change and, as suggested above, such reviews should take into account the views of foster parents themselves. Over and above the general baseline there are many additional costs to foster parents. These include pocket money, outings and fares as well as hidden items of household expenditure such as the extra cost of heating and lighting, wear and tear on furniture and fittings, cleaning and laundry. All these items should be taken into account when fixing the rate.

372. At present, in addition to boarding out allowances, grants are frequently paid for a variety of needs such as holidays and school uniform, but the system is often obscure and uncertain for both foster parents and social workers. The result is that discrepancies in payment can occur even within quite small geographical areas, the amount that is paid seeming to depend on the initiative and knowledge of the social worker and the determination of the foster mother. Many of these needs should be regarded as part of the basic requirement in fixing the ordinary allowance which would partially obviate the use of discretion in making payments. There would, however, continue to be a need for some special grants such as for a particularly expensive holiday.

373. In addition to the basic comprehensive allowance and to grants for special items, the system must allow for extra payments to foster parents taking children with special needs, such as those who are handicapped or very disturbed. Such children make great demands on foster parents and may, for instance, necessitate their employing domestic help in order to free themselves for the children's care. In addition, the wear and tear on clothes, furniture and fittings is likely to be greater than with a less handicapped child. Where foster parents take a succession of children for short periods this can cost more than having one child continuously for the same length of time; in addition such foster parents sometimes need time to 'refuel' themselves between placements, although their continuing financial commitments remain the same. In many situations the use of a telephone is an invaluable aid to both foster parents and social workers in keeping in close contact; it may be appropriate for an agency in some instances to provide this facility. Occasionally a local authority may be able to offer special housing facilities that would enable foster parents to meet a particular need.

374. All foster parents need to know as far ahead as possible what their income is likely to be in order to budget adequately, and it should be

remembered, for instance, that holiday accommodation usually has to be paid for well in advance. This implies a clear understanding by foster parents of the regular boarding out rates and of the availability of special payments. It is important that each agency makes it clear to everyone involved that they wish foster parents to receive their entitlements. It is indicative of poor practice if the official attitude to foster parents seems to be parsimonious and lacking in trust and sensitivity, and payments systems can be complicated, inaccurate and often lead to long delays. The wide spread use of financial procedures for either buying children's clothes with official orders or vouchers or only in the presence of a social worker, seems to suggest a lack of trust in foster parents and certainly shows a lack of sensitivity to the feelings of foster children in such a situation. Foster parents who make purchases for their foster children from their own pockets should not have to wait many months before reimbursement.

375. Foster agencies should look carefully at their procedure for the payment of allowances, since what can appear to be convenient to administrators, treasurers, and computer programmers can cause a great deal of suffering and hardship to foster parents. Procedures for the payment of allowances should be as streamlined as possible to avoid unnecessary delay. Local payments should always be possible for emergency situations. The method of payment by cheque, giro, postal order or cash should bear in mind the foster parents' preferences as well as the administrative convenience to the department. An essential consideration in all types of payment, however, should be the avoidance of delay which leads to foster parents waiting for long periods. In the case of short stay foster parents there is a very strong case for some payments to be made in advance, and this facility should also be available for other foster parents in special need. It is good practice for all payments to be accompanied by an explanatory slip which itemises in detail for the foster parent, the payment and its composition. Such a practice often prevents overpayments and their resulting problems. Foster parents may be able to assist the administrative process by giving information direct to the administrators about any important changes in the movements of children in their care.

376. Because of its very flexible nature, foster care obviously presents difficulties to the administrator and particularly to the administrator dealing with foster parent allowances. A good relationship between the foster parents and the agency, based if possible on a personal relationship, is one way of overcoming these difficulties. By knowing about and understanding the agency and its staff, foster parents will have an appreciation of the administrative problems that boarding out allowances present.

Chapter 19
The agency

What is the purpose of administration?

377. The organisation and administration of a fostering service is a complex task. It will automatically reflect the effectiveness of the overall structure of the agency of which it is a part. Fostering is one part of a community-based service to families and children and, whilst fostering schemes must be child focussed, the child's needs cannot be seen in isolation from the people who play an important part in his life. The primary aim of a fostering scheme will be to provide the best available service for the individual child in care, taking into consideration all the other alternatives. The fostering service has to be organised not just to administer the mechanics of foster care but also to support and encourage its participants in their various roles. The child is the hub of a wheel and if too many of the supporting spokes become damaged the wheel will collapse.

Who is involved?

378. The variety of spokes in the foster care wheel include the following: the child's own family, his foster family, residential staff, the child's social worker, the agency's fostering service, both its professional and administrative membership, the child's doctor, school, employer, friends and all the people to whom he looks for support at times of stress. It is essential for all those involved in the provision of a fostering service to understand its aims, their part in the scheme of things and the role and function of the other participants. Any service which is tailored to meet individual needs must be able to balance the singular, irregular and often illogical demands of people with the regular and normally logical demands of an efficient administration. Foster care is a rewarding task but it carries with it many frustrations, and if the child is to benefit it is essential that all those involved find it is a satisfying job. There must be job satisfaction for the foster mother, the foster father, the foster brothers and sisters and extended foster family, for the social workers and administrators and for the secretarial, clerical, reception and telephonist staff of the fostering agency. Any organisation which creates or exacerbates frustration in this group of care givers will inevitably fail to provide the best possible service for the child.

How does fostering fit into the general structure?

379. Much responsibility for the effectiveness of a fostering service will rest upon the structure of the total organisation to which it belongs, and the support this structure gives to those who work within it. Fostering services are provided within a variety of organisational structures—voluntary and statutory social service agencies which differ according to the range of services provided, their size, style of management, local needs and demands upon their resources. Where they are provided within Social Services Departments, the functioning of this specialist service demands very careful consideration.

380. One of the main purposes of setting up these departments was to enable family situations to be assessed as a whole and appropriate help to be given on a co-ordinated basis. Children in care, including foster children, are part of family situations and in planning for their future the circumstances of their whole family are relevant. For this reason it is essential that plans for children are developed within the area team, which is aware of the general family needs and of the total resources available for meeting them. As far as the individual child is concerned, it may for instance be more appropriate for resources to be put into preventive work, or for day care facilities to be provided instead of reception into care. Once the child has been received into care, it may then be possible to develop a plan for the whole family which will facilitate the child's early return home rather than his remaining in either residential care or foster care on a long term basis.

381. Within this overall setting, however, fostering is a specialist social work skill and foster parents need to feel that they have a special place in the structure of the agency. How can social workers and their supervisors and consultants obtain and retain the necessary skills in these departments, and how can the agency provide an adequate service for all those concerned? Members of the Working Party visited several Social Services Departments and discussed this issue with staff in these departments and elsewhere. In some instances attempts to preserve specialist skills are made by establishing specialist units. In some situations specialist skills are retained and made available from consultative posts. The advantages of these solutions are obvious but it was also found that they sometimes presented problems: specialist units can become isolated from the communities they serve as well as from the pressure and overall needs of the department in which they function, and as a result the contribution

which they make can be undermined. The use of consultants may also fail unless these posts carry with them some executive authority, and link in with and represent fostering where overall departmental decisions are made concerning the allocation of resources and formulation of policy. In other instances, when fostering is undertaken as part of a general caseload in an area team, a lack of knowledge and skill combined with insufficient time often handicaps good practice.

382. Owing to the variety of departmental structures that exist and the differing capabilities of staff, it is not possible to suggest any blueprint for an ideal organisation. In any case it is important that once local attempts at solution are made, they should be allowed to develop as people and circumstances change. It is possible, however, to recommend certain principles which should form the basis of providing a foster care service within a Social Services Department:

  i. Fostering must form part of the overall pattern of service offered by a department. Such service should be developed in accordance with explicit aims and objectives.

 ii. There should be a commitment to provide adequate resources for its maintenance and development in terms of finance, staffing, skill, standards and supervision.

iii. The headquarters management team must contain someone with adequate understanding and status to ensure that this commitment is incorporated into managerial action.

 iv. Where specialist staff or units are appointed to maintain and develop expertise in fostering, their work must be integrated with that of area social work teams so that the child's needs are considered in the family context and in the light of all the departmental resources available.

  v. Where fostering is undertaken as part of general caseload, both the social worker concerned and her supervisor must be given opportunities of developing sufficient expertise for good practice.

 vi. There must be a regular assessment of the agency's need for foster homes. Machinery should exist to ensure operational co-ordination between areas in order to promote the best use of available foster homes.

vii. Providing continuity of care is of paramount importance for all children in care, and there should never be a change of social worker solely for reasons of organisational convenience.

viii. The administrative system must be organised to meet the needs of all those concerned with the fostering service.

ix. There must be good links between fostering, adoption, residential care and day care services.

x. Good relationships and adequate communication regarding fostering and foster children must exist between the Social Services Department and the Finance, Legal and Education Departments of the local authority. Similar links with the services of the Area Health Authority, the Probation Service and the Police are also essential.

xi. The procedures of the fostering service should be reviewed regularly (preferably annually) to ensure that they are still serving the purpose for which they were originally designed. Such review should take into account the views of foster parents as well as those of the agency staff.

383. An efficient administrative system geared to meet the needs of both the foster parents and the social worker is indispensable. A summary of these needs can be expressed diagramatically as on page 161.
The services to meet these needs will involve administrative staff in area offices, and personnel at headquarters. In planning and reviewing departmental procedures it is essential to ensure that an integrated system for fostering is provided within the department's overall structure.

Professional supervision

384. Foster care agencies are responsible for the quality of service they provide and should monitor the effectiveness of their service, both in respect of individual cases and in general terms. Social workers cannot operate in isolation and must have professional as well as administrative support. It is the task of their supervisors to ensure that they understand the structure of the agency and are familiar with policies and procedures. In particular they must know what decisions they are empowered to make and which must be referred to senior staff in the agency. Reminders about

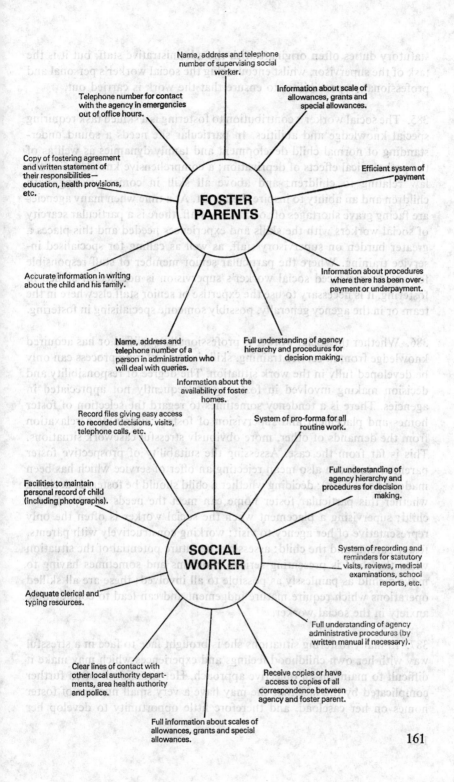

FOSTER PARENTS

Name, address and telephone number of supervising social worker.

Information about scale of allowances, grants and special allowances.

Telephone number for contact with the agency in emergencies out of office hours.

Efficient system of payment

Copy of fostering agreement and written statement of their responsibilities—education, health provisions, etc.

Accurate information in writing about the child and his family.

Information about procedures where there has been over-payment or underpayment.

Name, address and telephone number of a person in administration who will deal with queries.

Full understanding of agency hierarchy and procedures for decision making.

SOCIAL WORKER

Information about the availability of foster homes.

Record files giving easy access to recorded decisions, visits, telephone calls, etc.

System of pro-forma for all routine work.

Full understanding of agency hierarchy and procedures for decision making.

Facilities to maintain personal record of child (including photographs).

System of recording and reminders for statutory visits, reviews, medical examinations, school reports, etc.

Adequate clerical and typing resources.

Full understanding of agency administrative procedures (by written manual if necessary).

Clear lines of contact with other local authority departments, area health authority and police.

Receive copies or have access to copies of all correspondence between agency and foster parent.

Full information about scales of allowances, grants and special allowances.

161

statutory duties often originate with the administrative staff, but it is the task of the supervisor, whilst encouraging the social worker's personal and professional responsibility, to ensure that the work is carried out.

385. The social worker's contribution to fostering is a skilled task requiring special knowledge and abilities. In particular she needs a sound understanding of normal child development and family dynamics as well as of the pathological effects of deprivation; a comprehensive knowledge of the law relating to children; and above all skill in communicating with children and an ability to inspire their trust. At a time when many agencies are facing grave shortages of social work staff, there is a particular scarcity of social workers with the skills and experiences needed and this places a greater burden on supervisory staff, as well as calling for specialised in-service training. Where the particular senior member of staff responsible for an inexperienced social worker's supervision is not herself skilled in fostering, it is necessary to use the expertise of senior staff elsewhere in the team or in the agency generally, possibly someone specialising in fostering.

386. Whether the social worker is professionally qualified or has acquired knowledge from in-service training, skills in the fostering process can only be developed fully in the work situation. The degree of responsibility and decision making involved in fostering is frequently not appreciated in agencies. There is a tendency sometimes to regard the selection of foster homes and placement and supervision of foster children as a relaxation from the demands of other, more obviously stressful casework situations. This is far from the case. Assessing the suitability of prospective foster parents (which can also mean rejecting an offer of service which has been made in good faith); deciding whether a child should be fostered; deciding whether this particular foster home can meet the needs of a particular child; supervising a placement when the social worker is often the only representative of her agency to visit; working constructively with parents, foster parents and the child; assessing the future potential of the situation when the child is presenting serious problems and sometimes having to move a child as painlessly as possible to all involved; these are all skilled operations which require mature judgement and can lead to considerable anxiety in the social worker.

387. In many fostering situations she is brought face to face in a stressful way with her own childhood feelings and experiences which may make it difficult to maintain an objective approach. Her situation is often further complicated by the fact that she may have a very small number of foster homes on her caseload, and therefore little opportunity to develop her

skills. A prime requisite is that she should receive good supervision and support in extending these skills from a senior member of staff experienced in fostering, who can understand her feelings and, in sharing her anxieties, can help her to keep them within acceptable bounds. The supervisor's task includes helping the social worker to be at the centre of tension in conflicting relationships without identifying with any one party; enabling the social worker to judge the appropriate moment for active intervention; helping her recognise and cope with her prejudices; understanding her feelings and identifications, so that she can separate out her identification with the child from that with her own childhood. Supervision should enable the social worker to make a plan which not only considers the management aspects of the case but also plans for direct social work treatment.

Decision-making

388. All decisions should be based upon reliable information and sound professional judgement, but it is essential to recognise that decisions regarding a child's future must never be left to the individual social worker on her own. In addition to the support and involvement of the supervisor, there is considerable advantage in the appropriate use of case conference type discussions in the process of decision-making. The practice of using small case committees for decisions about accepting or rejecting foster parent applications and the placement of a particular child with selected foster parents, enables the cumulative knowledge and experience of the agency in fostering to be used and consistency in agency standards to be maintained. The use of group discussions for statutory reviews, drawing on the experience of a wider circle of people both inside and outside the agency with knowledge of the child, has been referred to in Chapter 14. Such reviews may lead for example to decisions that a child should be fostered, or that there should be an important change in the fostering situation. Both of these group decision-making procedures are recommended as aids to good practice. In addition to promoting appropriate care for a child they also have special value in enabling practice to be analysed and such an analysis can be used in developing policy.

389. Decisions about children in care must obviously be child centred, but it should also be borne in mind that these decisions have implications for the agency in terms of its legal, financial and administrative responsibilities. It is therefore important that agencies look at the areas of work which involve decision-making and consider who should be involved, how such decisions are made, who needs to be told about such decisions and

how the action following such decisions is monitored. The danger of decisions being made in isolation or by default is considerable, and leads to inconsistency, failure to fulfil departmental policy and failure to carry out legal requirements. It also often creates a lack of confidence in the agency and the service provided, not only by such vital people as the staff and foster parents but also by the general public.

390. The execution of decisions needs to be emphasised, and monitoring of decisions must be built into the department chain of accountability. The individual social worker, acting on behalf of the agency within a statutory framework, must clearly understand the lines of accountability as also must all the other participants in the fostering situation. Decisions are sometimes not translated into action because no record has been made of them. Any decision needs to be clearly recorded, and there must be effective channels of communication to inform all those who participate in decision making, as well as others who may be affected by the decisions. This process requires good clerical staff and professional workers and an administration in tune with the social work task. Monitoring decisions will depend upon how the agency builds in support and supervision but it is vital that this is not overlooked.

The law and statutory functions

391. Everyone involved in providing fostering services needs to have some knowledge and understanding of the law relating to children. Child care law is however complex, covering such important issues as the admission of children to care, parental rights, the selection and approval of foster parents and regulations concerning boarding out and foster homes. Appendix III lists some of the most relevant legislation and all those involved in fostering should in particular be knowledgable about the details of the Boarding Out Regulations. It is obviously the responsibility of each agency to ensure that its workers are equipped to undertake the tasks allocated to them, and in fostering this includes a working knowledge of child care law. As this is not the basic equipment of all social workers, departments need to consider the provision of facilities to enable their staff to gain and develop this information and knowledge. It is appropriate here to mention the use and value of departmental manuals and to stress once more the value of good supervision, access to internal and external training courses and the importance of each department using efficiently the knowledge and expertise located within its own organisation amongst staff at all levels.

164

Record keeping and information systems

392. The whole question of record keeping and documentation for any child in care is a complex one, since the case record serves many purposes and each department tends to have its own individual style of record keeping. Both administrators and social workers faced with a child's case record often have great difficulty in locating the information that they require. Consideration should always be given to why records are kept, what they should contain, who should have the responsibility for maintaining their accuracy, where they should be located in the organisation and who should have access to them.

393. One of the most important functions of the case record is to provide a source of information for the child in care about himself and his family. For children who have been subjected to numerous moves and who have experienced many changes of caretaker and social worker, the accuracy and completeness of departmental records is particularly important.

394. The case record is also an essential social work tool. It enables the social worker to chart the progress of a child and plan for his future. It enables her to evaluate the effectiveness of her own individual action in relation to the child and it provides information from which vital decisions can be made.

395. Records also enable information to be passed to other people involved with the child. Residential staff, foster parents, the staff in other areas and agencies, doctors, health visitors, teachers, magistrates, etc., should all have the information necessary fort carrying out their individual tasks in the interest of the child. In passing on information agencies will need to consider the ethical principles of confidentiality, and try to ensure that these are shared by all involved if the rights of the individual and his family are to be safeguarded.

396. Another important function of case records is to provide a record for the department concerning the performance of its statutory functions and the execution of its agreed policy, and to provide a basis for monitoring the quality and quantity of the service provided. Individual case records are also an important tool to administrative staff in carrying out their specific tasks, particularly their financial duties related to the assessment and collection of parental contributions and the payment of fostering fees. Records are in addition kept to provide statistics, both internal statistics for forward planning and research as well as national statistics used by government departments.

G

397. Methods for keeping case records vary and views on the best methods differ. In most social work agencies there tends to be a proliferation of forms, which are not always easy to use either in collecting information or acting on it. Vital information for all aspects of an agency's work is usually contained on admission-into-care forms. If information is not recorded at this point it may be lost for ever. Other vital forms for a child's record are review forms which describe his development and progress as well as that of his family, foster parent application forms and forms which indicate a change of circumstances for the child, his family or other important people in his life.

398. Often the only record that refers specifically to the foster family is the original application form which is aimed at giving an objective picture of the family at that time. Family attitudes, capacities and sometimes their physical surroundings and health change over the years and affect the placement of foster children. These changes should, however, be recorded separately from the child's records, as well as included in them, and should be used as a means of reassessment, particularly if there are problems in the fostering situation or a new child is to be placed. Such records can also show that foster parents are, for example, in need of a rest between placements, and can be invaluable to a new social worker taking over supervision of a foster home. A formal regular review is one way of ensuring that knowledge of particular foster families is kept up to date. These reviews could be a basis for an assessment of the foster care resources of the department.

399. It is the responsibility of the agency to provide a monitoring system which ensures that statutory regulations are complied with. Check lists and reminders about recording, statutory requirements and work to be done are valuable aids to social work practice. Written descriptions of situations and relationships are much used in case recording, and where this style of record keeping is used it should be succinct and informative. Social workers have to decide what it is they wish and need to communicate and then do so briefly. This is essential if records are to be kept up to date and if other people are to be able to make constructive use of them. In order to ensure efficient and up to date record keeping, professional staff must have access to adequate clerical and secretarial support.

400. Social workers also need to understand that records serve an administrative purpose, and to appreciate that often information which starts with them must flow quickly and smoothly into the administrative machine to enable administrative staff to carry out their functions.

Breakdown in communication and record systems and the failure of administrative and social work staff to work together, can lead to administrative errors which often affect relationships inside and outside the department and may have a negative effect upon the child and his welfare. The classic example of this failure in a fostering service is the overpayment or underpayment of boarding out allowances, which often leads to great complications.

401. In large decentralised departments, consideration should be given to the location of records and how information is transferred from one part of the organisation to another. The unnecessary duplication of records in various parts of an organisation can often be avoided by effective exchanges of information on weekly or monthly returns and the use of comprehensive card indexes.

402. In the new, large and often complexly organised social services departments, there can be breakdowns in communication which may result in key workers not having adequate knowledge of the administrative systems and procedures of the department. In some instances too much information leads to this breakdown in communication. Many agencies overcome this problem by producing procedural manuals and weekly or monthly bulletins of important information. Procedural manuals can be particularly useful for administrative staff, social workers and foster parents, but it must be stressed that they should be updated and reviewed on a regular basis.

403. Regular review of the philosophies, policies and procedures of the agency is an essential ingredient of fostering practice. The basis of a good system of foster care is the capacity of its participants to understand each others functions and the ease with which all concerned communicate with one another. Without such collaboration they cannot work together to ensure the well-being of the child.

Chapter 20
The future

404. This Guide presupposes that foster care will continue to be amongst the range of resources available to agencies responsible for the care of children. The Working Party which prepared the Guide has drawn out some basic principles and has given guidance on their implications for the practice of foster care. Many of its recommendations assume high standards of policy and practice and within the short term these standards may not always be attainable. But it is necessary to have ideals and at the same time to be clear as to the reasons which impede the progress towards their attainment. There can be limitations of time, of knowledge, of skill or of other resources.

405. A major resource in a foster care service is that of manpower, and the implication of this guide in terms of the quality and quantity of the manpower required are not inconsiderable. Foster parents, social workers and administrators are needed to maintain an effective service, and it is not easy to provide additional agency staff at a time when the social services are under unprecedented pressure. Such pressure, in part, is arising from the inevitable mismatch between the public expectation of service and the amount of resources available. There are resource implications in the recommendations of this Guide, but much of what is suggested could be put into immediate effect and could result in present resources being differently deployed so as to maximise existing expertise and skill. For example at the level of the individual interview or visit, there could be an examination of the way in which time is currently being spent to see if better use could be made of the same input of work. Agency philosophies could be examined and made explicit, administrative procedures could be reviewed. Staff with a specific interest and skill in working with children could be diverted to this work, and might replace those whose best work might be done with other client groups.

406. Fostering is commended as a means of care not because it is seen as being relatively inexpensive, but because, at its best, it provides a valuable service to children and their families. 'At its best' is the crucial test, for clearly a foster home placement does not automatically provide the right environment for a child. It is right for him only to the extent

that it succeeds in offering the compensatory experience he requires. To provide such an experience is not an easy task and the demand of time and skill from social workers and foster parents requires, in turn, adequate support from the policy makers, supervisory staff and administrators. If the future is to see an extension and improvement in the use of foster care, then attention has to be given to a wide range of issues. Some improvements will come about through more consistent adherence to proven principles, such as for example the need for deliberate and shared planning. Others will come from the application of existing knowledge in the attempt to close the gap between theory and practice. Monitoring and research will lead us on to new knowledge as to 'what is' and 'what ought to be'.

407. The issues specific to fostering which require attention include a continuing study as to the purpose of foster care. The expansion of fostering, particularly to those for whom foster care has not traditionally been seen as appropriate, will necessitate foster parents working very closely with and within the care agency. Included in this group of children will be those with physical, mental and behavioural disabilities which handicap them in their capacity to live normal lives. This work has role and status implications for foster parents and affects material and financial provisions. There is a great need to monitor new developments, and the evaluation of some of the experimental schemes now in operation should provide useful additional pointers to future developments. In this, as in many other areas, there is an urgent need to test assumptions and to analyse practice—both through replicating studies already available and in breaking new ground. For example, the effects of new legislation and of the resulting policies should be submitted to detailed monitoring and assessment. This should be a pre-requisite to further practice guidance.

408. Problems related to the acquisition and retention of specialist skills in child care practice, particularly within the context of multi-purpose social service organisations, are only now beginning to be tackled. Although there is an important organisational aspect to this, the issue fundamentally relates to training requirements. What kind and amount of child care knowledge and skill should be acquired at the level of basic professional training, and what provision of advanced training should there be? How much could and should be part of in-service training and staff development programmes generally? And what national standards, if any, could be set in that respect? What are the training needs of foster parents, alone or jointly with social workers? Much work needs to be done in this area. In addition there are other issues, perhaps less talked

about but also important, which require attention; for example, the need for a revised set of boarding out regulations and ways and means of extending protection of a recognised standard of care for children placed privately in foster homes.

409. These matters illustrate that this Guide is but one stage in a continuing process of concern with practice in foster care. It is hoped that it will be of immediate and continuing use in its own right, although it will need to be revised from time to time. The Working Party also hope that the Guide will stimulate central and local government, voluntary organisations, training bodies and professional associations to give attention to those issues outside its remit but which bear directly on the focus of its concern.

410. In considering the issues specific to fostering, it is important not to overlook the relationship between these and the general issues of policy and practice in the field of child care. Whilst this Guide has been concerned only with some aspects of one segment of child care practice, it is imperative that foster care should always be placed in the total context of the caring situation. Specific projects or undertakings are useful in allowing an 'in depth' look at a particular area of concern, but any such project in itself is not enough. The number and variety of projects that have been or are being undertaken in the child care field, the need for a continuing emphasis on prevention and the necessity to determine priorities, all point to the desirability of a comprehensive review of child care policy. It is hoped that the near future will see such a review, and that it will also be possible to see the production of a training manual on overall child care practice in the social services field.

411. Finally, it is worth restating that the needs of children in care cannot be fulfilled solely through endeavours in the specific field of the personal social services. Concern with the child's emotional, physical, social and intellectual needs demands a network of complementary services aimed at promoting the care of children and their family life. Fostering needs to be set in a wider child care context, but that total service, in its turn, must be related to the provision of other personal social services and to the wider social policies which underpin them.

Appendices

Appendices

172

Appendix I

The following summaries have been provided by Miss Celia Downes, a member of the Working Party. She wishes to acknowledge the assistance of Dr. John Bowlby and Mr. James Robertson and Mrs. Joyce Robertson in preparing this material.

This is an individual statement based on one specific theoretical viewpoint and is part of the ongoing discussion referred to in paragraph 6. (The whole of Chapter 3 of the Guide is particularly relevant in conjunction with this).

SOME ASPECTS OF A CHILD'S EMOTIONAL DEVELOPMENT AND THE IMPLICATIONS OF THESE FOR FOSTERING PRACTICE

Summaries such as these need to be followed with caution. Firstly, they are highly selective and have deliberately included more detail for the period between six months and four years, because this is a particularly important time in the development of a child's capacity to relate to others. Secondly, even where development has proceeded without interruption, there will be quite considerable variations in the age at which various aspects of emotional development are observed.

When a child has had experiences that have severed his primary emotional attachment or have hindered its formation, then the general effect is that the child is likely to be at an earlier developmental stage than his chronological age would indicate. Consequently his needs may well be that of a younger child and one can expect him to react to subsequent separations as a younger child would do. This point is of extreme importance, for example when young teenagers are being placed with foster parents, for the chronological expectations do not always match the social and emotional behaviour of many of the children in care.

As in the rest of the text, the term "mother" has been used when aspects of a child's normal development are being considered. This could equally well be father or whoever has his care long enough for a relationship of primary significance to form.

I. DURING THE PERIOD 0—6 MONTHS

Some aspects of a child's emotional development

Provided he has one person who will adapt with sensitivity to his rhythm of hunger and sleep, and how he is feeling, he will quickly adapt to his mother's particular rhythms.

He experiences generalised distress and satisfaction—relying on his mother to respond to his distress signals.

By three months he will recognise his mother, smile at her, hold babbling conversations —people are beginning to have meaning.

By four months he will be differentiating his mother from other members of the family.

Provided he has continuous personal care from one person, by the end of this period he will:

1. Begin to control and co-ordinate his impulses.

2. Begin to acquire some sense of himself as a person.

3. Begin to distinguish himself from what is happening around him.

Implications when he is separated from the person to whom he is primarily attached, without adequate substitute care

He will experience distress and will look blank and unresponsive. He will not be able to rely on people responding to his signals so is likely to have less trust than before. His developing capacity to form emotional attachments may be delayed.

Factors likely to reduce stress at this time

A satisfactory substitute caretaker who has had the opportunity to reduce the baby's sense of discontinuity of care to a minimum, e.g. opportunity to observe and familiarise herself with his feeding routine, how he was being held, changed, bathed, his sleeping pattern and what position he sleeps in, and his particular responses to stimuli, discomfort, etc., and ways of communicating.

Retention of familiar possessions, e.g. clothes, nappies, bottle, comfort blanket, dummy, etc., and if possible cot and bedding.

If a satisfactory caretaker is provided he will respond to her, having a sense of security and personal care, but he will still have to re-learn the meaning of her different responses to his signals and how best he can communicate with her.

II. DURING THE PERIOD 6 MONTHS—2 YEARS

Some aspects of a child's emotional development

He will develop an intense personal attachment to the person who is mainly responsible for his care.

As he gets more mobile his explorations cover an ever widening area, but within a safe radius of his mother. He cannot conceptualise time beyond very short periods of hours, or at the most, one or two days, nor hold on to memories of people in their absence for long.

Sometimes he experiences his mother as comforting, sometimes as frustrating his wishes. He gradually begins to integrate these two separate experiences of his mother and relate to her as a whole person.

He begins to develop a personal source of guilt and a sense of other people's feelings.

He begins to grasp some of the things his parents say he may do or not do, but can only hold on to these when they are present.

Implications when he is separated from the person to whom he is primarily attached, without adequate substitute care

He may experience intense anxiety, leading through the cycle of protest, despair and detachment to a loss of trust in himself and others.

He may experience himself as totally helpless or totally responsible for what has happened. He no longer has the resources to make sense of the world.

Rather than relating to his mother or caregiver as a whole person, he may see her as all good or all bad, and invest someone else with the opposite quality, e.g. a 'good' foster mother and a 'bad' mother. He may lose some or all of his capacity for concern, guilt or affection.

Factors likely to reduce stress at this time

He needs one familiar caretaker, preferably one known to his mother, who has become familiar by the time of his placement.

Although children under two will respond to someone talking to them, it will be primarily to the underlying feeling being conveyed rather than the words. Preparation for separation will involve enabling the child to become familiar with the place and people who will care for him, in the company of his parents or present caretaker.

Nothing but the quality of mothering-type care will serve to reassure him, and within this context familiar food, routines, environment and possessions are important, plus unaltered toilet demands.

He will rapidly transfer his affection to his new foster parent, and this will provide him with the security to cope with separation without being overwhelmed by anxiety.

175

III. DURING THE PERIOD 2—4 YEARS

Some aspects of a child's emotional development

A child's primary attachment will still be intense, but his subsidiary attachments, usually to other members of his family, will now be strongly developed as well.

He begins to hold on to the memory of his parents for short periods in their absence.

Play and make-belief are important in his continuing struggle to make sense of the world.

From about three years onwards, he starts being able to play with other children as contrasted with playing 'in parallel' in the presence of other children at an earlier stage.

There is likely to be a phase when he loves one parent while he is hostile with the other, and the feelings may be accompanied by a sense of sexual excitement.

By the end of this period, he has a growing identification with adults. He becomes aware of sexual differences and begins to accept his own sexual identity.

He can hold on to his parents' commands and prohibitions for a short time when they are not present.

Implications when he is separated from the person to whom he is primarily attached, without adequate substitute care

Separation will continue to result in overwhelming anxiety (see points mentioned under 6 months—2 years). He will soon find it difficult to maintain his primary emotional attachment to his absent parent. He will be very uncertain about time and distance and whether places and people who are not here have disappeared or been destroyed by him. He may become confused as to what he is or is not allowed to do.

Factors likely to reduce stress at this time

If preparation for placement and introductions take place within a trusting relationship with his parents and, where possible, his social worker and his new foster parents, he will at this age have far more resources of his own to help him cope, e.g. memory, language, and a beginning conception of his own feelings and of time and distance.

Detailed care should be taken not to vary his food, routine, sleeping habits and what his parents do and do not allow him to do, and to know his likes and dislikes.

Familiar simple words and games can be played to make sense of the experience around placement. All meetings, visits and preparation will need to happen with very short gaps between events if they are to make sense to him.

Talking about his parents and previous caretakers, using photographs and taking him back to see familiar people and places will help him hold on to his sense of identity.

Given this kind of care, he may be able to maintain his primary attachment to an absent parent for a limited period, but will often experience a conflict of loyalty in the process. Although the accompanying feelings of sadness and anger will be distressing for adults, they will become an important resource for him in forming new relationships.

176

IV. DURING THE PERIOD 5 YEARS—PUBERTY

Some aspects of a child's emotional development

The continuous focus of a child's mind will still be on his family even though he may spend an increasing amount of his time with other people.

As he becomes more self-reliant, so his mastery and control of himself in relation to the external world increases. He knows his likes and dislikes and anticipates events so that he can control them. Identification with adults and other children is important for his development. He gains skill and knowledge in the company of other children—and his achievement is important to his acceptance by the group. By the age of eight and nine, friends become very important. His sense of right and wrong stays with him in the absence of his parents. Because he holds memories of people he has lost, he may need to go through a period of mourning before he can make new relationships.

Implications when he is separated from people to whom he is primarily attached, without adequate substitute care

Separation and loss will create anxiety and he may show this by impulsive, uncontrolled behaviour, such as outbursts of anger or stealing. This behaviour may often become intelligible as part of the protest phase of separation,—when the child endeavours to recover the lost person. He may behave in such a way that he alienates caring people, and repeatedly provokes rejection.

He may be frightened by his behaviour and unable to talk about his fears of being unwanted and unlovable. He may turn inwards and seek comfort in masturbation.

He may be confused about the adults with whom he can identify, this may lead him to make exaggerated claims about his family.

Factors likely to reduce stress at this time

He is likely to need help in exploring his feelings about the people he is leaving and for his parents, if he is to be free to relate to new caretakers.

Anxiety may be kept at a manageable level by careful preparation for the placement, within the context of a trusting relationship with a social worker who can help him link what is happening now with what has happened previously.

The conflict of loyalties and problems of identity can be reduced by not placing him in a foster home that is culturally very far from his own.

His familiar possessions and routines are still important in diminishing disruption, but he may be too anxious to help himself, e.g. by telling his new foster mother that he likes going to sleep with the light on.

He will be anxious about his standing with the children of his new foster family, and he and his foster family need help with this.

The significance of a change of school should be fully appreciated, and introduction to a new school made carefully.

Although decisions about a move must ultimately still be made by adults, he will be able to have an increasing contribution to make planning these.

V. DURING THE PERIOD PUBERTY AND ADOLESCENCE

Some aspects of a child's emotional development

With the physical changes of puberty and changes in the way he thinks of his body come a resurgence of instinctive drives including sexual feelings which he may have difficulty in managing, resulting in extreme swings of mood and behaviour.

He may temporarily lose confidence in his ability to relate to adults and may rely heavily on his peer-group.

Provided he can feel sure enough about himself and his family, open self-determined rebellion or reaction is a possibility for him.

In middle to late adolescence, he will be turning his attention outwards and making attempts to separate from his family of origin, as a step towards setting up a new family of his own.

Implications when he is separated from the person to whom he is primarily attached without adequate substitute care

This will threaten his identity even more than would normally happen—he may lose all conception of himself as a person.

His sexuality may be inhibited or promiscuous—he may become confused about his sexual identity and sexual role.

He may have difficulty in controlling violent outbursts and other anti-social behaviour.

He may mask his anxiety through withdrawal and passivity or through feverish activity, e.g. running away.

Factors likely to reduce stress at this time

All the points mentioned under the earlier period 5—puberty still apply.

Although the ultimate decision about placement must be taken by adults, the process must increasingly be one of joint decision-making.

His need for acceptance by his foster family will be great, and this will include the material signs of belonging, such as clothes, their acceptance of his friends, and their acceptance of his strong and prolonged conflict of loyalties.

His social worker and foster parents need to recognise with him the anger or depression which may underlie his difficult behaviour.

178

References and suggestions for further study

These summaries draw heavily on:

RAYNER, ERIC, *Human development*, London, Allen and Unwin, 1971.

This book is strongly recommended for those who wish to understand these concepts in more depth and provides many suggestions for further reading.

In addition the following would provide material for further study:

ROBERTSON, JOYCE, Mothering as an influence on early development, *The Psyco-analytic Study of the Child*, Vol. XVII, 1962

ROBERTSON, JOYCE, Mother-Infant interaction from birth to twelve months: Two case studies, *Determinants of Infant Behaviour III*, London, Methuen, 1963.

These two discuss aspects of development in the first year with relevance to social work practice.

BOWLBY, JOHN, *Attachment and Loss* Vol. I—Attachment (especially Chapters 11, 14, 15 and 16), London, Hogarth Press and Harmondsworth, Middlesex, Penguin Books, 1969.

BOWLBY, JOHN, *Attachment and Loss* Vol. II—Separation (especially Chapters 1, 7, 9 and 14. Chapter 14 is particularly clear on some of the implications of the availability of attachment figures), London, Hogarth Press and Harmondsworth, Middlesex, Penguin Books, 1973.

ROBERTSON, JAMES AND JOYCE, Young Children in Brief Separation. A Fresh Look, *The Psycho-analytic Study of the Child*, Vol. XXVI, London, Hogarth Press and Tavistock Child Development Research Unit, 1971.

Film series of the same title relating to the above paper:	Tavistock Institute of Human Relations
Film 1 (1967) Kate, 2 yrs. 5 months.	In fostercare for 27 days.
Film 2 (1968) Jane, 17 months.	In fostercare for 10 days.
Film 3 (1969) John, 17 months.	For 9 days in a residential nursery.
Film 4 (1971) Thomas, 2 yrs. 4 months.	In fostercare for 10 days.
Film 5 (1973) Lucy, 21 months.	In fostercare for 19 days.

These are relevant to the period 6 months to about 5 years when the child's capacity to relate is normally at the height of his development.

ERIKSON, E. H., *Childhood and Society* (especially Part 3), London, Hogarth Press and Harmondsworth, Middlesex, Penguin Books, 1950.

ERIKSON, E. H., *Identity: youth and crisis* (especially pages 115-128), London, Faber and Faber, 1968.

Are relevant to the early school years.

ERIKSON, E. H., *Identity: youth and crisis* (especially pages 128 and 141 and Chapter VI "Towards contemporary issues: Youth"), London, Faber and Faber, 1968.

On adolescence.

Appendix II

The following text and chart have been produced by Dr. Mary Sheridan, at the request of the Working Party, as a guideline for social workers in their observation of young children's development and for discussion with foster parents about their general progress. The intention is to aid social workers in the early recognition of danger signals so that they may discuss the situation within their agency and, where appropriate, refer children for more specialised help.

DEVELOPMENTAL CHART

Ages and Stages in the Development of Babies and Young Children

There is general agreement that the younger the age at which children with physical, mental, emotional or social difficulties are discovered, fully assessed and treated, the more hopeful is the prognosis for their recovery or habilitation. Identification of children in need of help depends upon the recognition of the earliest signs of deviation from normal development. Hence it is essential that all professional workers in child care should be familiar with the accepted "milestones" (or as I prefer to call them "stepping-stones") of development, especially in relation to their everyday spontaneous behaviour.

The testing procedures outlined in the accompanying modified version of my STYCAR developmental sequences (reprinted here with permission of HMSO and NFER) require only a minimum amount of common play material and can be observed in any reasonably-sized, quiet, well-lighted, homely place. They do, however, call for an open mind, an observant eye, an attentive ear and considerable experience of young children.

In order to elicit reliable information and prevent invalid conclusions, it is important that the professional worker concerned should *personally* observe and record the child's behaviour in the various testing situations. The manner of the child's response is usually more illuminating than the mere fact that he is able to make the expected response. The child's caregiver's report of his capabilities or incapabilities in everyday situations should always be treated with respect and carefully recorded, particularly if she voices any suspicion that his reactions are in any way abnormal, but in order to prevent any future misunderstanding, the fact that this is hearsay evidence and not personal observation should be noted.

CHILDREN'S BASIC NEEDS

All children, normal and abnormal, have certain *physical needs*, without which life itself cannot continue, and certain *psychological needs* without which an individual cannot attain contentment, self-reliance and good relationships with other people.

Basic physical needs relate mainly to structural and functional healthy development:

Shelter and protective care;
Food, warmth and clothing;
Fresh air and sunlight;
Provisions for periods of activity and rest;
Prevention of illness and accidental injury;
Training in habits and skills necessary for the maintenance of life and health.

180

Basic psychological needs relate to intellectual, emotional and social development, because these processes are so closely interwoven that it is only possible to provide for them adequately in unison. They include:

Affection and continuity of individual care;

Security rooted in stable personal relationships, in familiar environmental conditions and in a feeling of belonging;

A sense of personal identity, of dignity as a human being, and of self-respect derived from the knowledge of being loved and valued for oneself alone;

Opportunity to learn from experience;

Opportunity to achieve success in some field of endeavour, however small;

Opportunity to achieve independence, physical, mental and financial;

Opportunity to take responsibility, however slight, and to be of service to others.

HEREDITY, ENVIRONMENT AND INDIVIDUALITY

In common with other living creatures, every child is subject to three influences. Broadly speaking—

Heredity determines the limits of each individual child's capacity to achieve optimal structural and functional maturity.

Environment determines the extent to which each individual child can fulfil his potential capacity.

Individual dynamics determine the quality of drive, concentration and performance.

The body is the instrument of all activity, emotion supplies the necessary energy, while intellect exercises control and forward planning.

It is in the nature of the developing body to be continually active, of the developing mind to be intensely curious and of the developing personality to seek good relationships with other people.

Consequently any inactive, incurious or unforthcoming child is in need of full physical and mental assessment and careful follow-up to ensure that he is not sick or suffering from environmental deprivation or defending himself against some intolerable stress. At the other end of the behavioural spectrum it is equally important to refer for further investigation children who show purposeless overactivity, obsessional inquisitiveness, incorrigible rebelliousness or relentless demand for attention.

GROWTH AND DEVELOPMENT are not identical.

Growth is increase in size. Its progressions are mainly structural and measurable.

Development is increase in complexity. It involves both structure and function. Its numerous simultaneous progressions are closely related but immeasurably variable.

Normally growth and development of body, intellect and personality progress harmoniously and with relative predictability.

Abnormally they are dissociated, producing widespread individual disharmonies between physical, mental and social development with uncertain final results.

HUMAN BIOLOGICAL CHARACTERISTICS

The four outstanding biological achievements of homo sapiens which mark his superiority over all other animals are:

first his upright posture, which facilitates locomotion and enables him to assume, adapt and maintain an enormous variety of effective attitudes, while leaving his hands free for more precise activities;

second his adjustable visual focus, uniquely flexible digits and ability to construct and use hand tools;

third his possession of spoken language;

fourth his evolution of complex cultural societies for the benefit of the individuals who comprise them, and for protection of the young during their relatively prolonged period of dependency.

A child's developmental progress may conveniently be observed within the context of these biological parameters.

THE FOUR PARALLELS OF HUMAN DEVELOPMENT

ONE: Motor, involving body postures and large movements which combine competent forward planning in time and space with high physical skills and economy of effort.

TWO: Vision and fine movement, combining competence in seeing and looking (for far and near) with manipulative skills.

THREE: Hearing and speech, combining competence in hearing, listening and communication.

FOUR: Social behaviour and spontaneous play, combining competence in organisation of the self, i.e. self-identification, self-care and self-occupation; with increasing voluntary acceptance of everyday social demands.

CHILDREN with SPECIAL NEEDS

i.e. handicapped, disadvantaged and vulnerable children.

Broadly speaking, the disabilities of handicapped children are the result of some disordered condition within themselves; the disabilities of disadvantaged children are the result of unfavourable conditions in their environment; while other children are unusually vulnerable to the effects of constitutional weakness or stressful experience.

A handicapped child may be defined as one who suffers from any continuing disability of body, intellect or personality which is likely to interfere with his normal growth and development or his capacity to learn.

A disadvantaged child is one who suffers from a continuing inadequacy of material, affectional, educational or social provisions, or who is subject to detrimental environmental stresses of any other sort, which are likely to interfere with the growth and development of his body, intellect or personality and thus prevent him from achieving his inherent potential.

182

Vulnerable children. Certain groups of children by reason of constitutional weakness, previous illness or detrimental emotional or social experience are more likely to suffer permanent damage from environmental stresses of all sorts than are the majority of their age peers. These children "at risk" may be divided into five groups. Children in the first groups present unsatisfactory medical or social histories. Children in the fifth group appear to be normal at first, but manifest signs of deviant development later. For practical purposes the five groups may be conveniently considered as follows:—

Group 1:   Adverse family, medical or social history.
Group 2:   Prenatal hazards.
Group 3:   Perinatal dangers.
Group 4:   Postnatal mishaps.
Group 5:   Developmental warning signals.

Community provisions for children with special needs additional to those provided for all children in the community are medical, educational and social. They include—

Early identification;

Full assessment of disabilities and of assets;

Prompt medical and surgical treatment;

Help and guidance for the parents to enable them to care for their handicapped child as long as possible in his own home;

Appropriate early training, education and vocational guidance;

Supervision and periodic assessment throughout childhood and adolescence;

Final placement in the community or in special care.

The role of the worker in child care must therefore include early recognition of danger signals, prompt referral for full investigation and regular supervision of all children with special needs.

Developmental Alerting Signals in Identification of Children in Special Need

Mother's or care-giver's suspicions that the child is not seeing, hearing, moving his limbs, playing with toys, taking notice of his surroundings or relating to people like other children of his age.

N.B. She is usually right.

Observed indications of developmental disorder.

Delayed motor development in whole body or in one or more limbs.

Lack of normal visual alertness for near and far.

Inattention to everyday sounds particularly voice.

Delayed development of vocalisation or speech.

Lack of interest in people and playthings.

Abnormal social behaviour of any sort.

N.B. If any of these conditions are present, or suspected, it is essential to refer the child immediately for paediatric investigation.

SUPERVISION OF CHILDREN'S DEVELOPMENT

The social worker's responsibilities in this sphere relate to both the child and his caregiver.

Observation of Caregiver

A good caregiver creates a satisfactory emotional and material environment; is affectionate, stable but not overindulgent. She must first of all know how to supply the child's basic physical and psychological needs and how to teach him everyday skills. Inadequate physical care, poor nutrition or limited opportunities for learning in the early months and years of life can permanently affect future performance.

Observation of the Child

The characteristics of a child who is healthy and progressing favourably in mind and body are—

he is happy, friendly and secure;

he looks well;

he keeps well;

he eats well;

he sleeps well;

he plays energetically and sensibly;

he likes going to school.

DEVELOPMENT and LEARNING

The essential provisions for satisfactory learning in childhood include *early training*, suitable *education* at school, and appropriate *vocational guidance*.

Early Training

Early training depends upon adequate stimulation. The natural *teachers* are parents. The natural *place* is the ordinary family home. The natural *tools* of learning are playthings. Knowledgeable observation of a child's spontaneous play provides useful indications of his progress in the four main biological parameters.

Play is as necessary to a child as food, warmth and protective care. It represents for him:

Apprenticeship to everyday living, providing practice in basic skills;

Research, i.e. adventure, observation, speculation and discovery;

Occupational therapy, i.e. relief from stress or boredom;

Chosen recreation, i.e. fun.

In his play, a child exercises his body, looks, listens and reaches out, experiments with people and things, stores his memory, studies causes and effects, reasons out problems, builds up a useful vocabulary and adapts his social behaviour to the cultural usages of his environment. Consequently, the provision of suitable *playthings, playspace, playtime* and *playfellows* for all young children and particularly for young, handicapped or disadvantaged children is of primary importance.

184

Provisions for Play

Playthings must be appropriate for stage of growth and development, neither too few, nor too many; *playspace* is needed for 'free-ranging' activities shared with others, but every child should also have a small personal 'territory' which is indisputably his own, so that he may learn the distinction between what is "mine" and what is "not mine" and thus also respect the ownership of others; *playtime* must be adequate for fulfilment of interest, without premature interruption causing frustration, or fading of purpose due to boredom; *playfellows* are required at all stages—encouraging adults for infants and toddlers, very small family-type collectives when powers of communications are improving; larger peer-groups at nursery-school age, when individual interests and social understanding are rapidly extending, and finally, at school age, in a circle of *chosen friends*, marking the beginnings of full social integration.

Types of Play

Six main types of play are usually described, i.e. *active, exploratory, imitative, constructive* (or end-productive), *make-believe* and *games-with-rules* (win/lose play). They emerge in orderly developmental sequence as the child learns to use his sensory and motor equipment and his powers of communication and creativity. Expected ages and stages of the first four types are outlined in the accompanying charts. There is no need to discuss them further.

Make-believe (or pretend) play, however, merits additional explanation. It usually begins a month or two before the age of two and is elaborated thereafter for many years. It presumes previous acquisition of all the foregoing varieties of play. Its appearance is highly significant since it can only evolve when the child has acquired some understanding of the world around him and possesses a code of communication. Having learned reasons for the activities he has observed and imitated, a child now deliberately invents increasingly complex make-believe situations in order to put into practice and enjoy his various already acquired skills, insights and sentiments. At the same time, while offering his personal comments upon the passing scene, he improves his general knowledge, cultivates his social interests and, most importantly, refines his communications. Observation of a young child's spontaneous make-believe play is therefore one of the most revealing indications of his general level of intelligence, and of his past experience, his present views about life, and his powers of forward planning.

Games-with-Rules (or win/lose play) beginning about $4\frac{1}{2}$ years, presuppose a high degree of skill in all the foregoing types and a well-developed sense of fair play. They continue through life in the sophisticated games and sports which interest older children and adults and which, to be rewarding, must be played strictly according to an agreed set of regulations.

Between 7 and 12 years, leisure-time activities become more selectively sex-determined. Outdoor games, including make-believe activities and games with rules in particular, tend to be played in exclusive masculine gangs and feminine groups until, from the early teens onwards, boys and girls re-discover mutual interests in highly organized sports, hobbies and the creative arts.

Playthings. Simple traditional playthings like rattles, balls, building blocks, dolls, wheeled toys and the common domestic objects from which ordinary family children derive so much pleasure and profit, remain of fundamental importance to early learning. A few soft toys are generally acceptable, but clock-work and other 'finished' commercial toys are seldom appropriate. There is no need to stress the importance of ensuring that all playthings are washable and flameproof, safe to handle, throw and suck, but impossible to swallow.

185

The use of common outdoor playground equipment should be encouraged, provided adequate supervision is available. Children of every age enjoy tricycles, pedal cars, climbing frames, slides, trampolines, swings, paddling pools, boating ponds and sand-pits. Outdoor activities promote good health, self-reliance and comradeship.

Suitable educational placement forms an integral part of provisions for treatment and social welfare of disadvantaged and handicapped children. Their schooling remains a primary consideration in the planning of necessary clinic attendance or hospital admission. For the same reason the geographical location of a foster home needs to be reasonably accessible to the child's special school, clinic or hospital.

Vocational Guidance

It is necessary for all of us who are concerned with the health, education and welfare of disadvantaged children to bear constantly in mind that childhood itself is a temporary phase in the life of any individual human being. Vocational guidance therefore should be based on realistic evaluation of a child's physical capacity, mental ability and social competence. Our ultimate goal is to do our best to equip him in body, mind and person-ality to become a happy, self-reliant and useful adult member of the social group to which he belongs.

USE OF ACCOMPANYING CHART

The ages and stages set out in the accompanying chart are only approximate. The words "pass" and "fail" in relation to the testing situations are inappropriate. Every child is different and can only be judged to respond, or not to respond in manner which might reasonably be expected of most healthy and contented children of his chrono-logical age. Few children will respond unequivocally to every item listed for his age level, during a single visit of observation, while many children who subsequently prove to have average abilities will respond to some items at an earlier or later age than indicated. A useful working rule is to expect a child to demonstrate adequate response to about two-thirds of the items listed in each of the four parameters for children in his age group.

Case Recording

In order to prevent any present or future misunderstanding it is exceedingly important to record separately what is *reported* to the professional worker and what he or she personally *observes*. Home visits at regular intervals, provide a useful means of assessing and recording developmental progress, although they cannot be relied upon to foretell a child's ultimate attainments.

Within these limitations the charts offer to professional workers, in plain words and tabulated form, information derived from many years' research work with normal, disadvantaged and handicapped young children, in the hope that it will be helpful in supervising the progress of children with special needs, and in their guidance of foster parents and others concerned with the health and welfare of young children in the community.

Note The references in the text relate to the H.M.S.O. publication "The Developmental Progress of Infants and Young Children" (Reports on Public Health and Medical Subjects No. 102—Third Edition 1975) and an extended illustrated version of the

STYCAR Sequences and a special wall chart published by the National Foundation for Educational Research (NFER), Jennings Buildings, Thames Avenue, Windsor, Berks SL4 1QS.

Colour-slide and audio-tape lectures for all key ages from birth to 5 years (spoken by MDS) are available for hire or sale from the Medical Recording Service Foundation (MRSF), Writtle, Chelmsford, Essex CM1 3EH.

A set of coloured films on child development and play prepared in collaboration with Professor Neil O'Doherty (Dublin) is also available for sale or hire from Guild Sound and Vision, Woodstone House, Oundle Road, Peterborough PE2 9PZ.

AGE	POSTURE AND LARGE MOVEMENTS	VISION AND FINE MOVEMENTS
1 month	Lies back with head to one side; arm and leg on same side outstretched, or both arms flexed; knees apart, soles of feet turned inwards. Large jerky movements of limbs, arms more active than legs. At rest, hands closed and thumb turned in. Fingers and toes fan out during extensor movements of limbs. When lifted or pulled to sit head falls loosely backwards. Held sitting, head falls forward, with back in one complete curve. Placed downwards on face, head immediately turns to side. Held standing on hard surface, presses down feet, straightens body and often makes reflex "stepping" movements.	Turns head and eyes towards light. Stares expressionlessly at brightness window or blank wall. Notices silent dangling toy shaken in line vision at 6-8 inches and follows its slo movement with eyes from side towards mi line. Gazes at mother's nearby face when she fee or talks to him with increasingly alert faci expression.
3 months	Now prefers to lie on back with head in mid-line. Limbs more pliable, movements smoother and more continuous. Waves arms symmetrically. Hands now loosely open. Brings hands together from side into mid-line over chest or chin. Kicks vigorously, legs alternating or occasionally together. Held sitting, holds back straight, except in lumbar region, with head erect and steady for several seconds before bobbing forwards. Placed downwards on face lifts head and upper chest well up in mid-line, using forearms as support, and often scratching at table surface; legs straight, buttocks flat. Held standing with feet on hard surface, sags at knees.	Visually very alert, particularly interested nearby human faces. Moves head deliberately to look around hi Follows adult's movements near cot. Follows dangling toy at 6-10 inches above fa through half circle from side to side, a usually also vertically from chest to brow. Watches movements of own hands before fa and beginning to clasp and unclasp han together in finger play. Recognises feeding bottle and makes eag welcoming movements as it approaches h face.
6 months	Lying on back, raises head from pillow. Lifts legs into vertical and grasps foot. Sits with support in cot or pram and turns head from side to side to look around him. Moves arms in brisk purposeful fashion and holds them up to be lifted. When hands grasped braces shoulders and pulls himself up. Kicks strongly, legs alternating. Can roll over, front to back. Held sitting, head is firmly erect, and back straight. May sit alone momentarily. Placed downwards on face lifts head and chest well up supporting himself on extended arms. Held standing with feet touching hard surface bears weight on feet and bounces up and down actively.	Visually insatiable: moves head and ey eagerly in every direction. Eyes move in unison: squint now abnormal. Follows adult's movements across room. Immediately fixates interesting small obje within 6-12 inches (e.g. toy, bell, wooden cub spoon, sweet) and stretches out both hands grasp them. Uses whole hand in palmar grasp. When toys fall from hand over edge of c forgets them.

188

HEARING AND SPEECH	SOCIAL BEHAVIOUR AND PLAY

Startled by sudden loud noises, stiffens, quivers, blinks, screws eyes up, extends limbs, fans out fingers and toes, and may cry.
Stops whimpering to sound of nearby soothing human voice, but not when screaming or feeding.
Cries lustily when hungry or uncomfortable.
Utters little guttural noises when content.
(Note:—Deaf babies also cry and vocalise in this reflex way, but if very deaf do not usually show startle reflex to sudden noise. Blind babies may also move eyes towards a sound-making toy.)

Sucks well.
Sleeps much of the time when not being fed or handled.
Expression still vague, but becoming more alert, progressing to social smiling about 5-6 weeks. Hands normally closed, but if opened, grasps examiner's finger when palm is touched. Stops crying when picked up and spoken to.
Mother supports head when carrying, dressing and bathing.

Sudden loud noises still distress, provoking blinking, screwing up of eyes, cry and turning away.
Definite quietening or smiling to sound of mother's voice before she touches him, but not when screaming.
Vocalises freely when spoken to or pleased.
Cries when uncomfortable or annoyed.
Often licks lips in response to sounds of preparation for feeding.
Shows excitement at sound of approaching footsteps, running bath water, voices, etc.
(Note:—Deaf baby, instead, may be obviously startled by M's sudden appearance beside cot).

Fixes eyes unblinkingly on mother's face when feeding.
Beginning to react to familiar situations—showing by smiles, coos, and excited movements that he recognises preparation for feeds, baths, etc.
Responds with obvious pleasure to friendly handling, especially when accompanied by playful tickling and vocal sounds.
Holds rattle for few moments when placed in hand, but seldom capable of regarding it at same time.
Mother supports at shoulders when dressing and bathing.

Turns immediately to mother's voice across room.
Vocalises tunefully and often, using single and double syllables, e.g. ka, muh, goo, der, adah, k-leh.
Laughs, chuckles and squeals aloud in play.
Screams with annoyance.
Shows evidence of response to different emotional tones of mother's voice.

Hands competent to reach for and grasp small toys.
Most often uses a two-handed scooping-in approach, but occasionally a single hand.
Takes everything to mouth.
Beginning to find feet interesting and even useful in grasping.
Puts hands to bottle and pats it when feeding.
Shakes rattle deliberately to make it sound, often regarding it closely at same time.
Still friendly with strangers but occasionally shows some shyness or even slight anxiety, especially if M is out of sight.

189

AGE	POSTURE AND LARGE MOVEMENT	VISION AND FINE MOVEMENTS
9 months	Sits alone for 10-15 minutes on floor. Can turn body to look sideways while stretching out to grasp dangling toy or to pick up toy from floor. Arms and legs very active in cot, pram and bath. Progresses on floor by rolling or squirming. Attempts to crawl on all fours. Pulls self to stand with support. Can stand holding on to support for a few moments, but cannot lower himself. Held standing, steps purposefully on alternate feet.	Very observant. Stretches out, one hand leading, to grasp small objects immediately on catching sight of them. Manipulates objects with lively interest passing from hand to hand, turning over, etc. Pokes at small sweet with index finger. Grasps sweets, string etc, between finger and thumb in scissor fashion. Can release toy by pressing against firm surface, but cannot yet put down precisely. Searches in correct place for toys dropped within reach of hand. Looks after toys falling over edge of pram or table. Watches activities of adults, children and animals within 10-12 feet with eager interest for several seconds at a time.
12 months	Sits well and for indefinite time. Can rise to sitting position from lying down. Crawls rapidly, usually on all fours. Pulls to standing and lets himself down again holding on to furniture. Walks round furniture stepping sideways. Walks with one or both hands held. May stand alone for few moments. May walk alone.	Picks up small objects, e.g. blocks, string, sweets and crumbs, with precise pincer grasp of thumb and index finger. Throws toys deliberately and watches them fall to ground. Looks in correct place for toys which roll out of sight. Points with index finger at objects he wants to handle or which interest him. Watches small toy pulled along floor across room 10 feet away. Out of doors watches movements of people, animals, motor cars, etc., with prolonged intent regard. Recognises familiars approaching from 20 feet or more away. Uses both hands freely, but may show preference for one.
15 months	Walks unevenly with feet wide apart, arms slightly flexed and held above head or at shoulder level to balance. Starts alone, but frequently stopped by falling or bumping into furniture. Lets himself down from standing to sitting by collapsing backwards with bump, or occasionally by falling forward on hands and then back to sitting. Can get to feet alone. Crawls upstairs. Kneels unaided or with slight support on floor and in pram, cot and bath. May be able to stoop to pick up toys from floor.	Picks up string, small sweets and crumbs neatly between thumb and finger. Builds tower of two cubes after demonstration. Grasps crayon and imitates scribble after demonstration. Looks with interest at pictures in book and pats page. Follows with eyes path of cube or small toy swept vigorously from table. Watches small toy pulled across floor up to 12 feet. Points imperiously to objects he wishes to be given. Stands at window and watches events outside intently for several minutes.

190

HEARING AND SPEECH	SOCIAL BEHAVIOUR AND PLAY
Vocalises deliberately as means of inter-personal communication. Shouts to attract attention, listens, then shouts again. Babbles tunefully, repeating syllables in long strings (mam-mam, bab-bab, dad-dad, etc.) Understands "No-No"; and "Bye-Bye". Tries to imitate adults' playful vocal sounds, e.g. smacking lips, cough, brr etc.	Holds, bites and chews biscuits. Puts hands round bottle or cup when feeding. Tries to grasp spoon when being fed. Throws body back and stiffens in annoyance or resistance. Clearly distinguishes strangers from familiars, and requires reassurance before accepting their advances. Clings to known adult and hides face. Still takes everything to mouth. Plays peek-a-boo. Holds out toy held in hand to adult, but cannot yet give. Finds partially hidden toy. May find toy hidden under cup. Mother supports at lower spine when dressing.
Knows and immediately turns to own name. Babbles loudly, tunefully and incessantly. Shows by suitable movements and behaviour that he understands several words in usual context (e.g. own and family names, walk, dinner, pussy, cup, spoon, ball, car.) Comprehends simple commands associated with gesture (Give it to Daddy. Come to Mummy. Say bye-bye, clap hands, etc.) Imitates adult's playful vocalisations with gleeful enthusiasm. May hand E common objects on request, e.g. spoon, cup, ball, shoe.	Drinks from cup with little assistance. Chews. Holds spoon but usually cannot use it alone. Helps with dressing by holding out arm for sleeve and foot for shoe. Takes objects to mouth less often. Puts wooden cubes in and out of cup or box. Rattles spoon in cup in imitation. Listens with obvious pleasure to percussion sounds. Repeats activities to reproduce effects. Gives toys to adult on request and sometimes spontaneously. Finds hidden toy quickly. Likes to be constantly within sight and hearing of adult. Demonstrates affection to familiars. Waves "bye-bye" and claps hands in imitation or spontaneously. Child sits, or sometimes stands without support, while Mother dresses.
Jabbers loudly and freely, using wide range of inflections and phonetic units. Speaks 2-6 recognisable words and understands many more. Vocalises wishes and needs at table. Points to familiar persons, animals, toys, etc. when requested. Understands and obeys simple commands (e.g. Shut the door. Give me ball. Get your shoes).	Holds cup when adult gives and takes back. Holds spoon, brings it to mouth and licks it, but cannot prevent its turning over. Chews well. Helps more constructively with dressing. Indicates when he has wet pants. Pushes large wheeled toy with handle on level ground. Seldom takes toys to mouth. Repeatedly casts objects to floor in play or rejection usually without watching fall. Physically restless and intensely curious. Handles everything within reach. Emotionally labile. Closely dependent upon adult's reassuring presence. Needs constant supervision to protect C from dangers of extended exploration and exploitation of environment.

191

AGE	POSTURE AND LARGE MOVEMENT	VISION AND FINE MOVEMENTS
18 months	Walks well with feet only slightly apart, starts and stops safely. Runs stiffly upright, eyes fixed on ground 1-2 yards ahead, but cannot continue to run round obstacles. Pushes and pulls large toys, boxes, etc. round floor. Can carry large doll or teddy-bear while walking and sometimes two. Backs into small chair or slides in side-ways. Climbs forward into adult's chair then turns round and sits. Walks upstairs with helping hand. Creeps backwards downstairs. Occasionally bumps down a few steps on buttocks facing forwards. Picks up toy from floor without falling.	Picks up small sweets, beads, pins, threads etc., immediately on sight, with delicate pincer grasp. Spontaneous scribble when given crayon and paper, using preferred hand. Builds tower of three cubes after demonstration. Enjoys simple picture book, often recognising and putting finger on coloured items on page. Turns pages 2 or 3 at a time. Points to distant interesting objects out of doors.
2 years	Runs safely on whole foot, stopping and starting with ease and avoiding obstacles. Squats to rest or to play with object on ground and rises to feet without using hands. Walks backwards pulling large toy. Pulls wheeled toy by cord. Climbs on furniture to look out of window or open doors, etc. and can get down again. Walks upstairs and down holding on to rail or wall: two feet to a step. Throws small ball without falling. Walks into large ball when trying to kick it. Sits astride large wheeled toy and propels forward with feet on ground.	Picks up pins and thread, etc., neatly and quickly. Removes paper wrapping from small sweet. Builds tower of six cubes (or 6+). Spontaneous circular scribble and dots when given paper and pencil. Enjoys picture books, recognising fine details in favourite pictures. Turns pages singly. Recognises familiar adults in photograph after once shown. Hand preference becoming evident.
2½ years	Walks upstairs alone, but downstairs holding rail, two feet to a step. Runs well straight forward and climbs easy nursery apparatus. Pushes and pulls large toys skillfully, but has difficulty in steering them round obstacles. Jumps with two feet together. Can stand on tiptoe if shown. Kicks large ball. Sits on tricycle and steers with hands, but still usually propels with feet on ground.	Picks up pins, threads etc., with each eye covered separately. Builds tower of seven (or 7+) cubes and lines blocks to form "train". Recognises minute details in picture books. Paints strokes, dots and circular shapes on easel. Recognises himself in photographs when once shown.

HEARING AND SPEECH	SOCIAL BEHAVIOUR AND PLAY

ontinues to jabber tunefully to himself at play.
ses 6-20 recognisable words and understands many
ore.
choes prominent or last word addressed to him.
emands desired objects by pointing accompanied
loud, urgent vocalisation or single words.
njoys nursery rhymes and tries to join in.
ttempts to sing.
nows his own or doll's hair, shoe, nose.

Lifts and holds cup between both hands.
Drinks without spilling.
Hands cup back to adult. Chews well.
Holds spoon and gets food to mouth.
Takes off shoes, socks, hat.
Indicates toilet needs by restlessness and vocalisation.
Bowel control usually attained.
Explores environment energetically.
No longer takes toys to mouth.
Remembers where objects belong.
Casts objects to floor in play or anger less often.
Briefly imitates simple activities, e.g. reading book,
kissing doll, brushing floor.
Plays contentedly alone, but likes to be near adult.
Emotionally still very dependent upon familiar
adult, especially M.
Alternates between clinging and resistance.

---

ses 50 or more recognisable words and understands
any more.
uts 2 or more words together to form simple
ntences.
efers to himself by name.
alks to himself continually as he plays.
choolalia almost constant, with one or more
ressed words repeated.
onstantly asking names of objects.
oins in nursery rhymes and songs.
hows correctly and repeats words for hair, hand,
et, nose, eyes, mouth, shoe on request.

Lifts and drinks from cup and replaces on table.
Spoon-feeds without spilling.
Asks for food and drink. Chews competently.
Puts on hat and shoes.
Verbalises toilet needs in reasonable time.
Dry during day.
Turns door handles. Often runs outside to explore.
Follows M round house and copies domestic
activities in simultaneous play.
Constantly demanding M's attention.
Clings tightly in affection, fatigue or fear.
Tantrums when frustrated but attention readily
distracted.
Demands own possessions with determination.
As yet no idea of sharing.
Plays near other children but not with them.
Resentful of attention shown to other children.

---

ses 200 or more recognisable words but speech
hows numerous infantilisms.
nows full name.
alks intelligibly to himself at play concerning
vents happening here and now.
choolalia persists.
ontinually asking questions beginning "What?",
"Where?"
ses pronouns, I, me and you.
tuttering in eagerness common.
ays a few nursery rhymes.
njoys simple familiar picture book.

Eats skilfully with spoon and may use fork.
Pulls down pants or knickers at toilet, but seldom
able to replace.
Dry through night if lifted.
Very active, restless and rebellious.
Throws violent tantrums when thwarted or unable to
express urgent needs and less easily distracted.
Emotionally still very dependent upon adults.
Prolonged domestic make-belief play (putting dolls
to bed, washing clothes, driving motor-cars, etc.)
but with frequent reference to friendly adult.
Watches other children at play interestedly and
occasionally joining in for a few minutes, but little
notion of sharing playthings or adult's attention.

193

AGE	POSTURE AND LARGE MOVEMENT	VISION AND FINE MOVEMENTS
3 years	Walks alone upstairs with alternating feet and downstairs with two feet to step. Usually jumps from bottom step. Climbs nursery apparatus with agility. Can turn round obstacles and corners while running and also while pushing and pulling large toys. Rides tricycle and can turn wide corners on it. Can walk on tiptoe. Stands momentarily on one foot when shown. Sits with feet crossed at ankles.	Picks up pins, threads, etc. with each e covered separately. Builds tower of nine cubes, also (3½) bridge three from model. Can close fist and wiggle thumb in imitatio R and L. Draws man with head and usually indication features and one other part. Matches two or three primary colours (usual red and yellow correct, but may confuse bl and green). Paints "pictures" with large brush on easel. Cuts with scissors.
4 years	Turns sharp corners running, pushing and pulling. Walks alone up and downstairs, one foot per step. Climbs ladders and trees. Expert rider of tricycle. Hops on one foot. Stands on one foot 3-5 seconds. Arranges or picks up objects from floor by bending from waist with knees extended.	Picks up pins, thread, crumbs, etc., with ea eye covered separately. Builds tower of 10 or more cubes and seve "bridges" of three on request. Draws man with head, legs, features, trun and (often) arms. Draws very simple house. Matches and names four primary colou correctly.
5 years	Runs lightly on toes. Active and skilful in climbing, sliding, swinging, digging, and various "stunts". Skips on alternate feet. Dances to music. Can stand on one foot 8-10 seconds. Can hop 2-3 yards forwards on each foot separately. Grips strongly with either hand.	Picks up minute objects when each eye covered separately. Writes a few letters spontaneously. Draws recognisable man with head, trun legs, arms and features. Draws simple house with door, windows, ro and chimney. Names four primary colours and matches 10 12 colours.

194

HEARING AND SPEECH	SOCIAL BEHAVIOUR AND PLAY
arge intelligible vocabulary but speech still shows any infantile phonetic substitutions. ives full name and sex, and (sometimes) age. ses plurals and pronouns. till talks to himself in long monologues mostly oncerned with immediate present including make-elieve activities. arries on simple conversations, and verbalises past xperiences. sks many questions beginning "What?" "Where?", "Who?". istens eagerly to stories and demands favourites ver and over again. nows several nursery rhymes.	Eats with fork and spoon. Washes hands, but needs supervision in drying. Can pull pants and knickers down and up, but needs help with buttons. Dry through night. General behaviour more amenable. Affectionate and confiding. Likes to help with adult's activities in house and garden. Makes effort to keep his surroundings tidy. Vividly realised make-believe play including invented people and objects. Enjoys floor play with bricks, boxes, toy trains and cars, alone or with siblings. Joins in play with other children in and outdoors. Understands sharing playthings, sweets, etc. Shows affection for younger siblings. Shows some appreciation of past and present.
peech completely intelligible. Shows only a few fantile substitutions usually k/t/th/f/s and r/l/w/y roups. ives connected account of recent events and xperiences. ives name, sex, home address and (usually) age. ternally asking questions "Why?", "When?", How?" and meanings of words. istens to and tells long stories sometimes confusing ct and fantasy.	Eats skilfully with spoon and fork. Washes and dries hands. Brushes teeth. Can undress and dress except for back buttons, laces and ties. General behaviour markedly self-willed. Inclined to verbal impertinence when wishes crossed but can be affectionate and compliant. Strongly dramatic play and dressing-up favoured. Constructive out-of-doors building with any large material to hand. Needs other children to play with and is alternately co-operative and aggressive with them as with adults. Understands taking turns. Shows concern for younger siblings and sympathy for playmates in distress. Appreciates past, present and future.
peech fluent and grammatical. Articulation correct xcept for residual confusions of s/f/th and r/l/w/y roups. oves stories and acts them out in detail later. ives full name, age and home address. ives age and (usually) birthday. sks meaning of abstract words.	Uses knife and fork. Washes and dries face and hands, but needs help and supervision for rest. Undresses and dresses alone. General behaviour more sensible, controlled and responsibly independent. Domestic and dramatic play continued from day to day. Plans and builds constructively. Chooses own friends. Co-operative with companions and understands need for rules and fair play. Appreciates meaning of clocktime in relation to daily programme. Tender and protective towards younger children and pets. Comforts playmates in distress.

195

Appendix III

STATUTES

Extracts from various Acts of Parliament which relate to the contents of the Gujde.

NOTE: These extracts are quoted for general guidance only and must not be treated as a complete and authoritative statement of the law. The Acts in question should be referred to for the precise effect of their provisions.

(Account has been taken of the Children Act 1975 but it should be noted that certain provisions of this Act may not yet have been brought into force.)

A. England and Wales

1. Reception of children into the care of local authorities.
2. Committal of children to the care of local authorities.
3. General duty of local authorities regarding children in care.
4. Boarding out of children in care.
5. Assumption by local authorities of parental rights over children in their care.
6. Miscellaneous matters. (Including miscellaneous powers and duties of local authorities in relation to children).
7. Children in the care of voluntary organisations.

1. Reception of children into the care of local authorities

The enactment whereby a child may be received into the care of a local authority is the Children Act, 1948.

CHILDREN ACT, 1948—Section 1 (As amended by the Children Act, 1975)
Duty of local authority to provide for orphans, deserted children, etc.

(1) Where it appears to a local authority with respect to a child in their area appearing to them to be under the age of 17—

    (a) that he has neither parent nor guardian or has been and remains abandoned by his parents or guardian or is lost; or

    (b) that his parents or guardian are, for the time being or permanently, prevented by reason of mental or bodily disease or infirmity or other incapacity or any other circumstances from providing for his proper accommodation, maintenance and upbringing; and

    (c) in either case, that the intervention of the local authority under this section is necessary in the interests of the welfare of the child,

it shall be the duty of the local authority to receive the child into their care under this section.

(2) Where a local authority have received a child into their care under this section, it shall, subject to the provisions of this Part of this Act, be their duty to keep the child in their care so long as the welfare of the child appears to them to require it and the child has not attained the age of 18.

196

(3) Nothing in this section shall authorise a local authority to keep a child in their care under this section if any parent or guardian desires to take over the care of the child, and the local authority, shall, in all cases where it appears to them consistent with the welfare of the child so to do, endeavour to secure that the care of the child is taken over either—

(a) by a parent or guardian of his, or

(b) by a relative or friend of his, being, where possible, a person of the same religious persuasion as the child or who gives an undertaking that the child will be brought up in that religious persuasion.

(3A) Except in relation to an act done—

(a) with the consent of the local authority, or

(b) by a parent or guardian of the child who has given the local authority not less than 28 days notice of his intention to do it,

subsection (8) (penalty for taking away a child in care) of section 3 of this Act shall apply to a child in the care of a local authority under this section (notwithstanding that no resolution is in force under section 2 of this Act with respect to the child) if he has been in the care of that local authority throughout the preceding six months; and for the purposes of the application of paragraph (b) of that subsection in such a case a parent or guardian of the child shall not be taken to have lawful authority to take him away.

(3B) The Secretary of State may by order a draft of which has been approved by each House of Parliament amend subsection (3A) of this section by substituting a different period for the period of 28 days or of six months mentioned in that subsection (or the period which, by order under this section, was substituted for that period).

(4) Where a local authority receive a child into their care under this section who is then ordinarily resident in the area of another local authority,—

(a) that other local authority may at any time not later than 3 months after the determination (whether by agreement between the authorities or in accordance with the following provisions of this sub-section) of the ordinary residence of the child, or with the concurrence of the first mentioned authority at any subsequent time, take over the care of the child; and

(b) the first mentioned authority may recover from the other authority any expenses duly incurred by them under Part II of this Act in respect of him (including any expenses so incurred after he has ceased to be a child and, if the other authority take over the care of him, including also any travelling or other expenses incurred in connection with the taking over).

Any question arising under this sub-section as to the ordinary residence of a child shall be determined by the Secretary of State and in this section any reference to another local authority includes a reference to a local authority in Scotland.

(5) In determining for the purposes of the last foregoing subsection the ordinary residence of any child, any period during which he resided in any place as an inmate of a school or other institution, or in accordance with the requirements of a supervision order or probation order or supervision requirement or the conditions of a recognisance, or while boarded out under this Act, the Poor Law Act, 1930, the Children and Young Persons Act, 1933, the Poor Law (Scotland) Act, 1934, or the Children and Young Persons (Scotland) Act 1937, or Part II of the Social Work (Scotland) Act 1968 by a local authority or education authority shall be disregarded.

H

2. Committal of children to the care of local authorities.

(i) The Children and Young Persons Act 1969 provides for an order to be made by the juvenile court placing a child in the care of a local authority.

CHILDREN AND YOUNG PERSONS ACT, 1969—Section 1 (As amended by the
Children Act 1975)
Care proceedings in
juvenile courts

(1)   Any local authority, constable or authorised person who reasonably believes that there are grounds for making an order under this section in respect of a child or young person may, subject to section 2(3) and (8) of this Act, bring him before a juvenile court.

(2)   If the court before which a child or young person is brought under this section is of opinion that any of the following conditions is satisfied with respect to him, that is to say—

    (a) his proper development is being avoidably prevented or neglected or his health is being avoidably impaired or neglected or he is being ill-treated; or

    (b) it is probable that the condition set out in the preceding paragraph will be satisfied in his case, having regard to the fact the court or another court has found that the condition is or was satisfied in the case of another child or young person who is or was a member of the household to which he belongs; or

    (bb) it is probable that the conditions set out in paragraph (a) of this subsection will be satisfied in his case, having regard to the fact that a person who has been convicted of an offence mentioned in Schedule 1 to the Act of 1933 is, or may become, a member of the same household as the child;

    (c) he is exposed to moral danger; or

    (d) he is beyond the control of his parent or guardian; or

    (e) he is of compulsory school age within the meaning of the Education Act 1944 and is not receiving efficient full-time education suitable to his age, ability and aptitude; or

    (f) he is guilty of an offence, excluding homicide,

and also that he is in need of care or control which he is unlikely to receive unless the court makes an order under this section in respect of him, then, subject to the following provisions of this section and sections 2 and 3 of this Act, the court may if it thinks fit make such an order.

(3)   The order which a court may make under this section in respect of a child or young person is—

    (a) an order requiring his parent or guardian to enter into a recognisance to take proper care of him and exercise proper control over him; or

    (b) a supervision order; or

    (c) a care order (other than an interim order); or

    (d) a hospital order within the meaning of Part V of the Mental Health Act 1959; or

    (a) a guardianship order within the meaning of that Act.

(4)   In any proceedings under this section the court may make orders in pursuance of paragraphs (c) and (b) of the preceding subsection but subject to that shall not make more than one of the orders mentioned in the preceding subsection,

198

without prejudice to any power to make a further order in subsequent proceedings of any description; and if in proceedings under this section the court makes one of those orders and an order so mentioned is already in force in respect of the child or young person in question, the court may discharge the earlier order unless it is a hospital or guardianship order.

(5)   An order under this section shall not be made in respect of a child or young person—

    (a) in pursuance of paragraph (a) of subsection (3) of this section unless the parent or guardian in question consents;

    (b) in pursuance of paragraph (d) or (e) of that subsection unless the conditions which, under section 60 of the said Act of 1959, are required to be satisfied for the making of a hospital or guardianship order in respect of a person convicted as mentioned in that section are satisfied in his case so far as they are applicable;

    (c) if he has attained the age of sixteen and is or has been married.

(6)   In this section "authorised person" means a person authorised by order of the Secretary of State to bring proceedings in pursuance of this section and any officer of a society which is so authorised, and in sections 2 and 3 of this Act "care proceedings" means proceedings in pursuance of this section and "relevant infant" means the child or young person in respect of whom such proceedings are brought or proposed to be brought.

(ii) Other sections within the 1969 Act which relate to Section 1 are:

CHILDREN AND YOUNG PERSONS ACT, 1969

—Section 2.   Provisions supplementary to Section 1.

—Section 7.   Alterations in treatment of young offenders, etc.

—Section 11A. Local authority functions under certain supervision orders (as inserted by paragraph 68 of Schedule 3 of the Children Act, 1975).

—Section 15. Variation and discharge of supervision orders.

—Section 16. Provisions supplementary to Section 15.

—Section 21. Variation and discharge of care orders (as extended by paragraph 69 of Schedule 3 of the Children Act, 1975.)

—Section 23. Remand to care of local authorities etc.

—Section 24. Powers and duties of local authorities etc. with respect to persons committed to their care.

—Section 27. Review of (case of child in care (see also Appendix III. A6 (iv))

(iii) In addition children may be committed to the care of local authorities under the following enactments:

MATRIMONIAL PROCEEDINGS (MAGISTRATES' COURTS) ACT, 1960

—Section 2.   Order by magistrates' court in matrimonial proceedings.

FAMILY LAW REFORM ACT, 1969

—Section 7.   Committal of wards of court to care of local authority.

GUARDIANSHIP ACT, 1973

—Section 2.   Jurisdiction and order on applications under Section 9 of Guardianship of Minors Act, 1971.

MATRIMONIAL CAUSES ACT, 1973

—Section 43. Power to commit children to care of local authority.

CHILDREN ACT, 1975

—Section 17. Care etc. of child on refusal of adoption order

—Section 36. Care etc. of child on revocation of custodianship order.

3. General duty of local authorities regarding children in care.

CHILDREN ACT, 1948

—Section 12. (As amended by the Children Act, 1975). General duty of local authority.

(1)   In reaching any decision relating to a child in their care, a local authority shall give first consideration to the need to safeguard and promote the welfare of the child throughout his childhood; and shall so far as practicable ascertain the wishes and feelings of the child regarding the decision and give due consideration to them, having regard to his age and understanding.

(1A)   If it appears to the local authority that it is necessary for the purpose of protecting members of the public, to exercise their powers in relation to a particular child in their care in a manner which may not be consistent with their duty under the foregoing subsection, the authority may, notwithstanding that duty, act in that manner.

(2)   In providing for a child in their care, a local authority shall make such use of facilities and services available for children in the care of their own parents as appears to the local authority reasonable in his case.

4. Boarding out of children in care.

(i) Section 13(1)(a) of the Children Act, 1948 enables a local authority to board out a child in their care.

CHILDREN ACT, 1948

—Section 13. (As substituted by Section 49 of the Children and Young Persons Act, 1969).

Provision of accommodation and maintenance for children in care.

(1)   A local authority shall discharge their duty to provide accommodation and maintenance for a child in their care in such one of the following ways as they think fit, namely,

(a) by boarding him out on such terms as to payment by the authority and otherwise as the authority may, subject to the provisions of this Act and regulations thereunder, determine; or

(b) by maintaining him in a community home or in any such home as is referred to in section 64 of the Children and Young Persons Act, 1969; or

(c) by maintaining him in a voluntary home (other than a community home) the managers of which are willing to receive him;

or by making such other arrangements as seem appropriate to the local authority.

(2)   Without prejudice to the generality of sub-section (1) of this section, a local authority may allow a child in their care, either for a fixed period or until the local authority otherwise determine, to be under the charge and control of a parent, guardian, relative or friend.

200

(3)   The terms, as to payment and other matters, on which a child may be accommodated and maintained in any such home as is referred to in section 64 of that Act shall be such as the Secretary of State may from time to time determine.

(ii) Regulations as to the boarding out by a local authority of a child in their care or by a voluntary organisation are made under section 14 of the Children Act, 1948.

CHILDREN ACT, 1948

—Section 14.   Regulations as to boarding out.

(1)   The Secretary of State may by regulations make provision for the welfare of children boarded out by local authorities under paragraph (a) of sub-section (1) of the last foregoing section.

(2)   Without prejudice to the generality of the last foregoing sub-section regulations under this section may provide—

    (a) for the recording by local authorities of information relating to persons with whom children are boarded out as aforesaid and persons who are willing to have children so boarded out with them;

    (b) for securing that children shall not be boarded out in any household unless that household is for time being approved by such local authority. as may be prescribed by the regulations;

    (c) for securing that where possible the person with whom any chid is to be boarded out is either of the same religious persuasion as the child or gives an undertaking that the child will be brought up in that religious persuasion;

    (d) for securing that children boarded out as aforesaid, and the premises in which they are boarded out, will be supervised and inspected by a local authority and that the children will be removed from those premises if their welfare appears to require it.

(iii) The regulations which at present regulate boarding out are:

THE BOARDING OUT OF CHILDREN REGULATIONS, 1955—SI 1955 No. 1377

These are not quoted in full because the whole of the Regulations are appropriate to the content of the Guide and should be carefully studied and acted upon.

There is also published an explanation of the Boarding Out Regulations:

MEMORANDUM ON THE BOARDING OUT REGULATIONS, 1955
(H.M.S.O., London, 1955 SO Code No. 34-372)

5. Assumption by local authorities of parental rights over children in their care.

CHILDREN ACT, 1948

—Section 2.   (As substituted by the Children Act, 1975)
                Assumption by local authority of parental rights and duties

(1)   Subject to the provisions of this Part of this Act, if it appears to a local authority in relation to any child who is in their care under the foregoing section—

    (a) that his parents are dead and he has no guardian or custodian; or

    (b) that a parent of his—

        (i) has abandoned him, or

        (ii) suffers from some permanent disability rendering him incapable of caring for the child, or

        (iii) while not falling within sub-paragraph (ii) of this paragraph, suffers from a mental disorder (within the meaning of the Mental Health Act, 1959), which renders him unfit to have the care of the child, or

(iv) is of such habits or mode of life as to be unfit to have the care of the child, or

(v) has so consistently failed without reasonable cause to discharge the obligations of a parent as to be unfit to have the care of the child; or

(c) that a resolution under paragraph (b) of this subsection is in force in relation to one parent of the child who is, or is likely to become, a member of the household comprising the child and his other parent; or

(d) that throughout the three years preceding the passing of the resolution the child has been in the care of a local authority under the foregoing section, or partly in the care of a local authority and partly in the care of a voluntary organisation, or partly the one and partly the other,

the local authority may resolve that there shall vest in them the parental rights and duties with respect to that child and, if the rights and duties were vested in the parent on whose account the resolution was passed jointly with another person, they shall also be vested in the local authority jointly with that other person.

(2) In the case of a resolution passed under paragraph (b), (c) or (d) of subsection (1) of this section, unless the person whose parental rights and duties have under the resolution vested in the local authority has consented in writing to the passing of the resolution, the authority, if that person's whereabouts are known to them, shall forthwith after the passing of the resolution serve on him notice in writing of the passing thereof.

(3) Every notice served by a local authority under subsection (2) of this section shall inform the person on whom the notice is served of his right to object to the resolution and the effect of any objection made by him.

(4) If, not later than one month after notice is served on a person under sub-section (2) of this section, he serves a counter-notice in writing on the local authority objecting to the resolution, the resolution shall, subject to the provisions of subsection (5) of this section, lapse on the expiry of fourteen days from the service of the counter-notice.

(5) Where a counter-notice has been served on a local authority under sub-section (4) of this section, the authority may not later than fourteen days after the receipt by them of the counter-notice complain to a juvenile court having jurisdiction in the area of the authority, and in that event the resolution shall not lapse until the determination of the complaint; and the court may on hearing of the complaint order that the resolution shall not lapse by reason of the service of the counter-notice:

Provided that the court shall not so order unless satisfied—

(a) that the grounds mentioned in subsection (1) of this section on which the local authority purported to pass the resolution were made out, and

(b) that at the time of the hearing there continued to be grounds on which a resolution under subsection (1) of this section could be founded, and

(c) that it is in the interests of the child to do so.

(6) While a resolution passed under subsection (1)(b), (c) or (d) of this section is in force with respect to a child section 1(3) of this Act shall not apply in relation to the person who, but for the resolution, would have the parental rights and duties in relation to the child.

202

(7)   Any notice under this section (including a counter-notice) may be served by post, so however that a notice served by a local authority under subsection (2) of this section shall not be duly served by post unless it is sent by registered post or recorded delivery service.

(8)   A resolution under this section shall cease to have effect if—

(a) the child is adopted;

(b) an order in respect of the child is made under section 14 or 25 of the Children Act, 1975; or

(c) a guardian of the child is appointed under section 5 of the Guardianship of Minors Act, 1971.

(9)   Where, after a child has been received into the care of a local authority under the foregoing section, the whereabouts of any parent of his have remained unknown for twelve months, then, for the purposes of this section, the parent shall be deemed to have abandoned the child.

(10) The Secretary of State may by order a draft of which has been approved by each House of Parliament amend subsection (1)(d) of this section to substitute a different period for the period mentioned in that paragraph (or the period which, by a previous order under this subsection, was substituted for that period).

(11) In this section—

"parent", except in subsection (1)(a), includes a guardian or custodian;

"parental rights and duties", in relation to a particular child, means all rights and duties which by law the mother and father have in relation to a legitimate child and his property except the right to consent or refuse to consent to the making of an application under section 14 of the Children Act, 1975 and the right to agree or refuse to agree to the making of an adoption order or an order under section 25 of that Act.

CHILDREN ACT, 1948

—Section 3.   (As amended by the Children and Young Persons Act, 1969 and the Children Act, 1975).

Effect of assumption by local authority of parental rights.

(6)   A resolution under the said section two shall not relieve any person from any liability to maintain, or contribute to the maintenance of the child.

(7)   A resolution under the said section two shall not authorise a local authority to cause a child to be brought up in any religious creed other than that in which he would have been brought up but for the resolution.

(8)   Any person who—

(a) Knowingly assists or induces or persistently attempts to induce a child to whom this subsection applies to run away, or

(b) without lawful authority takes away such a child, or

(c) knowingly harbours or conceals such a child who has run away or who has been taken away or prevents him from returning,

shall be liable on summary conviction to a fine not exceeding £400 or to imprisonment for a term nor exceeding three months or to both.

This subsection applies to any child in the care of a local authority under section 1 of this Act with respect to whom a resolution is in force under section 2 thereof and for whom accommodation (whether in a home or otherwise) is being provided by the local authority in pursuance of Part II of this Act; and references in this subsection to running away or taking away or to returning are references to running away or taking away from, or to returning to, a place where accommodation is or was being so provided.

CHILDREN ACT, 1948

—Section 4A (as inserted by section 58 of the Children Act, 1975) provides for a right of appeal to the High Court against decisions in juvenile courts upholding or rescinding resolutions passed by local authorities assuming parental rights and duties in respect of children in their care.

CHILDREN ACT, 1948

—Section 4B (as inserted by section 58 of the Children Act, 1975) extends to proceedings involving resolutions as to parental rights and duties the concept of separate representation of the child.

CHILDREN ACT, 1975

—Section 67. Recovery of children in care of local authorities.

This section provides local authorities with new powers of recovery of children in care under section 1 of the Children Act, 1948 who are subject to a resolution as to parental rights and duties under section 2 of that Act and are absent from premises at which they are required by a local authority to live.

6. Miscellaneous matters

(Including miscellaneous powers and duties of local authorities in relation to children)

(i) Duty of local authorities to make available such advice, guidance and assistance as may promote the welfare of children by diminishing the need to receive them into or keep them in care, or to bring them before a juvenile court.

CHILDREN AND YOUNG PERSONS ACT, 1963

—Section 1. Extension of power to promote welfare of children.

(ii) Parental contributions towards child in care.

CHILDREN AND YOUNG PERSONS ACT, 1963

—Section 86. Contributions to be made by parents of children and young persons committed to the care of fit persons or to approved schools.

—Section 87. Enforcement of duty of parents, etc. to make contributions.

CHILDREN ACT, 1948

—Section 23. Contributions in respect of child in care of local authority.

—Section 24. Persons liable to make contributions.

CHILDREN AND YOUNG PERSONS ACT, 1963

—Section 30. Recovery of arrears of contributions.

CHILDREN AND YOUNG PERSONS ACT, 1969

—Section 62. Contributions in respect of children and young persons in care.

(iii) Custodianship

Part II of the Children Act, 1975 provides a means by which, as an alternative to adoption, relatives and others looking after children on a long-term basis can apply for and obtain the legal custody of the children. For England and Wales, this is achieved in sections 33 to 46 by enabling the courts to make what are described as 'custodianship orders' vesting the legal custody of the child in the applicant, who becomes known as the child's 'custodian'. The term 'legal custody' is defined in section 86 as so much of the parental rights and duties as relate to the person (i.e. not the property) of the child, including the place and manner in which his time is spent. The custodian will not have the right to arrange for a child's emigration nor to agree to a child's adoption. (Schedule 3, paragraph 7, amends the Marriage Act 1949 to enable a custodian to consent to the marriage of a child under 18.)

Section 33 provides, with certain restrictions, for the court, on the application of any person who is not the mother or father of a child, to make a custodianship order vesting the legal custody of the child in the applicant.

Section 34 enables a court to make supplementary orders about access and maintenance on the application of the custodian or the child's mother or father.

Section 36 safeguards the position of children on the revocation of a custodianship order.

Section 39 requires persons who apply for a custodianship order to give notice to the local authority who must then investigate the application and report to the court.

Section 41 contains restrictions, pending a court decision, on the child's removal where the applicant has provided a home for three years.

Section 42 enables the court to order the child's return and to enforce that order, if need be.

(iv) Review of care orders

Section 27(4) of the CHILDREN AND YOUNG PERSONS ACT, 1969 (as substituted by paragraph 71 of Schedule 3 of the Children Act, 1975) places on a local authority a duty to review the case of each child in their care in accordance with regulations made by the Secretary of State. These regulations may provide for the manner in which cases are to be reviewed, the considerations to which the local authority are to have regard in reviewing cases, the time for first review and the frequency of subsequent reviews.

(v) Conflict of interest between parent and child

Sections 32A and 32B of the CHILDREN AND YOUNG PERSONS ACT, 1969 (inserted by section 64 of the Children Act, 1975) concerns the situation where there may be a conflict of interest between parent and child or young person and the safeguarding of interests of child or young person where section 32A order made. Section 65 of the Children Act, 1975 amends section 28 of the LEGAL AID ACT, 1974 to enable the parents as well as the child to qualify for legal aid in these cases.

7. Children in the care of voluntary organisations

(i) Definition of voluntary organisation. The definition of a voluntary organisation appears in several statutes, e.g.:

CHILDREN ACT, 1975

—Section 107. Interpretation.

"voluntary organisation" means a body, other than a public or local authority, the activities of which are not carried on for profit.

(See also Section 59 of the CHILDREN ACT, 1948 and Regulation 32 in the BOARDING OUT OF CHILDREN REGULATIONS, 1955 (SI 1955 No. 1377)).

(ii) Restriction on removal of child from care of voluntary organisation.

Section 33A of the CHILDREN ACT, 1948 (inserted by section 56(2) of the Children Act, 1975) provides:

33A (1) Section 3(8) of this Act shall apply in relation to children who are not in the care of local authorities under section 1 of this Act but who are in voluntary homes or are boarded out, as it applies by virtue of subsection (3A) of the said section 1 to children in the care of the local authority, except that in the case of a child who is not in the care of a local authority the references in subsection (3A) to a local authority shall be construed as references to the voluntary organisation in whose care the child is.

    (2)   For the purposes of this section—

        (a) a child is boarded out if he is boarded out, by the voluntary organisation in whose care he is, with foster parents to live in their home as a member of their family;

        (b) "voluntary home" includes a controlled community home and an assisted community home.

(iii) Transfer of parental rights and duties.

Section 60 of the CHILDREN ACT, 1975 enables a local authority to pass a resolution transferring parental rights and duties in respect of a child in the care of a voluntary organisation who is not in the care of a local authority, to that organisation provided that the conditions necessary for the assumption of parental rights and duties set out in the amended section 2 of the Children Act, 1948 are satisfied (see Appendix III A5).

    (1)   Where it appears to a local authority as respects a child in the care of a voluntary organisation which is an incorporated body—

        (a) that the child is not in the care of any local authority; and

        (b) that a condition specified in section 2(1) of the Children Act, 1948 is satisfied; and

        (c) that it is necessary in the interests of the welfare of the child for the parental rights and duties to be vested in the organisation,

the authority may, subject to subsections (5) and (6), resolve that there shall vest in the organisation the parental rights and duties with respect to that child.

    (2)   While a resolution under this section is in force the parental rights and duties shall vest in the organisation in whose care the child is when the resolution is passed.

    (3)   If, immediately before the resolution is passed, the parental rights and duties are vested in the parent in relation to whom the resolution is passed jointly with any other person, then on the passing of the resolution the parental rights and duties shall vest jointly in that other person and the organisation in whose care the child is.

(4)   In determining, for the purposes of subsection (1) of this section, whether the condition specified in section 2(1)(b)(i) of the Children Act, 1948 is satisfied, if the whereabouts of any parent of the child have remained unknown for twelve months, that parent shall be deemed to have abandoned the child.

(5)   A resolution under subsection (1) may not be passed by a local authority in respect of any child unless—

(a)   the child is living in the area of the authority either in a voluntary home or with foster parents with whom he has been boarded by the organisation in whose care he is; and

(b)   that organisation has requested the authority to pass the resolution.

(6)   The parental rights and duties which may vest in an organisation by virtue of this section do not include the right to consent or refuse to consent to the making of an application under section 14 and the right to agree or refuse to agree to the making of an adoption order or an order under section 25; and regulations made under section 33(1) of the Children Act, 1948 shall apply to the emigration of a child notwithstanding that the parental rights and duties relating to the child are vested in the voluntary organisation.

(7)   Subsection (8) of section 2 of the Children Act, 1948 shall apply in relation to a resolution under subsection (1) as if it were a resolution under the said section 2.

Other sections of the CHILDREN ACT, 1975 which relate include:

Section 61 which enables a local authority, at any time after the passing of a resolution transferring parental rights and duties to a voluntary organisation, to pass a further resolution vesting those powers in itself if it considers that the interests of the welfare of the child require that those powers should no longer be vested in the voluntary organisation.

Section 62 which sets out the effect of resolutions transferring or withdrawing parental rights and duties to or from voluntary organisations.

Section 63 which applies to resolutions transferring or withdrawing parental rights and duties, the rights of objection and complaint to a juvenile court against the passing or termination of those resolutions.

(iv) Boarding out of children by voluntary organisations

CHILDREN ACT, 1948

—Section 33.   Powers of Secretary of State as to voluntary organisations.
Section 33(3) provides for the Boarding Out Regulations to apply to children boarded out by voluntary organisations.

(3)   The power conferred by Part II of this Act on the Secretary of State to make regulations as to the boarding out of children by local authorities shall extend also to the boarding out of children by voluntary ogranisations;

Provided that in the provisions of the said Part II conferring that power any reference to the supervision and inspection by a local authority of boarded out children and the premises in which they are boarded out shall, in relation to children boarded out by voluntary organisations, be deemed to be a reference to supervision and inspection either by a local authority or, where it is so provided by or under the regulations, by a voluntary organisation.

207

B. Scotland

1. Reception of children into the care of local authorities

SOCIAL WORK (SCOTLAND) ACT, 1968

—Section 15.   (As amended by the Children Act, 1975). Duty of local authority to provide for orphans, deserted children, etc.

(1)   Without prejudice to the generality of the foregoing provisions of this Part of this Act, where it appears to a local authority with respect to a child in their area appearing to them to be under the age of seventeen—

(a)   that he has neither parent nor guardian or has been and remains abandoned by his parent or guardian or is lost; or

(b)   that his parent or guardian is, for the time being or permanently, prevented by reason of illness or mental disorder or bodily disease or infirmity or other circumstances from providing for his proper accommodation, maintenance and up-bringing; and

(c)   in either case, that the intervention of the local authority under this section is necessary in the interests of the welfare of the child,

it shall be the duty of the local authority to receive the child into their care under this section.

(2)   Where a local authority have received a child into their care under this section, it shall, subject to the provisions of this Part of this Act, be their duty to keep the child in their care so long as the welfare of the child appears to them to require it and the child has not attained the age of eighteen.

(2A)   In reaching any decision relating to a child in their care, a local authority shall give first consideration to the need to safeguard and promote the welfare of the child throughout his childhood; and shall so far as practicable ascertain the feelings and wishes of the child regarding the decision and give due consideration to them, having regard to his age and understanding;

(3)   If, at the time when a child is received into the care of a local authority under this section, the whereabouts of any parent or guardian of his are unknown, it shall be the duty of the local authority to take all reasonable steps to discover them; and nothing in this section shall authorise a local authority to keep a child in their care under this section if any parent or guardian desires to take over the care of the child, and the local authority shall, in all cases where it

208

appears to them consistent with the welfare of the child so to do, endeavour to secure that the care of the child is taken over either—

(a) by a parent or guardian of his, or

(b) by a relative or friend of his, being where possible, a person of the same religious persuasion as the child or who gives an undertaking that the child will be brought up in that religious persuasion.

(3A) Subsection (8) (penalty for taking away a child in care etc.) of section 17 of this Act shall apply to a child in the care of a local authority under this section, notwithstanding that no resolution is in force under section 16 of this Act with respect to the child, if he has been in the care of that local authority throughout the preceding six months; and for the purposes of the application of paragraph (b) of that subsection in such a case a parent or guardian of the child shall not be taken to have lawful authority to take him away.

Provided that that subsection shall not by virtue of this subsection apply in relation to an act done—

(a) with the consent of the local authority, or

(b) by a parent or guardian of the child who has given the local authority not less than 28 days' notice of his intention to do it.

(3B) The Secretary of State may by order, a draft of which has been approved by each House of Parliament, amend subsection (3A) of this section by substituting a different period for the period of 28 days or of six months mentioned in that subsection (or for the period which by a previous order under this subsection, was substituted for that period).

(4) Where a local authority receive a child into their care under this section who is then ordinarily resident in the area of another local authority, that other local authority may within three months after the determination (whether by agreement between the authorities or under section 86 of this Act) of the ordinary residence of the child, or with the concurrence of the first-mentioned authority at any subsequent time, take over the care of the child; and a local authority shall not exercise their right to take over the care of a child under this subsection unless they are satisfied that the taking over will not be detrimental to his welfare.

(5) Where under the last foregoing subsection a local authority take over the care of a child from another local authority, that other authority shall where possible inform the parent of the child that the care of the child has been so taken over.

2. Committal of children into the care of local authorities.

MATRIMONIAL PROCEEDINGS (CHILDREN) ACT, 1958

—Section 10.   Power of court in actions of divorce etc. to commit care of child to local authority or an individual.

GUARDIANSHIP ACT, 1973

—Section 11.   Jurisdiction and orders relating to care and custody of children.

3. Children subject to compulsory measures of care.

SOCIAL WORK (SCOTLAND) ACT, 1968

—Section 44(5)   Child subject to a supervision requirement made by a children's hearing shall for certain purposes of the 1968 Act, viz sections 16 to 18, 20, 24 to 26, 28 and 29 be in the care of the local authority for the area of the children's hearing.

4. General duty of local authorities regarding children in care.

SOCIAL WORK (SCOTLAND) ACT, 1968

—Section 20.　　(as amended by the Children Act, 1975) Duty of local authority to further the best interests of a child in their care and to afford opportunity for this proper development.

(1)　Where a child is in the care of a local authority under any enactment the local authority shall, in reaching any decision relating to the child, give first consideration to the need to safeguard and promote the welfare of the child throughout his childhood; and shall so far as practicable ascertain the wishes and feelings of the child regarding the decision and give due consideration to them, having regard to his age and understanding.

(2)　In providing for a child in their care as aforesaid, a local authority shall make such use of facilities and services available for children in the care of their own parents as appears to the local authority reasonable in his case.

(3)　Where a local authority allow the care of a child to be taken over under section 17(3) or 18(3) of this Act, their duties in respect of the child under this section shall not be affected by that take-over.

5. Boarding out of children in care

(i) Local authorities' power to board out children in their care

SOCIAL WORK (SCOTLAND) ACT, 1968

—Section 21.　　Mode of provision of accommodation and maintenance.

(1)　Subject to the provisions of this section, a local authority shall discharge their duty to provide accommodation and maintenance for a child in their care—

    (a)　by boarding him out on such terms as to payment by the authority and otherwise as the authority may, subject to the provisions of this Act and regulation thereunder, determine; or

    (b)　by maintaining the child in a residential establishment.

(2)　Nothing in the foregoing subsection shall be construed as preventing a local authority from making use, in the case of any child, of any such facilities and services as are referred to in subsection (2) of the last foregoing section, and for that purpose arranging for his accommodation and maintenance in any suitable manner not specified in the last foregoing subsection.

Arrangements may be made by a local authority under this section for boarding out a child in England or Wales or for maintaining him in any accommodation in England or Wales which a local authority in those countries is authorised to use for that purpose by virtue of section 13 of the Children Act, 1948.

(ii) Regulations as to boarding out are made under Section 5 of the Social Work (Scotland) Act, 1968.

SOCIAL WORK (SCOTLAND) ACT, 1968

—Section 5(3).　　Powers of Secretary of State (Regulations as to boarding out)

(3)　Without prejudice to the generality of the foregoing subsection, regulations under this section may make provision for the boarding-out of persons by local authorities and voluntary organisations, whether under any enactment or otherwise, and may provide—

    (a)　for the recording by local authorities and voluntary organisations of information relating to persons with whom persons are boarded out as aforesaid, and to persons who are willing to have persons boarded out with them;

210

(b) for securing that persons shall not be boarded out in any household unless that household is for the time being approved by such local authority or voluntary organisation as may be prescribed by the regulations;

(c) in the case of a child, for securing that, where possible, the person with whom any child is to be boarded out is either of the same religious persuasion as the child or gives an undertaking that the child shall be brought up in that religious persuasion;

(d) for securing that persons boarded out as aforesaid, and the places in which they are boarded out, shall be supervised and inspected by a local authority or voluntary organisation, as the case may be, and that those persons shall be removed from those places if their welfare appears to require it.

(iii) The regulations which at present regulate boarding out are:

THE BOARDING OUT OF CHILDREN (SCOTLAND) REGULATIONS, 1959

SI 1959 No. 835 (S44)

These are not quoted in full because the whole of the Regulations are appropriate to the content of the Guide and should be carefully studied and acted upon.

6. Assumption by local authorities of parental rights over children in their care.

SOCIAL WORK (SCOTLAND) ACT, 1968

—Section 16.   (As amended by the Children Act, 1975) Assumption by local authorities of parental rights

(1)   Subject to the provisions of this Part of this Act, a local authority may resolve

(a) that there shall vest in them the relevant parental rights and powers with respect to any child who is in their care under section 15 of this Act; or

(b) that there shall vest in a voluntary organisation which is an incorporated body, or a trust within the meaning of section 2(a) of the Trusts (Scotland) Act, 1921, the relevant parental rights and powers with respect to any child who is in the care of that organisation,

if it appears to the local authority—

(i) that the parents of the child are dead and that he has no guardian; or

(ii) that there exists in respect of a parent or guardian of the child (the said parent or guardian being hereafter in this Part of this Act referred to as the person on whose account the resolution was passed) any of the circumstances specified in subsection (2) of this section; or

(iii) that a resolution under this subsection is in force in terms of sub-paragraph (ii) above in relation to one parent of the child and that parent is, or is likely to become, a member of the household comprising the child and his other parent; or

(iv) that throughout the three years preceding the passing of the resolution the child has been in the care of a local authority under section 15 of this Act, or in the care of a voluntary organisation or partly the one and partly the other.

(2)   The circumstances referred to in sub-paragraph (ii) of subsection (1) of this section are that the person on whose account the resolution was passed—

(a) has abandoned the child; or

(b) suffers from some permanent disability rendering him incapable of caring for the child; or

211

(c) while not falling within paragraph (b) of this subsection, suffers from a mental disorder (within the meaning of the Mental Health (Scotland) Act, 1960) which renders him unfit to have the care of the child; or

(d) is of such habits or mode of life as to be unfit to have the care of the child; or

(e) has so persistently failed without reasonable cause to discharge the obligations of a parent or guardian as to be unfit to have the care of the child.

(3) In this section "the relevant parental rights and powers" means all the rights and powers in relation to the child (other than the right to consent or refuse to consent to the making of an application under section 14 or 15 of the Children Act, 1975 and the right to agree or refuse to agree to the making of an adoption order)—

(a) where the resolution was passed by virtue of circumstances specified in sub-paragraph (i) of subsection (1) of this section, which the deceased parents would have if they were still living;

(b) where the resolution was passed by virtue of circumstances specified in sub-paragraph (ii) of that subsection, of the person whose account the resolution was passed;

(c) where the resolution was passed by virtue of circumstances specified in sub-paragraph (iii) of that subsection, of the parent other than the one on whose account the previous resolution was passed;

(d) where the resolution was passed by virtue of circumstances specified in sub-paragraph (iv) of that subsection, of the parents or guardian of the child.

(4) A local authority shall not pass a resolution under paragraph (b) of subsection (1) of this section unless—

(a) it is satisfied that the child is not in the care of any local authority under any enactment; and

(b) it is satisfied that it is necessary in the interests of the welfare of the child for the parental rights and powers to be vested in the voluntary organisation; and

(c) the child is living in the area of the local authority either in a residential establishment or with foster parents with whom he has been boarded out by the voluntary organisation in whose care he is; and

(d) that organisation has requested the local authority to pass the resolution.

(5) In the case of a resolution passed under subsection (1) of this section, by virtue of circumstances specified in sub-paragraph (ii), (iii) or (iv) thereof, unless the person whose parental rights and powers have under the resolution vested in the local authority or in the voluntary organisation as the case may be, has consented in writing to the passing of the resolution, the local authority, if that person's whereabouts are known to them, shall forthwith after the passing of the resolution serve on him notice in writing of the passing thereof.

(6) Every notice served by a local authority under subsection (5) of this section shall inform the person on whom the notice is served of his right to object to the resolution and of the effect of any objection made by him.

212

(7)   If, not later than one month after notice is served on a person under subsection (5) of this section, he serves a counter-notice in writing on the local authority objecting to the resolution, the resolution shall, subject to the provisions of subsection (8) of this section, lapse on the expiry of fourteen days from the service of the counter-notice.

(8)   Where a counter-notice has been served on a local authority under subsection (7) of this section, the authority may, not later than fourteen days after the receipt by them of the counter-notice, make a summary application in respect thereto to the sheriff having jurisdiction in the area of the authority and in that event the resolution shall not lapse until the determination of the application; and the sheriff may, on the hearing of the application, order that the resolution shall not lapse by reason of the service of the counter-notice:

Provided that the sheriff shall not so order unless satisfied—

(a)   that it is in the interests of the child to do so; and

(b)   that the grounds mentioned in subsection (1) of this section on which the local authority purported to pass the resolution were made out; and

(c)   that at the time of the hearing there continued to be grounds on which a resolution under subsection (1) of this section could be founded.

(9)   While a resolution passed under subsection (1) of this section by virtue of circumstances specified in sub-paragraph (ii), (iii) or (iv) thereof is in force with respect to a child, that part of subsection (3) of section 15 of this Act from the words "and nothing in this section shall authorise" onwards shall not apply in relation to the person who, but for the resolution, would have the relevant parental rights and powers in relation to the child.

(10)   Any notice under this section (including a counter-notice) may be served by post, but a notice served by a local authority under subsection (5) of this section shall not be duly served by post unless it is sent by registered post or recorded delivery service.

(11)   A resolution under this section shall cease to have effect if—

(a)   the child becomes the subject of an adoption order within the meaning of Schedule 2 to the Children Act, 1975; or

(b)   an order in respect of the child is made under section 14 or section 25 of the Children Act, 1975; or

(c)   a person is appointed, under section 4(2A) of the Guardianship of Infants Act, 1925, to be the guardian of the child; or

(d)   it is a resolution under paragraph (b) of subsection (1) of this section and a resolution is passed under subsection (1) of section 16A of this Act in respect of the child.

(12)   If the whereabouts of any parent or guardian of a child have remained unknown for twelve months, and throughout that period the child has been in the care of a local authority under section 15 of this Act, or in the care of a voluntary organisation, or partly the one and partly the other, then for the purposes of this section that parent or guardian shall be deemed to have abandoned the child.

213

(13) The Secretary of State may by order, a draft of which has been approved by each House of Parliament, amend sub-paragraph (iv) of subsection (1) of this section to substitute a different period for the period of three years mentioned in that sub-paragraph (or for the period which, by a previous order under this subsection, was substituted for that period).

SOCIAL WORK (SCOTLAND) ACT, 1968

—Section 17.   (As amended by the Children Act, 1975)

Effect of assumption by local authorities of parental rights

(3) A resolution under section 16 of this Act shall not prevent the local authority from allowing, either for a fixed period or until the local authority otherwise determine, the care of the child to be taken over by, and the child to be under the control of, a parent, guardian, relative or friend in any case where it appears to the authority to be for the benefit of the child.

(4) Where a resolution under section 16 of this Act is in force in respect of a child and the child has ceased to be in the care of the local authority by whom the resolution was passed, then (without prejudice to the provisions of section 15 of this Act if those provisions apply) the local authority by whom the resolution was passed shall have power to receive the child back into their care in any circumstances in which it appears to them that their intervention under this subsection is necessary in the interests of the welfare of the child.

(5) Where a local authority receive a child into their care under the last foregoing subsection, the provisions of this Act, except subsection (4) of section 15 thereof, shall apply as if the child had been received into their care under the said section 15.

(6) A resolution under the said section 16 shall not relieve any person from any liability to maintain, or contribute to the maintenance of, the child.

(7) A resolution under the said section 16 shall not authorise a local authority to cause a child to be brought up in any religious persuasion other than that in which he would have been brought up but for the resolution.

(8) Any person who—

(a) Knowingly assists or induces or persistently attempts to induce a child to whom this section applies to run away, or

(b) without lawful authority takes away such a child, or

(c) knowingly harbours or conceals such a child who has run away or who has been taken away or prevents him from returning,

shall be liable on summary conviction to a fine not exceeding fifty pounds or to imprisonment for a term not exceeding six months or to both such fine and such imprisonment.

(9) Where a local authority have, in accordance with subsection (3) of this section, allowed any person to take over the care of a child with respect to whom a resolution under the said section 16 is in force and have by notice in writing required that person to return the child at a time specified in the notice (which, if that person has been allowed to take over the care of the child for a fixed period, shall not be earlier than the end of that period) any person who harbours or conceals the child after that time or prevents him from returning as required by the notice shall be liable on summary conviction to a fine not exceeding fifty pounds or to imprisonment for a term not exceeding six months or to both such fine and such imprisonment.

214

(10) Where an offence under subsection (8) or (9) of this section has been or is believed to have been committed, a constable, or any person authorised by any court or by any justice of the peace, may take and return the child to the local authority or voluntary organisation in whom are vested the parental rights and powers relating to the child.

7. Miscellaneous matters (including miscellaneous powers and duties of local authorities in relation to children)

(i) Duty of local authority to make available such advice, guidance and assistance as may promote the welfare of children

SOCIAL WORK (SCOTLAND) ACT, 1968

—Section 12. General duty to make available advice, guidance and assistance and power to provide assistance to children in kind or in cash where such assistance may diminish need to receive a child into care.

—Section 24. Financial assistance towards expenses of maintenance, educational training of persons over school age and who are or have been in care.

—Section 25. Power of local authority to guarantee indentures and other deeds of apprenticeship etc., of persons in their care.

—Section 26. After-care of children formerly in care of local authorities or voluntary organisations.

(ii) Parental contributions towards children in care

SOCIAL WORK (SCOTLAND) ACT, 1968

—Section 78. Duty to make contributions in respect of children in care.

—Section 80. Enforcement of duty to make contributions.

—Section 81. Provisions as to decrees for aliment.

—Section 82. Recovery of arrears of contributions.

—Section 83. Variations of trusts.

(iii) Custodianship

In Part II of the CHILDREN ACT, 1975 sections 47 to 55 relate to custody in Scotland. The following sections may be of particular interest:

—Section 47. Granting of custody.

—Section 48. Miscellaneous provisions relative to custody.

—Section 49. Notice to local authority of certain custody applications.

—Section 50. Payments towards maintenance of children.

—Section 51. Restriction on removal of child where applicant has provided home for three years.

—Section 52. Return of child taken away in breach of section 51.

(iv) Review of case of child in care

Section 80 of the Children Act, 1975 inserts a new section after section 20 of the SOCIAL WORK (SCOTLAND) Act, 1968. The new section places a duty on a local authority to review the case of every child who has been in care throughout the preceding six months and in respect of whom during that period they have not held such a review.

(v) Safeguarding of interests of children

Section 66 of the Children Act, 1975 inserts a new section 34A in the SOCIAL WORK (SCOTLAND) ACT, 1968 whereby the chairman or sheriff may consider the appointment of a person to represent the interests of a child in certain proceedings.

215

Section 78 of the Children Act, 1975 inserts a new section after section 18 of the SOCIAL WORK (SCOTLAND) ACT, 1968 concerning the appointment of a person to represent the interests of the child involved in proceedings in Scotland relating to the assumption of parental rights.

8. Children in the charge of voluntary organisations

(i) Definition of voluntary organisation

The definition of a voluntary ogranisation appears in several statutes, e.g.:

CHILDREN ACT, 1975

—Section 107. Interpretation.

"voluntary organisation" means a body, other than a public or local authority, the activities of which are not carried on for profit.

(See also Section 94 of the Social Work (Scotland) Act, 1968 and the Boarding Out of Children (Scotland) Regulations, 1959 (SI 1959 No. 835 (S.47))—Regulation 19).

(ii) Restriction on removal of child from care of voluntary organisation

Section 81 of the Children Act, 1975 inserts a new section after section 25 of the SOCIAL WORK (SCOTLAND) ACT, 1968, as follows:

25A (1) Section 17(8) of this Act shall apply in relation to a child who is not in the care of a local authority under section 15 of this Act but who is in the care of a voluntary organisation, as it applies by virtue of subsection (3A) of the said section 15 to a child in the care of a local authority except that, in the case of a child who is not in the care of a local authority, references in subsection (3A) to a local authority shall be construed as references to the voluntary organisation in whose care the child is.

(2) For the purposes of this section, a child is in the care of a voluntary organisation if the voluntary organisation is providing accommodation for the child in a residential establishment or has boarded out the child.

(iii) Transfer of parental rights and duties

Section 16 of the SOCIAL WORK (SCOTLAND) ACT, 1968 (as amended by Section 74 of the Children Act, 1975) provides for a local authority to vest in a voluntary organisation the relevant parental rights and powers with respect to any child who is in the care of that organisation.

(See Appendix III B.6. for full extract of new section).

A new section 16A of the SOCIAL WORK (SCOTLAND) ACT, 1968 (inserted by section 75 of the Children Act, 1975) concerns the duty of local authority in Scotland to assume parental rights and powers vested in a voluntary organisation.

Section 17 (effect of assumption of parental rights) of the SOCIAL WORK (SCOTLAND) ACT, 1968 (as amended by section 76 of the Children Act, 1975) concerns the return of children taken away in breach of section 17(8) or (9) of the 1968 Act. (See appendix III B.6)

(iv) Boarding out of children by voluntary organisations.

SOCIAL WORK (SCOTLAND) ACT, 1968

—Section 5. Powers of the Secretary of State.

This section provides for the boarding out regulations made by the Secretary of State to apply to voluntary organisations as well as to local authorities. (The section is quoted in full in Appendix III B.5 (ii).)

216

Appendix IV

Suggestions for further reading

The following are the Working Party's suggestions for further reading. There is, however, an extensive list of publications in the field of child care and the Library of the Department of Health and Social Security is able to supply a list of books and articles relating to the fostering of children. It also publishes a monthly bulletin on current literature on the personal social services, and training officers in particular may like to draw on these sources when compiling programmes for their local use.

ADAMSON, G., *The Caretakers*, London, Bookstall Publications, 1973.

ALDGATE, J., *A study of factors that influence the stay of children in the care of two local authorities in Scotland*. PhD Thesis, University of Edinburgh (Unpublished), 1975.

AINSWORTH, M., *Deprivation of maternal care: a re-assessment of its effects*. (*Public Health Papers No. 14*). Geneva, World Health Organisation, 1962.

ASSOCIATION OF BRITISH ADOPTION AGENCIES, *Meeting children's needs through adoption and fostering*. London, Association of British Adoption Agencies, 1975.

ASSOCIATION OF BRITISH ADOPTION AGENCIES, *Ending the waiting*. (A series of discussion papers on substitute family care). 1. Which children and what plan? London, Association of British Adoption Agencies, 1975.

BERRY, J., *Social work with children: helping children directly*. British Journal of Social Work, London 1971, Vol. 1, No. 3, 1971.

BOWLBY, J., *Maternal care and mental health* (World Health Organisation Monograph Series, No. 2). Geneva, World Health Organisation, 1951.

BOWLBY, J., *Attachment and loss, Vol. 1: Attachment* (International Psycho-Analytical Library, No. 79). London, Hogarth Press and Harmondsworth, Middlesex, Penguin Books, 1969.

BOWLBY, J., *Attachment and loss, Vol. 2: Separation* (International Psycho-Analytical Library, No. 95). London, Hogarth Press and Harmondsworth, Middlesex, Penguin Books, 1973.

BRITISH ASSOCIATION OF SOCIAL WORKERS, *The featuring of children in care in publicity for substitute families—guidelines for practice*. Social Work Today, Birmingham, 1975, Vol. 6, No. 17, 1975.

CHARNLEY, J., *The art of child placement*. University of Minneapolis, 1955.

CLARKE, E., *My mother who fathered me*. London, Allen and Unwin, 1957.

COMMUNITY RELATIONS COMMISSION, REFERENCE AND COMMUNITY SERVICES, *Fostering black children: a policy document on the needs of ethnic minority group children*. London, Community Relations Commission, 1975.

DINNAGE, R. AND PRINGLE, M. L. K., *Foster home care: Facts and Fallacies*. London, Longmans, in association with the National Bureau for Co-operation in Child Care (now National Children's Bureau), 1967.

ERIKSON, E. H., *Childhood and Society*. London, Hogarth Press and Harmondsworth, Middlesex, Penguin Books, 1969.

ERIKSON, E. H., *Identity: youth and crisis*. London, Faber and Faber, 1971.

GEORGE, V., *Foster care. Theory and practice*. London, Routledge and Kegan Paul, 1970.

GIBB, J. AND THORPE, R., *The natural parent group*. Social Work Today, Vol. 6, No. 13, 1975.

GOLDSTEIN, J., FREUD, A. AND SOLNIT, A. J., *Beyond the best interests of the child*. New York, Free Press, London, Collier, McMillan, 1973.

217

HEINICKE, C. M. AND WESTHEIMER, I. J., *Brief separations*. London, Longmans, 1965.
HOLGATE, E. (EDITOR), *Communicating with children* (Collected papers). London, Longmans, 1972.
HOLMAN, R., *The child and the Child Care Officer*. Case Conference, Vol. 13, No. 2, 1966.
HOLMAN, R., *The place of fostering in social work*. British Journal of Social Work, London, 1975, Vol. 5, No. 1, 1975.
JENKINS, R., *Long term fostering*. Case Conference, Vol. 15, No. 9, 1969.
JENKINS, S. AND NORMAN, E. *Filial deprivation and foster care*. New York, Columbia University Press, 1972.
JOLOWICZ, ALMEDA R., *The hidden parent—Some of the effects of the concealment of the parents' life upon the child's use of a foster home*. Department of Public Affairs, Minsola, New York.
KLINE, D. and OVERSTREET, H. M. F. *Foster care of children: nurture and treatment*. New York and London, Columbia University Press, 1972.
LEEDING, A. E. *Child care manual for social workers*. London, Butterworth, 1971.
MANDELL, B. R., *Where are the children? A class analysis of foster care and adoption*. Lexington, Mass., Lexington Books, D. C. Heath, 1973.
NEILSON, J., *Older children need love too*. London, Association of British Adoption Agencies, 1974.
PARKER, R. A., *Decisions in child care—a study of prediction in fostering* (N.I.S.W. Training Series, No. 8), London, Allen and Unwin, 1966.
PATTERSON, S., *Dark strangers*. London, Tavistock Publications, 1963.
PETTES, D. E., *Supervision in social work: a method of student training and staff development* (N.I.S.W. Training Series, No. 10), London, Allen and Unwin, 1967.
PORTSMOUTH POLYTECHNIC and PORTSMOUTH DEPT. OF SOCIAL SERVICES, *Portsmouth Fostering Study*, Portsmouth, Portsmouth Polytechnic Department of Social Studies, 1973.
PRINGLE, M. L. K., *The needs of children*, London, Hutchinson, 1974.
RAYNER, E., *Human development*, London, Allen and Unwin, 1971.
ROBERTSON, JAMES and JOYCE, *Young children in brief separation. A fresh look*, London, Hogarth Press and Tavistock Child Development Research Unit, 1971.

Films of same title relating to the above paper. Tavistock Institute of Human Relations.

Film 1 (1967) Kate, 2 yrs. 5 months.	In fostercare for twenty-seven days.
Film 2 (1968) Jane, 17 months.	In fostercare for ten days.
Film 3 (1969) John, 17 months.	For nine days in a residential nursery.
Film 4 (1971) Thomas, 2 yrs. 4 months.	In fostercare for ten days.
Film 5 (1973) Lucy, 21 months.	In fostercare for nineteen days.

ROWE, J. and LAMBERT, L., *Children who wait*, London Association of British Adoption Agencies, 1973.
RUTTER, M., *Maternal deprivation re-assessed*, Harmondsworth, Middlesex, Penguin Books, 1972.
SAWBRIDGE, P., *Finding homes for children: a glimpse of American practice*, London, International Social Services (G.B.), 1973.
SHERIDAN, M. D., *The handicapped child and his home*, London, National Children's Home, 1973.
STEVENSON, O., *Someone else's child*. London, Routledge and Kegan Paul, 1965.
THORPE, R., *Mum and Mrs. So and So*, Social Work Today, Birmingham, 1974, Vol. 4, No. 22, 1974.

THORPE, R., *The social and psychological situations of the long term foster child with regard to his natural parents*, PhD Thesis, University of Nottingham (unpublished), 1974.

TOD, R. (editor), *Social work in foster care—collected papers*, London, Longmans, 1971.

TRASLER, G., *In place of parents: a study of foster care*, London, Routledge and Kegan Paul, 1960.

VANN, J., *The child as a client of the social services department*, British Journal of Social Work, London, 1971, Vol. 1, No. 2, 1971.

WALTON, R. and HEYWOOD, M., *Success and failure in long term fostering placement: Project to validate Parker's prediction study*, Social Work: London, 1970, April, Vol. 27, No. 2, 1970.

WEINSTEIN, E. A., *The self image of the foster child*, New York, Russell Sage Foundation, 1960.

WINNICOTT, C., *Child care and social work* (A collection of papers written between 1954 and 1963), Welwyn, Herts, Codicote Press, 1964.

WINNICOTT, D., *The maturational processes and the facilitating environment*, London, Hogarth Press, 1965.

WINNICOTT, D., *The child, the family and the outside world*, Harmondsworth, Middlesex, Penguin Books, 1964.

WINNICOTT, D., *The family and individual development*, London, Tavistock Publications, 1965.

Appendix V

Organisations and individuals who submitted comments to the working party

The Working Party is indebted to the following organisations and individuals who have assisted with written and oral comments.

Aberdeen Foster Parent Group
Adoption Resource Exchange
Alloa Foster Parent Group
Association of British Adoption Agencies
Association for Child Psychology and Psychiatry (Scottish Branch)
Association of County Councils (Scotland)
Association of Directors of Social Services
Association of Directors of Social Services (Northern Branch)
Association of Directors of Social Work
Association of Educational Psychologists
Association of Head Mistresses
Association of Teachers in Social Work Education

Bath Association of Foster Parents
Berkshire County Council
Blackburn and District Foster Parents Association
Board for Social Responsibility
Bolton Metropolitan Foster Parent Association
British Association of Social Workers
British Association of Social Workers—Scottish Committee
British Paediatric Association
Bromsgrove Foster Parent Association

Camden Foster Parent Association
Camden London Borough Council
Central Council for Education and Training in Social Work
C.H.E. Croydon Group
Children's Regional Planning Committee—Area 1
Children's Regional Planning Committee—Area 6
Children's Regional Planning Committee—Area 10
Children's Regional Planning Committee—Area 12
Church of England Children's Society
Clackmannan County Council
Community Relations Commission
Co-ordination Meeting in Fostering Subjects
Coventry Foster Parents Association
Croydon Foster Parents
Croydon London Borough Council
Crusade of Rescue

Department of Health and Social Security, Medical Division
Department of Health and Social Security, Nursing Division

220

Department of Health and Social Security, Social Work Service
Doncaster and District Foster Parent Association
Dudley Metropolitan Borough Council
Dukeries Foster Parent Association
Dumbarton Burgh
Durham County Foster Parents Association

Ealing Foster Parent Group
Eastleigh and Southern Parishes Foster Parent Group
Edinburgh Foster Parent Group
Education Welfare Officers National Association
Essex County Council

Gingerbread
Gloucestershire Foster Parents Association
Guild of Service, Edinburgh

Health Visitors Association
Herefordshire Foster Parents Association
Hitchin Foster Parents Association

Lancashire County Council
Lancaster Diocesan Protection and Rescue Society
Leeds Metropolitan Borough Council
Leicester Foster Parents Association
Lewisham Foster Care Association
Lewisham London Borough Council
Liverpool Foster Parents Association
London Boroughs Association

Medical Group of the Association of British Adoption Agencies
Mothers In Action
Motherwell Foster Parent Group

National Association for Mental Health
National Association of Counsellors in Education
National Association of Head Teachers
National Association of Schoolmasters
National Children's Bureau
National Council of Voluntary Child Care Organisations
National Foster Care Association
National Society for the Prevention of Cruelty to Children
Newport and District Foster Parents Association
Northamptonshire County Council
North Humberside Adoptive and Foster Parents Association
Northern Ireland Foster Parent Group
North Tyne Foster Parent Group
Northumberland (Alnwick) Foster Parent Group
Nuneaton Area Foster Care Association

Parent to Parent Information on Adoption Services
Personal Social Services Council
Perth Association of Foster Parents
Peterborough Foster Parents

Race Relations Board
Royal Burgh of Dumfries
Royal College of Psychiatrists (Scottish Division)

Scottish Association of Voluntary Child Care Organisations
Scottish Council for Single Parents
Scottish Counties of Cities Association
Sefton Foster Care Association
Social Welfare Commission
Social Work Services Group (Scottish Education Department)
Solihull Foster Parents
Southampton Association of Foster Parents

Tower Hamlets Foster Parents Group
Tiverton and District Foster Parents

Warwickshire Foster Parents Group
Welsh Office Medical and Nursing Divisions
West Midlands Foster Parents Association
Wiltshire County Council
Wolverhampton Foster Parents Association

Mrs. Jane Aldgate
Dr. John Bowlby
Mrs. Vivienne Coombe
Dr. Christine Cooper
Mr. Robert Gee
Dr. Iris Knight
Dr. Alan Little
Dr. Marion Mackenzie
Dr. Mia Kellmer Pringle
Mr. Kenneth Pryce
Miss Christine Reeves
Mr. and Mrs. James Robertson
Professor Michael Rutter
Dr. Mary Sheridan
Dr. Rosamund Thorpe
Mrs. Clare Winnicott
Dr. Basil Wolman

In addition over 400 foster parents, foster children, children whose parents have fostered and other interested people responded to the general invitation to supply the Working Party with their views and experiences.

222

Index

223

224

Printed in England for Her Majesty's Stationery Office
by Knight & Forster Ltd., Water Lane, Leeds LS11 9UB

Dd 290597 K40 4/76